contents

Preface   vi

The Digital Cinematographer   2

This chapter is an introduction to cinematography as an art form
and production responsibility.

Visual Storytelling   16

This chapter explores the fine art of visual storytelling, focusing on
the concept development, script writing, and pre-production of an
animated film.

Directing the Camera – A Traditional
Filmmaking Perspective   54

This chapter provides the digital animator with an overview of the
camera from a traditional filmmaking perspective.

1
2
3

CONTENTS

The Virtual Camera 88

This chapter covers the bridge to digital directing; exploring the most common parameters of virtual camera as they are seen in today's high-end 3D animation software packages.

Introduction to Light and Color 130

This chapter explores the creation, appearance, and interaction of light and color.

Traditional Lighting Techniques 176

This chapter explores the traditional production tools and techniques used in filmmaking, including three-point lighting.

Virtual Lighting 226

This chapter explores the bridge between the color theory and real-world lighting techniques and their application in the digital environment.

Wrapping it Up — Materials and Textures   284

This chapter focuses on real-world surface reflection, color, and texture, and also discusses how to recreate their effects using materials and maps within the 3D environment.

8

Appendix   333
Index   334

preface

INTENDED AUDIENCE

Exploring Digital Cinematography is intended for students enrolled in two- and four-year college and graduate level programs. In particular, this text is designed for those interested in animation, special effects, and game art and design. Although there is vital information that beginners would find useful, it is geared toward students who have some familiarity with the 3D environment. This text also can benefit junior to mid-level industry professionals that would like to sharpen their cinematography skills.

BACKGROUND OF THIS TEXT

I have been entrenched in the 3D universe since 1993, but I have had little time to reflect on the people, courses, jobs, textbooks, Web sites, and so on that have shaped my development as a filmmaker. It was not until I became the chair of a newly formed animation program that I was afforded the luxury to analyze their greater meaning. In fact, this has become a key component of my job.

As I began to develop the program's curriculum, it became evident that I would need to establish the core competencies/qualities of a great animator/filmmaker before I could determine which courses, instructors, textbooks, software, and so on I would need to implement. What skills would best equip my future graduates to obtain their dream job? Which qualities would I look for if I were hiring for the next blockbuster feature film or real-time game? It was through this reverse-engineering process that I realized that the most successful animators are, in fact, three-headed monsters. That is not to say that they are the scary creatures that pop up in one of those early *Godzilla* movies—although I have seen some of those same personality traits at 3 AM before a deadline. What it means is that great animators need to have three very distinct qualities that are quite diverse and typically not found in one individual.

Simply put, the best animators are:
1. Fine Artists
2. Filmmakers
3. Technologists

Although some have one or even two of these qualities, only those who have the unique combination of all three will realize their full potential. You could be the best artist and filmmaker in the world, but if you can't find peace within some of the most technically complicated software packages around, your work will suffer. By contrast, you could be the chief code writer for Autodesk and have invented the zoom shot, but if your artistic skills leave a lot to be desired, the animation will suffer.

The reality is that the three-headed monster concept is a reflection of the 3D animation production process. In the end, every animator will have to flex their artistic, directorial, and technological muscles. Whether you are in the storyboarding phase or putting the finishing touches on special effects, you will need to make sure that this three-pillared foundation is solid. But although digital cinematography in an animated film *absolutely* requires the three-headed monster, it is for the most part overlooked or just plain ignored in curriculum today.

The term *cinematography*, in the classical sense, refers to the process (pre- through postproduction) of developing/producing all of the aspects that affect a motion picture's "look and feel." The cinematographer, or director of photography, makes all of the decisions that relate to the use of camera shots/angles/framing, lighting, and color, and he or she works closely with the director to develop the overall aesthetic of the film. Although this job function/production process has been around since the early days of the motion picture industry, it has not been widely adopted in the 3D animation industry, nor is it being taught at the university/college level—and it shows.

With ever-increasing competition for jobs in the industry, it has become critical, in my opinion, that these digital cinematography skills start being developed at the university/college level.

The aspects of digital cinematography that usually are discussed in the university setting are typically from a 3D perspective only. I am a strong believer that students should pull from reality whenever possible before making decisions in the virtual world. The "filmmaker" head of the three-headed monster should have a solid understanding of how lights and cameras work in the real world before he or she attempts to create a lighting setup in a 3D environment.

TEXTBOOK ORGANIZATION

Exploring Digital Cinematography is designed to balance out an animator's skill set, using the three-headed monster concept as its backbone. The book delves deeply in the areas of CG directing, lighting, and texturing; approaching each from an art, film, and technology point of view. This approach will build a solid foundation of art and filmmaking knowledge that is then translated into the 3D world. Furthermore, the text is packed with visual examples, meaningful exercises, production tips, and artist spotlights from some of the most talented artists in the industry.

Chapter 1 is an introduction to art of cinematography. Starting with a historical look at the birth of film, it follows the role of the cinematographer from the late nineteenth century through today.

Chapters 2, 3, and 4 explore the critical role of the camera and camera direction within the filmmaking process. These three chapters will not only guide you through the inner workings of the camera but also provide students with the real-world production techniques that all digital cinematographers should know.

Chapters 5, 6, and 7 explore the power of some of the cinematographer's most powerful assets; light and color. From color theory to common light setups, these chapters will guide the viewer through the often uncharted waters of digital lighting.

Chapter 8 wraps up the text with an introduction to 3D materials and textures. Although these are not often associated with traditional cinematography, one can only become an effective digital lighter by having a solid understanding of materials and texture maps.

INSTRUCTOR'S E.RESOURCE

This guide on CD was developed to assist instructors in planning and implementing their instructional programs. It includes sample syllabi for using this book in either an eleven- or fifteen-week semester. It also provides chapter review questions and answers, exercises, PowerPoint slides highlighting the main topics, and additional instructor resources.

ABOUT THE AUTHOR

Jason Donati is an award-winning animator and cinematographer. He is currently the Chair of Media Arts and Animation at The New England Institute of Art in Brookline, Massachusetts. Jason also has worked as a Creative Director for Kaon, Inc., where his team was responsible for the production of photorealistic 3D models and animation in the creation of interactive product tours for Fortune 500 consumer electronic companies. Before that, Jason was Director of 3D at Animation Technologies, Inc. in Boston, where he led a team of animators delivering cutting-edge visual solutions for medical and legal visualization purposes.

Jason's personal animated films have been showcased internationally at some of the most prestigious festivals and conferences in the industry, including SIGGRAPH 1999 (Los Angeles), SIGGRAPH 2000 (New Orleans), Ani Mundi 1999 (Rio De Janeiro, Brazil), Seoul Film Festival

1999 (Seoul, Korea), and ASIFA East 1999 and 2000 (New York City). He holds a BFA in Computer Animation from the University of Massachusetts Amherst and an MFA from the School of Film and Animation at the Rochester Institute of Technology. Jason is a longtime member of the Association of Computer Machinery (ACM/SIGGRAPH) as well as the Association Internationale du Film d' Animation (ASIFA East).

ACKNOWLEDGMENTS

First and foremost, this book is dedicated to my wife Michelle. Without her unwavering love, support, and guidance, this project simply would not have become a reality.

I would like to extend my sincerest gratitude to the two artists whose work has helped to shape the overall look and feel of this book. They both enthusiastically took on this project for one reason and one reason only: their love of 3D animation. Although they did not directly contribute to the written text, their passion, devotion, and creativity was and will continue to be a gigantic source of inspiration. With that said, I would like to thank Edward Brillant and Louis Tammaro for their contributions toward *Exploring Digital Cinematography*.

Many thanks to Shane Acker and Christopher Cordingley for their thoughtful insights and spectacular imagery in the Artist Spotlights.

Thank you to all the other amazing artists who contributed to the amazing collection of images seen throughout the book: Ron Alpert, Franco Galletta, Michael Gonsalves, and Dr. Rachelle "Derminator" Dermer.

Thanks to the amazing folks at The New England Institute of Art for their continual support and encouragement: Mary Cardaras, Rob Lehmann, Dr. John Gostan, Stephanie Vincent, Barbara Merandi, and to all the Media Arts and Animation faculty and students.

Thanks to all the incredible artists and instructors who have helped mold me into the animator I am today: Mike Krummhoefener, Patricia Galvis-Assmus, Skip Battaglia, and Marla Schweppe.

Special thanks to my entire family for always being there: Mom, Norm, Dad, Cindy, Amanda, and Jessica.

A big shout-out to the whole Lowell/Tewksbury crew for all the good times and laughs over the years: Chris, Becky, Matty, Jamie, and Sean.

And thank you to everyone at Thomson for their guidance and support throughout the production of my first book: Jim Gish, Nicole Bruno, and Roxanne Pleace.

QUESTIONS AND FEEDBACK

Thomson Delmar Learning and the author welcome your questions and feedback. If you have suggestions that you think others would benefit from, please let us know, and we will try to include them in the next edition.

To send us your questions and/or feedback, you can contact the publisher at:

Thomson Delmar Learning
Executive Woods
5 Maxwell Drive
Clifton Park, NY 12065
Attn: Media Arts & Design Team
800-998-7498

Or the author at:

jason@3DCinematography.com
http://www.3DCinematography.com

SPECIAL FEATURES

The following features can be used throughout this book.

▶ ## Objectives

Learning Objectives start off
each chapter. They
describe the competencies
the reader should achieve
on understanding the
chapter material.

objectives

- Explore the transition from a real-world camera to a virtual camera
- Understand the common parameters within the 3D camera
- Understand the basics of camera framing and composition
- Learn the fundamentals of virtual camera blocking
- Recognize the axis of action within any shot
- Explore advanced 3D techniques with camera shake and motion tracking

Insider Info

When discussing camera moves, it is important to understand the power of *Parallax*. Parallax is an optical phenomenon that results when a camera is in motion. From the viewer's standpoint, it can appear that stationary objects are actually in motion and change position relative to other stationary objects in the scene. How far these stationary objects are from the camera will determine how fast or slow they appear to move. For instance, if a camera is following a character walking across a street, objects that are near to the character, such as street signs or parking meters, will appear to move very quickly, whereas other objects further away, such as buildings or mountains, will appear to move much more slowly. Parallax is not only a visual clue to the audience as to the relative distances between objects but also a wonderful artistic tool to keep shots compelling.

▶ ## Insider Info

Insider Info provides valuable
industry knowledge, tips, and
techniques to the reader.

▶ ## Notes

Notes appear throughout
the text, offering additional
valuable information on
specific topics.

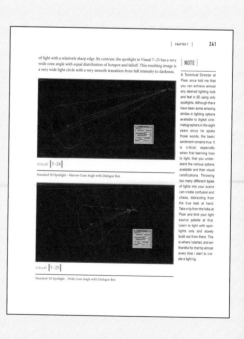

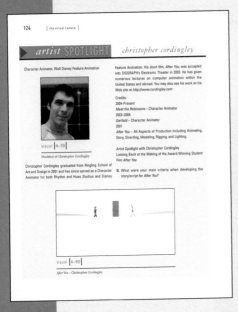

▶ Artist Spotlights

Artist Spotlights, located throughout the book, allow the reader to learn from some of the most successful animators in the industry. Each provide a behind-the-scenes look at their work, techniques used, and offer practical advice for aspiring digital cinematographer.

▶ Review Questions and Exercises

Review Questions and Exercises are located at the end of each chapter and allow readers to assess their understanding of the chapter. Exercises are intended to reinforce chapter material through practical application.

CHAPTER 1

objectives

- Explore the history of traditional cinematography
- Understand the Director of Photography's role within the filmmaking process
- Explore the production parallels between traditional and digital filmmaking
- Discover the two main production responsibilities for the digital cinematographer
- Understand the three-headed monster concept and its relationship to 3D animation

introduction

As we move rapidly into the digital age of filmmaking, celluloid is being replaced by 1s and 0s. Although the cinematographer's trade tools and equipment may be evolving, the foundational theories and concepts behind producing quality visual stories remains remarkably intact. However, with relatively new storytelling mediums such as 3D animation and the Internet, the digital cinematographer must be able to translate these traditional skills into the virtual environment. This chapter will serve as the introduction to cinematography as an art form and production responsibility.

THE DIGITAL CINEMATOGRAPHER

INTRODUCTION TO CINEMATOGRAPHY

Cinematography is the art and science behind the visual elements of filmmaking. Centered mostly on the camera operation and lighting setups, well-executed cinematography can be as critical to the film's overall impact as much as the script or the acting. In fact, in certain films, such as *The Godfather* and *The Purple Rose of Cairo*, the individual frames can be considered works of art. Gordon Willis, the visual mastermind behind both of those classics, may have put it best when he said, "A cinematographer is a visual psychiatrist, moving the audience to a movie, from here to there, to there to here, making them think the way you want them to think, painting pictures in the dark" (Fauer).

visual |1–1|

Digital Cinematography

History

The origin of cinematography must be traced back to the late nineteenth century and the birth of motion pictures. In 1888, Louis Aime Augustin Le Prine shot a three-second film titled *Leeds Bridge Traffic*, which is considered to be the oldest film footage in existence. Although technically it was a moving picture, it was far from what we think

visual |1–2|

Image from "A Trip to the Moon" by Georges Méliès circa 1902

of as a modern movie. During these early stages of production, filmmaking pioneers were more concerned with the science and technology behind the photographic and projection processes than with the actual images. It wouldn't be until the late 1890s and early 1900s, with works such as Georges Méliès' *A Trip to the Moon*, that its true artistic capabilities would be explored (Burns).

As filmmaking tools progressed, so did the potential to use these sequential images as a storytelling medium. The demand from the general public, which was in awe with the new art form, drove film screenings out of the local cafés and into large dedicated movie houses such as Vitascope Hall in New Orleans. This popularity led to the development of an entirely new industry, which would change the way that people spent their hard-earned entertainment dollar.

Within the next decade, the motion picture industry had grown by leaps and bounds and started to set up camp on the West Coast of the United States. Companies such as the Biograph Company and the Fox Film Company began to cultivate the many production resources that would be needed to mass-produce motion pictures, including writers, actors, directors, and camera operators.

DIRECTOR OF PHOTOGRAPHY

In the early stages of the movie industry, the director of the film not only would oversee the entire production but also would actually work the camera and lights. However, as scripts got longer, casts became larger, and budgets got bigger, the need for specialized roles and responsibilities began to emerge. One of the new job functions that was created was the *Director of Photography*, also known as the *DoP* or *DP*. Synonymous with the term cinematographer, the DoP's purpose is to oversee the visual content from both a technical and aesthetic standpoint. In accordance with the Director's overall artistic vision, the Director of Photography manages the camera and lighting crews; making critical decisions on all aspects of the production, including film stock, lenses, camera blocking, staging and movement, and lighting. Visual 1–3 illustrates the DoP's job responsibilities within the filmmaking process.

Director of Photography
(Cinematographer)

⟹ Camera Framing

⟹ Lighting

⟹ Lenses

visual | 1–3 |

Director of Photography's Job Responsibilities Flowchart

THE DIGITAL CINEMATOGRAPHER

First and foremost, *animation* is *filmmaking*. Although there certainly are some major differences in execution, the majority of the production steps required to make a traditional live-action film and an animated film are identical. The processes for *Gone with the Wind* and *Toy Story* were very similar. Starting with the scriptwriting process, the crew progressed through the *preproduction, production,* and *post-production* phases, which include storyboarding, lighting, and editing. Although some preproduction phases such as set design were produced in very different manners, the desired end results for each film were identical.

visual |1–4|

Filmmaking Production
Process

Filmmaking Process

➡ Pre-Production

➡ Production

➡ Post-Production

These days, now that a majority of the feature animation being produced is created in 3D, the similarities are even stronger. In fact, *3D animation* software manufactures have gone out of their way to make the production toolsets as close to their *real-world* equivalent as possible. The virtual cameras look like cameras and the spotlights look like spotlights, providing all of the same controls and options available to the live-action DoP.

visual |1–5|

3D Cameras and Lights

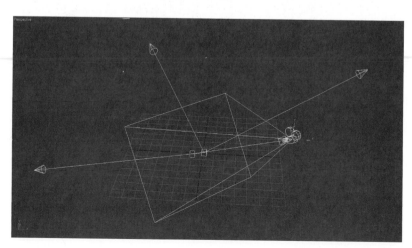

In 2003, Pixar Animation Studio's broke new ground in the animation world by officially assigning a Director of Photography role into the production of their feature film *Finding Nemo*. Actually, Pixar thought it was important enough to have two individuals working in that role; Sharon Calahan and Jeremy Lasky. Although Sharon was cited as early as 1998 for her cinematography work in *A Bug's Life*, this was the first time that the DoP credit was officially given.

The fact that high-end animation studios such as Pixar have put an increased emphasis on the role of the Director of Photography speaks volumes about the overall importance of camerawork and lighting. Therefore, it is critical, as an aspiring animator, that you take the time to study these aspects of the production process that are often overshadowed by modeling and animation. Although those are still foundational aspects of the craft, creating well-executed digital cinematography will only make them better.

THE THREE-HEADED MONSTER

Believe it or not, this is not the introduction to the character design process. That will come a little later down the road. The *three-headed monster* refers to the qualities that I would I look for if I were hiring for the next blockbuster feature film or blockbuster video game. What does that mean? Most successful animators are, in fact, three-headed monsters. That's not to say they are the scary creatures that appear in those early Godzilla movies, although I have seen some of those same personality traits at 3 AM before a deadline. What it really means is that great animators need to have three very distinct qualities typically not found in one individual.

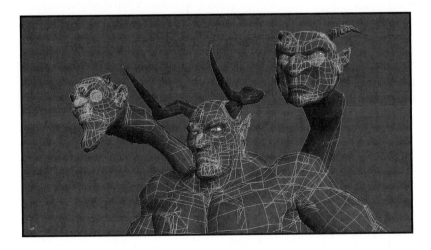

visual | 1–6 |

Three-Headed Monster
Wireframe

Simply put, the best 3D animators are:

1. Fine Artists

2. Filmmakers

3. Technologists

Although some animators have one or even two of these qualities, only those who have the unique combination of all three will realize their full 3D animation potential. You could be the best artist and filmmaker in the world, but if you can't find peace within some of the most technically complicated software packages around, your work will suffer. By contrast, you could be the chief code writer at Autodesk and have invented the Zoom shot, but if your artistic abilities leave a lot to be desired, then your animation will suffer.

visual | 1–7 |

Three-Headed Monster
Render

Don't get me wrong; there are certain situations, at the bigger production companies in particular, that allow, and even encourage, specialization and focus. However, I can assure you that even if you are hired as a technologist, a shader writer at Pixar for instance, your director will consider you infinitely more valuable if you also have artistic and filmmaking skills.

The reality is that the three-headed monster concept is a reflection of the 3D animation production process. In the end, every animator will have to flex his or her artistic, directorial, and technological muscles. Whether you are in the storyboarding phase or putting the finishing touches on a lighting rig, you'll need to make sure that your foundation is solid. The following chapters are dedicated to examining the major components of digital cinematography, camerawork, lighting, and texturing, from all three perspectives; bridging the gap between traditional live-action filmmaking and cutting-edge 3D animation.

SUMMARY

Cinematography is a vital part of the filmmaking process, from small-budget independent live-action films to blockbuster Hollywood animated features. Although the technology changes almost daily, the need for well-executed camerawork and lighting does not. In fact, the larger animation studios seem to be reverting to some of the traditional production roles and responsibilities that were developed at the dawn of filmmaking.

The most successful 3D animators are three-headed monsters. They possess a unique combination of artist talent, filmmaking abilities, and technical knowledge.

artist SPOTLIGHT   *edward brillant*

3D Artist, Tilted Mill Entertainment

visual |1–8|

Ed Brillant

Edward Brillant, a graduate of the Montserrat College of Art in 2000, started his career in 3D animation at the Massachusetts-based Deos Animation Studios, serving as Lead Modeler and Animator for nationally syndicated television programs such as *Ribert and Robert's Wonderworld* and *A Very Wompkee Christmas*. Then Edward worked as a lead artist creating models for 3D product visualization. Currently, Edward is a 3D Artist for Tilted Mill Entertainment, a game development company focused on the creation of high quality strategy and role-playing games for the PC. You can see his work on his Web site, *http://www.jumpinmyhead.com*.

Credits:
2006–Present
3D Artist – Caesar IV
2004–2006
Kaon Interactive –Lead Artist
2003–2004
Ribert and Robert's Wonderworld – Lead Modeler
2002–2003
A Very Wompkee Christmas – Animator

Q. With virtually no formal training in animation, you were able to break into the extremely competitive gaming industry as a 3D artist. What types of projects and resources could you recommend to those trying to achieve similar goals?

A. The most important thing is by far hard work. You will get what you put into it. If you only work a couple hours a night doing 3D, it's going to take that much longer than it would four or six hours. Not having any formal training, I had to sacrifice a lot to reach my goals. I'm not saying stop living but there is a degree of sacrifice in reaching any goals. I was lucky my wife was very supportive. I think another component was in 3D forums. They help give you guidance from more experienced artist. In doing so, you make connections with people that help build a network.

As far as projects, I would make a character from concept to fully rigged. From start to end they were far from perfect but I didn't let the mistakes get to me. I would learn from them. Even if I knew the model wasn't looking great I would make sure the next one did.

Q. The camera and lighting toolsets available within the high-end 3D software packages are directly related to their real-world counterparts. How important do you think understanding the traditional filmmaking process is to 3D animation production?

visual |1–9|

Ed Brillant – Gallery Image #1

A. It is very important in a 3D animation production to understand the real-world counterparts for many reasons. In some instances, you may be composting characters into live action and being able to match the real-world cameras is vital. And while making a 3D production using the same guidelines that are in the real world will keep you grounded in the real world. In a 3D production it is very easy to start making shots you wouldn't normally be able to do in the real world. Which is a great advantage, but often that freedom can also be a problem. Without at least an understanding of lighting and cameras things can quickly start to get out of hand and become chaotic. Leaving the viewer visually lost.

Q. Where do you see the animation and gaming industries heading in the next five years? What role will cinematography play in both?

A. In the next five years, I see a thinner line defining games from film. Games are steadily catching up to film in quality. More and more big-name directors are going to be going from film to games. In a movie, the filmmakers want their viewers to live through the story they are watching. The evolution to that would be to let the audience interact with the story. I believe gaming technology is growing and helping bridge that gap.

But, on the other hand, I think the animation industry is in fear of becoming over saturated. 3D animated films over the last five years have been growing exponentially. And with that you will have many studios cashing in on the 3D wave. So I think over the next five years you will see some good with the bad on the film side. You will see a larger quantity in animated movies with less higher-quality movies. But the high-end movies will be really something spectacular.

Q. What advice can you give to students who are creating their first animated film?

A. Take things slow and simple. Don't try and make that epic that you have been dreaming up for the past ten years. Start short and simple. No dialogue, tell your story with visuals, light, and camera movements. Then as you learn from the trials of a short film your next will be that much better. Then the epic will be nice and smooth. Wink!

Q. With ever-changing software tools and techniques, how do you ensure that you are staying current in the industry?

visual |1–10|

Ed Brillant – Gallery Image #2

A. Staying on top of things really isn't too hard to do. Finding a good 3D community really is key. Those communities help you find other sites as well as themselves to give you all the big news in the industry.

artist SPOTLIGHT   *louis tammaro*

3D Artist, Tilted Mill Entertainment

visual |1–11|

Louis Tammaro

Louis Tammaro, a graduate of Montserrat College of Art in 2000, with a Bachelor's degree in Illustration, started his career working in 2D. Louis did some illustrations for videogame Web sites, while teaching himself 2D animation. It wasn't until 2002 when Louis was introduced to 3D and videogame art. He spent the next couple of years teaching him self to model, texture, and rig characters, slowly building his skills and producing work that he would show potential employers in the gaming industry. His personal work can be seen at *http://www.visionsoftammaro.com*.

Credits:
2005–Present
3D Artist – Ceaser IV
2001–2002
Web site illustrations for videogame Web sites such as gamecubeland.com (now defunct).

Q. What aspects of your illustration degree were you able to draw from when learning how to animate?

A. I am more a modeler than an animator. You need to have a skill you want to develop, and it is very tough to learn every aspect of 3D. But the fundamentals of 3D all come back to 2D. You need to be able to draw, understand perspective and composition, as well as color theory, no getting around it. My job is to take the flat 2D screen and bring you into a three-dimensional world. Illustration has helped me greatly because, in Illustration, you must convey emotion to the viewer to support the text that accompanies the picture, whether it be in magazines or children's books.

Q. Cinematography is a critical component to filmmaking; traditional and animated. However, it is becoming increasingly important in the gaming industry. Explain the term "cinematics" and how the role of camerawork and lighting is dramatically changing the user's experience.

visual |1–12|

Louis Tammaro – Gallery Image #1

A. The term "cinematics" in the gaming industry refers to noninteractive scenes that move the story along. They can be real time (meaning in engine), or prerendered. In both scenarios, lighting and camerawork have become very important to make the gamers' experience deeper and more memorable.

As technology grows, developers are able to bring a more cinematic feel to their games. Developers want to invoke the same emotions in games as directors do in film. It is important to learn from film and study the techniques directors use to draw us in to their vision. The gaming industry gets closer to this every year. Gamers today want to be emotionally involved in the games they play.

Q. From a cinematography standpoint, what are some of the live-action films that have inspired the work that you create and why?

A. Wow, that is a tough one. I would start off with the work of Tim Burton. I feel he has a good sense of scene composition. Although it seems weird at first, you soon realize that his shots and lighting compliment his vision very well.

I will also say that *The Godfather* movies are a perfect example of excellent cinematography. Very dramatic, very deliberate, you feel as though you are sitting in the room with the family. You are part of their world.

Q. This textbook is based on the fact that the best computer animators are three-headed monsters: artists, filmmakers, and technicians. Explain how you were able to become all three.

visual | 1–13 |

Louis Tammaro – Gallery Image #2

A. Community. There is nothing better than having a community of people with knowledge to share with each other. Communities help you become a better artist, a better film maker and a better technician. Being self-taught in 3D, I have learned that you need to use the resources that are available to you to progress. Artists are a tight-knit group, and we love to see people reach that next level in their skill.

Q. Who are some of the 3D artists that inspire you and your work and why?

A. Steven Stahlberg for his narrative illustrations and his skill at realistic modeling. As a whole, the artists at Square Enix. The work they do for their franchises, like Final Fantasy, to me are what this industry is all about. Those artists are at the top of their game.

in review

1. Which Louis Aime Augustin Le Prine film is considered to be the oldest in existence?

2. What is the relationship between cinematography and the Director of Photography?

3. What are the main production responsibilities of the DoP?

4. Name the three main production stages that are similar in both live-action and animation filmmaking.

5. Who received the first DoP credit for a 3D animated film?

6. The most successful 3D animators have which three skill sets?

exercises

1. Using the Internet Movie Database (*http://www.imdb.com*), research your favorite live-action film of all time.

   a. Find out who the DoP was for that production and create a list of all the other films that they were involved in.

   b. Watch at least a couple of shots from those movies, if you haven't seen them already. Do you notice a pattern in the film's camerawork or lighting?

2. Excluding the films created by Pixar Animation Studios, find another animated feature that has used a DoP.

   a. What do you notice about the overall quality of the camerawork and lighting?

   b. Using the Internet Movie Database, research the background of that DoP, including schools attended and previously held positions in the field. Is this DoP a three-headed monster?

CHAPTER 2

objectives

- Discover the principles of visual storytelling
- Learn the process of concept development and idea generation
- Understand the three-act story structure and the Hero's Journey
- Avoid common student mistakes
- Explore the design phase of preproduction
- Understand the role and process of storyboarding

introduction

Visual Storytelling is the art of the stringing together individual images that, when viewed in succession, create a greater whole. Whether in a static medium like a comic book or in motion like an animation, each image builds on the last, continuously divulging information to the viewer.

This chapter will introduce the fine art of visual storytelling focusing on the concept development, script writing, and preproduction of a film—serving as a how-to, and how-not-to, guide for student filmmakers. The goal is to make the appropriate decisions up front that will translate into a solid foundation for amazing cinematography down the road.

VISUAL STORYTELLING

VISUAL STORYTELLING

Storytelling is as old as the human race. For thousands of years, we have used the art of storytelling to enlighten, inform, provoke, and entertain. Although storytelling has evolved along with our language, communication, and technology, the basic premise remains intact. Whether it is an old wives' tale passed down from generation to generation, an ancient cave drawing, or Pixar's next animated feature film, stories communicate ideas while engaging their audience.

visual |2–1|

Storyboards from the film Head Quarters © Jason Donati 1999

Stories can be told orally, textually, or visually. Although there are countless examples of amazing stories delivered in written or spoken form, we undeniably live in a visual society. From TV, the Internet, video games, and films, one can expect to get almost all of their information and entertainment visually. Certainly, there are advantages to telling stories visually, especially with the technological advances that have taken place over the past twenty years. For instance, the computer can now allow the ultimate visual storyteller, a filmmaker, to create hyperrealistic worlds and characters that we could only have dreamed about in years past.

visual |2–2|

Still from the film Head Quarters © Jason Donati 1999

But therein lies the challenge of *visual storytelling*. Can you possibly reach the same visual complexity and creativity that our imagination can achieve when reading novels or listening to the radio?

Peter Jackson, the director behind the 2001–2003 *Lord of the Rings* film trilogy, took that challenge head on. J.R.R. Tolkien's masterpiece had already captured the minds and imaginations of so many. Jackson decided that not only the tools, but also the talent, were available to recreate, visually, Tolkien's world. This triumph in visual storytelling was able to exceed viewer's expectations by recreating a universe so rich and complex that the average imagination could not compete. The end result was a series of films that transcended Tolkien's textual version by allowing the viewer complete immersion into the story. However, and this is a big "however," Peter Jackson had the luxury of starting with something that most student or amateur filmmakers do not: a near-perfect story.

Any seasoned director will tell you that a great film starts with a great story. Although amazing imagery is an important part of visual storytelling, it is just a part of the equation. In fact, if you break down the term "visual storytelling," it is comprised of three words: visual, story, and telling. These three words speak directly to the process of creating successful visual stories, and, in particular, films.

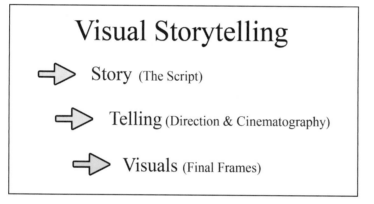

A solid story must be in place before anything else can transpire. The story is the brains of the operation and should dictate all *production* decisions thereafter. Once a story is in place, the visual *preproduction* portion of the visual storytelling equation can begin. This is when a majority of the design decisions are made, including *character design, set design,* and *color palettes.* The final part of the equation is the telling phase. Starting with the *storyboarding* process, the director begins to piece together the *action* of the film.

THE CREATIVE PROCESS

One of the most popular student filmmaker questions surrounding the creative process is, without a doubt, where do stories come from? The truth of the matter is that there is just no simple answer. As with any other art form, it is nearly impossible to nail down where the inspiration comes from or how to generate truly creative ideas on demand. It is a fluid process that usually occurs when the artist is not trying. For instance, Jimi Hendrix did not wake up one morning and decide that he was going to write a song called "Purple Haze." A combination of events inspired Jimi to play a certain note or series of notes in a particular way. This *spark* of creativity is what serves as the genesis of a great song, painting, and story. To try to manufacture this spark often creates works that seem forced or unfinished.

The harsh reality for students is that they typically have to generate creative ideas within a twelve- to fifteen-week semester system. In their later semesters, students have to produce a complete film. Up until then, the student has been doing small projects focusing mostly on technique. However, now the student is challenged to create a complete work, the purpose of which is not only to demonstrate all of the theory and techniques they have acquired along the way but to do so via a story. The story is the ultimate goal and the techniques exist to serve that goal. It becomes very easy for a student filmmaker to become enamored with a particular software feature or skill they have acquired and lose sight of the big picture; the film.

The Spark: Idea Generation, Inspiration, and Research

So where should you start? The answer is easy; you need the spark. You must find that initial moment of pure creativity that will inspire you to take that project to completion. In many ways, it is similar to falling in love. It is that initial burst of energy that makes you want to pursue the other person and spend as much time with them as possible to develop a relationship. In filmmaking, the relationship is between you and your film.

As I am sure you know by now, that spark does not often come easy. The first essential ingredient in creating that spark is time. I cannot reiterate this enough; creativity is a natural process that should not be forced. Therefore, you need to give yourself enough time for the spark to happen. In fact, if you are only starting to think about your film, and, more important, the story of the film, when you get to the first week of your studio class, you are already behind schedule. I encourage my students to start thinking about their film four or five semesters before their studio class.

The next important ingredients for *spark-generation* are inspiration and research. If you have allowed yourself enough time, this should be a welcome and eye-opening experience. The goal of this exercise is twofold. First, you should inundate yourself visually with as many student films as you can possibly watch. Second, you should analyze that visual data and decide what you liked and what you did not like, and why.

Phase one is to figure out how you can see other student's work. (Hint, hint. . . the Internet.) Do some research and figure out what the top fifty animation schools are in the world. This is a valuable exercise. I am constantly surprised to find out how many students do not know this information. The reality is that the students that are graduating from these schools, and, more specifically, the films that they are producing, are your competition.

Insider Info

Pixar's Web site (*http://www.pixar.com*) lists, what they consider to be, the top animation schools. In fact, at the time of publication, they have links to the schools' Web sites as well. This is an amazing resource. Also, check out the Animation World Network's Web site (*http://www.awn.com*) for a comprehensive list of all schools that have an animation program. If it is not on this list, it probably does not exist.

Once you figure out which schools are considered the best, visit their Web sites and navigate to the animation program's homepage. Ninety-nine out of one hundred schools will have some variation of a student gallery or links to individual student Web sites. Typically, the gallery will host the better work, but you may have to do some more digging to get that information. Look for a news section that might list recent student works that have won awards or that have been shown in festivals. Watch as many as you can. Take notes or bookmark the ones that you like and the ones that you do not like. Do not bother to analyze them too deeply at this point; just soak them in.

Here is a quick list of the schools, in no particular order, that you absolutely should investigate:

- Ringling School of Art and Design
- Sherridan College
- Vancouver Film School
- The New England Institute of Art (The Art Institutes)
- Rochester Institute of Technology
- School of Visual Arts
- Design Center
- California School of the Arts
- Pratt
- Savannah College of Art and Design (SCAD)

Phase two of this process is to step back and revisit the films that you thought were noteworthy. Spend some time analyzing those films that you thought worked well and some you thought did not. Try to notice the high-level patterns in these films. What do you notice about their overall length? How many characters did the films have? Did the stories try to accomplish too much or too little with the allotted time frame? Was the story confusing? If you take the time to go through this process, I am confident that you will come out feeling energized and more knowledgeable about the art of student filmmaking.

I cannot point to a surefire formula that will guarantee that spark of creative genius. By understanding what other films are out there, however, and by analyzing the common components that make up great stories, you can put yourself in a position to succeed. I am confident that you will come to the same conclusions that I did when I was in your shoes—the most memorable films were those that had a great story, not necessarily the ones that were the most technically sophisticated. In fact, you may have noticed that the story will override the visuals to a certain degree. Most people will conclude that an animation with an outstanding story and average visuals is better than the one with amazing visuals but no story. However, the pièces de résistance are the student films that are able to accomplish both at the same time. These films will garner the attention of film festivals and employers alike.

Setting Parameters without Hindering the Creative Process

Now that you have done your preliminary research, you probably have a bunch of story ideas that are bouncing around your head. These ideas are the raw chemicals that, if mixed correctly, can produce the spark. However, these chemicals, if mixed incorrectly, can produce nothing but smoke and fumes.

During this *brainstorming* phase, it is critical that you are able to balance creativity with reality. Although creating your student film will be one of the most autonomous creative endeavors you'll encounter in your career, it also will be one of the most restricting. This will be an amazing opportunity for you to control every aspect of the production, flexing every creative muscle in your filmmaking body. However, you will be the only one working on this film within a time frame that would make most seasoned veterans cry. Therefore, you must be able to be creative within the student filmmaking parameters. Without a doubt, this is downfall of most student films.

There are two major parameters that all students need to consider when developing the story for their film: *running time* and *characters*. If you are able to work within these parameters, your film will be a success.

Two Minutes and Two Characters

The time parameter refers to two things in the filmmaking process; the time that you have to produce the film and the total running time of the film that you wish to create.

The amount of time that you have to produce the film plus the number of people working on your film minus the desired quality you wish to achieve will equal the total running time of your film. Although MIT won't be banging down my door to present *The Donati Theorem* any time soon, it certainly tells volumes about the limitations of the process.

The Student Filmmaker Equation
(The Donati Theorem)

$$(T + P) - Q = R$$

T = Time to Produce the Film (Typically One Semester)
P = People Working on the Film (Usually Just One - YOU)
Q = Quality of the Film You Wish to Produce
R = Running Time of the Final Film

visual |2–4|

The Student Filmmaker
Equation – The Donati
Theorem

The amount of time and the number of people who are creating this film should be fixed at this point. Chances are that you, and you alone, will have about fifteen weeks or about three and a half months to produce the film. That may seem like a lot of time if you have never gone through this process before, but trust me, it is not. Start thinking about it in terms of the types of tasks that you need to accomplish. For instance, it took three years and 100–150 animators at Pixar to create *Toy Story*. With some rough math, you could extrapolate that it would have taken one person about three hundred–plus years to produce the same movie. I realize that I am being overly dramatic about this, but this is important information that does not often get communicated to students until it is too late in the process.

This information is not intended to intimidate but to empower. By framing your story ideas with these parameters in mind, you will save yourself headache and heartache down the road. Given that your time frame—a semester, for example—and manpower are fixed, you are left with the running time and quality as variables. Therefore, you can make some simple conclusions about the filmmaking process. The longer and more involved your story is, the more likely that the quality of the visuals will suffer. If your film is more compact, it will allow the quality of the visuals to increase.

Another variable in the running time is the overall complexity of your film. Certainly, it would be possible to have a long film in which absolutely nothing happens. However, I am going to assume that longer films are that way for a reason, and therefore that they are more complex. The major reason for complexity in student films is the number of characters they choose to include. Although I applaud their creativity and epic filmmaking visions, there is simply no time in student films for characters that do not push the story forward. There simply is not a lot of room for supporting roles and extras in the world of student filmmaking. Think about the time in effort you would have to put into designing, building, rigging, and animating a character, and if they are not going to really help to tell the story, then that time is lost. My rule of thumb

Insider Info

To see a perfect example of the Two-Minute/Two-Character principle in action, check out Christopher Cordingly's animation, *After You*. This amazing work was created during his senior year at The Ringling School of Art & Design. He still has a link to this movie from his student site, which can be found at Ringling's Web site, or via a Google search. To further illustrate the effectiveness of his film, it helped to him land a job after graduation as animator at Rhythm & Hues Studios out in Los Angles.

has been, and will always be, two minutes and two characters. If you go back to the research that you did of the most successful student films, I am sure that you will notice that most of them fit into that category.

I cannot reiterate this enough: It is better to take on something simple and compact and make it beautiful rather than to create a mediocre-looking epic.

STORY STRUCTURE

Once you have generated that initial spark, it is important to understand how to grow that into a complete story for your film. Although it is impossible to give a specific formula for coming up with the initial idea, a recipe for effective storytelling has been around for thousands of years.

Aristotle, the ancient Greek philosopher and author, is considered to be the mastermind behind the formula for storytelling, the *dramatic structure*. His analysis, which dates back to 300 BC, is the foundation for all storytelling mediums. Certainly, Aristotle had no idea what a computer was, let alone digital cinematography. However, his theories, which were focused on literature, poetry, and theater at the time, have proven to be extremely useful even within modern storytelling mediums such as film and television. His understanding of the human mind and its ability to process information led him to the conclusion that all *drama* (a Greek word for action) should be broken up into three distinct parts: a beginning, a middle, and an end.

These parts, also known as the *Three-Act Structure*, provide an invaluable road map for all storytellers. It serves as a framework for how and when the story information should flow through to the viewer. This is especially important for student filmmakers who are typically going through this process for the first time.

To help put the three-act structure into visual terms, try to relate it to a vicious dog. What the heck does a dog have to do with storytelling, you ask? Let me explain. The beginning can be thought of as the bite or the teeth of the story. It is the initial burst of drama that captures that viewer's attention, which is what the sharp teeth of a vicious dog's teeth would do. The middle can be considered the body of the story, where the majority of the story development and action takes place and is typically the longest of the acts. Last but not least, you can think of the end of the story as the tail. This is where the story builds to a climax and is resolved.

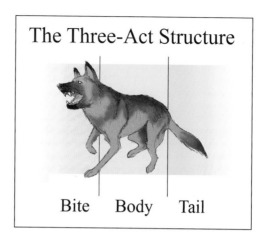

visual |2-5|

The Three-Act Structure as a Dog

Beginning – Act I

Act I, or the beginning of the story, is considered the *bite,* in which the basic information about the characters, settings, time frames, and, most important, the conflict is set up for the viewer. Keep in mind that stories are about *character development* and *conflicts.* Let's face it, if the viewer does not care about the characters, or if nothing happens to them, then there will be very little interest in the film. Therefore, the beginning serves as the introduction or handshake between the characters and the audience. The hope is to form a bond between the good guys or *protagonists* and a level of distaste for the bad guys or *antagonists.* This is achieved in many ways, including through their actions, *dialogue,* and appearance.

Act I should also introduce the conflict, which can be emotional, physical, or both. The conflict should be a single *inciting incident,* which will be the major source of motivation for the main character during the remainder of the story. Without conflict, there is no reason for telling the story and therefore no reason to for the viewer to watch. The beginning should leave the audience pondering questions such as, How is the main character going to react? What will the villain do? How will this get resolved?

The Three-Act Structure

Act I
(AKA the Beginning or Bite)

⇨ Basic Information About the Characters, Settings, Timeframes, etc. is Revealed

⇨ A Bond is Formed Between the Audience and the Protagonist

⇨ The Main Conflict is Introduced

visual |2-6|

Act I Components

Middle – Act II

Act II, or the middle portion, should be the *body* of your story. This is where the main character has decided that certain actions must be taken in order to reach their goal. Typically, the main character encounters many obstacles along the way to solve the conflict. These complications are often referred to as the *rising action* because the overall tension and drama is increased. The rising action culminates with a major turning point in the story—something occurs to alter the direction or focus of the main character. Whether it is a specific event, new piece of information, or an unexpected villain, this turning point often leads the main character to believe that the original goal is now impossible to achieve.

The Three-Act Structure

Act II
(AKA the Middle or Body)

⇨ The Main Character Decides that Actions Must be Taken to Reach Their Goal

⇨ Many Obstacles are Encountered (Rising Action) Along the Way

⇨ A Major Turning Point in the Story

End – Act III

Act III, or the ending, should serve as the *climax* and *resolution* to your story. This is typically the most powerful portion of the film in which the inevitable battle between good versus evil, or the protagonist versus antagonist, takes place. Everything in the film has built up to this moment as the main character puts everything on the line to achieve the goal. For better or for worse, a resolution occurs in which the audience discovers whether the main character will win or lose. Often a resolution can conclude one story but open the door to further questions or conflicts; this happens quite a bit with mystery and horror films.

The Three-Act Structure

Act III
(AKA the End or Tail)

⇨ The Climax and Resolution to the Story

⇨ The Most Powerful Portion of the Film in which the Inevitable Battle Between Good vs. Evil Unfolds

⇨ Win or Lose, there is a Sense of Closure

The Three Sentence Test

When teaching scriptwriting and storyboarding to animation students, I ask them to break down their stories into three sentences. Typically, this is not an assignment but something that I have them do on the spot. It forces them to think about the story in three distinct parts: the beginning, the middle, and the end. This test helps to identify quickly the portions of their story that are strong and those that need some work.

CHARACTER DEVELOPMENT

Building on Aristotle's Three-Act Structure, Joseph Campbell wrote *The Hero with a Thousand Faces* in 1949. A noteworthy author and mythologist, Campbell theorized that the most treasured stories throughout history, in every culture across the globe, all followed the same basic model. Although he still adhered to the Three-Act format, his book identified the common *character archetypes* and stages that he coined "The Hero's Journey."

1. Hero
2. Mentor
3. Threshold Guardian
4. Herald
5. Shapeshifter
6. Shadow
7. Trickster

The Hero's Journey

Forty years later, Christopher Vogler, a film producer, screenwriter, and Disney story analyst, would pen the famous seven-page memo that would further refine the concept of Hero's Journey. His memo to a Hollywood Studio, would serve as the impetus to translate Campbell's work into modern-day terms by applying them to filmmaking. The end result was a book, *The Writer's Journey: Mythic Structure for Writers,* that outlined twelve distinct steps.

ACT I – Beginning - Bite

1. Ordinary World
2. Call to Adventure
3. Refusal of the Call
4. Meeting with the Mentor
5. Crossing the First Threshold

ACT II – Middle - Body

6. Test, Allies & Enemies

7. Approach to the Inmost Cave

8. Ordeal

9. Reward

ACT III – End - Tail

10. The Road Back

11. Resurrection

12. Return with the Elixir

Some of the most popular films of the last thirty years have followed this model almost to the letter, including *Star Wars, The Lion King, Lord of the Rings,* and *The Matrix.* Although a two-minute student film will not be able to accomplish all of these stages, by understanding them and following the basic blueprint the student can create a stronger story and film.

Common Character Archetypes

In order to fully understand The Hero's Journey, you must be able to recognize the different character archetypes that are involved. It is important to note that an archetype is more of a function within the story rather than a personality type, as it only concerns itself with its relationship to the story and, in particular, with the Hero. Furthermore, a particular character can have multiple archetypes within the same storyline. Depending on who they are interacting with, a character could be a shadow to one character and a mentor to another. Below are brief descriptions of the most common archetypes as defined by Vogler.

Hero

The hero, or protagonist, is the principal character who must sacrifice, willingly or not, a great deal in order to resolve a conflict. Through adventures, encounters, and realizations while attempting to fix the problem, the hero should experience significant change by the end of the story. Therefore, the hero should get the majority of the screen time as the plot revolves around their journey. The audience should relate most with the hero because of their appearance, actions, and dialogue, and is perceived as the good guy.

Mentor

The mentor, often portrayed as a friend or relative, is the purveyor of wisdom, information, and guidance for the hero. This information, which can come in many different forms, typically is critical to the hero's ability to achieve his/her goal in the story.

Threshold Guardian

The threshold guardian's main purpose within the story is to stop the hero from reaching his goal. The hero is typically confronted by the threshold guardian before he leaves his home base or the ordinary world, and presents the first test that the hero must overcome on the journey.

Herald

The herald's purpose is to make announcements to the hero with regard to an important event or encounter. This information typically is regarded as the call to adventure and prompts the hero to make the journey. The herald may appear as either a friend or a foe.

Shapeshifter

A shapeshifter is a character that the hero encounters who may change shape as the story unfolds. The change might affect their appearance, personality, or alliance, and should not be trusted.

Shadow

The shadow is typically the villain, or antagonist, whose main purpose is to defeat the hero or thwart their ability to reach the goal. A final confrontation between the hero and the shadow will typically happen toward the end of the story. This confrontation, for better or worse, will determine the success of the hero's journey.

Trickster

The trickster understands how to use the strengths and weakness of other characters against them. The trickster typically is deceptive in nature and can be either an enemy or ally to the hero. In fact, the hero himself often can play the role of the trickster.

The Twelve Stages of The Hero's Journey

Christopher Vogler outlined these twelve distinct stages that the hero must pass through on the way to achieving their ultimate goal. Again, it is important to note that this format is geared toward the two-hour feature-length film and not to the two-minute student short. Therefore, it would be impossible to effectively cram all of these stages and characters into your animation. However, it is critical that you understand all of them and pick and chose the ones that you think would work best in your film.

Ordinary World

The journey starts off showing the hero living within the ordinary world. This typically is where the hero lives or spends most of his time. The purpose is to give the audience a sense of the hero's normal or everyday life, how he spends his time, and some clues to his personality. You can think of the journey as building a house. The ordinary world is similar to laying the concrete foundation of the film on which everything else is built. However, there should be an overriding sense from the hero that there is something missing or wrong lurking beneath the surface of his otherwise happy existence.

Call to Adventure

The call to adventure occurs when the hero is presented with a concrete challenge or crisis that had been alluded to in the previous stage of the journey. The hero realizes that he must move outside the comfort zone of his ordinary world to fix the problem. The call to adventure is usually presented to the hero via the herald, but it may be presented by anyone in the cast.

Refusal of the Call

The hero, after thinking about the challenges that lie ahead, is unsure of his abilities and refuses to proceed with the journey. The refusal may simply be internal dialogue or may be expressed to many people. However, the refusal leads to a sense of hopelessness, despair, and defeat.

Meeting with the Mentor

The hero has a meeting with the mentor, typically an older and wiser individual, who relays critical information, guidance, instruction, gifts, or powers. This meeting empowers the hero with the tools—physical, emotional, or both—to accept the challenge.

Crossing the First Threshold

With a new sense of hope and strength, the hero crosses the threshold from the ordinary world into the special world. Outside his comfort zone, the hero encounters the threshold guardian or guardians who try to immediately impede his progress and stop the journey all together. Typically, the hero will use some of the knowledge or power that was given by the mentor to overcome the threshold guardians.

Test, Allies & Enemies

The hero discovers the extent of the special world though his encounters with allies and enemies. The hero will be challenged and confronted by various characters that will test his abilities and knowledge along the way. However, the setback will only be temporary as he also will gain further valuable information or powers through various allies that will allow the journey to continue.

Approach to the Inmost Cave

After passing all of the tests along the way, the hero makes preparations to enter the inmost cave. This is the location in which the goal, problem, or conflict will be faced head-on. This is usually an extremely difficult and dangerous place to navigate, for example, the enemies' castle. The tension of the film should be at an all-time high as the hero and audience realize that a confrontation is inevitable.

Ordeal

The hero enters the inmost cave and faces his ultimate fear/enemy face to face. Typically, the hero is engaged in a fierce battle with the shadow, or antagonist character. Although the hero eventually overtakes his enemy, there often is a moment in which he is losing the battle, facing death and defeat.

Reward

Utilizing all of the knowledge and skills acquired during the journey, the hero is now able to defeat the antagonist and reap the rewards. This reward will solve the hero's problem or dilemma that initiated the journey and restore order to his life.

The Road Back

The hero, with reward in hand, is able to return to his ordinary world. However, he must travel back through the treacherous special world in which he came. More than likely, the hero will again face obstacles and tests along the way as additional antagonists may be in pursuit.

Resurrection

The journey's experiences, for better or for worse, have forever changed the hero. These changes can be physical, emotional, or both. Again, stories are about character development and change; this is the realization of that change for the hero and the audience.

Return with the Elixir

The hero crosses back over the threshold into the ordinary world. With the reward in hand, the hero is able to restore order and confidence to the people. All is well with the world.

UNDERSTANDING DIFFERENT POINTS OF VIEW

The old adage, that there are two sides to every story, is inaccurate from a filmmaking perspective. There actually are three sides or three points of view from which your can tell a story.

Point of view, or *POV,* is the vantage point from which a story is told. Every film has to consider from which perspective everything will be seen. For instance, think about a bank robbery. Depending on the point of view of the story, the film should be shot in very different manners, for example, what information about the situation is given to the viewer, the camera angles, and the pacing. The same bank robbery would be told very differently depending on if it was from the robber's, bank teller's, customer's, or security camera's perspective.

Objective POV

The *objective* point of view tells the story without any inference or bias. Similar to the security camera in the bank robbery example, the objective POV presents only the actions and dialogue as it is dictated by the film and nothing else.

Third-Person POV

A story with a *third-person* POV relies on a narrator who is not only able to witness all of the action and dialogue but also is able to communicate to the audience the thoughts and feelings of all the characters. This POV goes a step beyond the objective viewpoint and adds depth and insight without actively participating in the story.

First-Person POV

The *first person* POV builds on the third person viewpoint. In this case, the narrator is an active participant in the story; therefore, their opinions and perspective may be skewed toward the motivation of the character and should not always be trusted.

Expanding On the Concept

Once you feel comfortable with your story *concept,* it is time to develop it into a *script.* Chances are that your premise exists only in narrative form at this point. Although this is helpful for you to explain your story in general terms or to work out some of the major themes, it does not provide all of the necessary information needed to proceed into preproduction of the film.

Story Concept – 3-Headed Monster ??? *Need Title*

Time of day?

The Early Concept for an Animated Film

Bite
(Act I)

The animation starts with shots of the two different characters/species. The human-like character lives in a built hut made from trees and mud, and he is cooking a meager dinner from a small rabbit on an open fire. The cat-like character, which lives in a small cave, has hunted and killed a small creature, and is eating it raw. Around the same time, an earth-shaking noise startles them as they are eating. They both quickly emerge from their shelters and the look towards the mountain tops. While ~~are~~ obviously in very different locations/landscapes, they both are seeing large billows of smoke emitting from the same mountain peak. Both are intrigued since neither has been to the top of the mountains. There are quick shots of both as they ascend the mountain. When they reach the top, they see fire and smoke starting to spread across the vast mountaintop. Then the two species spot each other, thinking that the other has started this fire. They begin to battle each other, when from the treetops, a 3-headed monster comes crashing down, fire emitting from its mouth. The two species find cover together, and quickly realize they must work together to survive. With a brief nod from each, the two species dart at the beast and engage in a fierce battle, to which they eventually take down the beast. After the battle, the fires subside, and for the first time, they examine this newfound land on the mountain tops. Admiring its beauty, and realizing that this land is far superior then from which they came, they look at each other and decide to share it ~~with each other.~~ Although not friends, a mutual understanding is established. The last shot is the same as the first, but on the new land. The human character is cooking an elk, ~~or some bigger animal,~~ and is living in a significantly larger house made from stronger trees. The cat-like character is still living in a large cave and is cooking a much larger kill over an open fire.

Body
(Act II)

Too Quick?

Tail
(Act III)

How to show this with visuals?

For instance, this premise explains that the hero of the story, after seeing a distant plume of smoke, decides to climb to the top of the mountain to inspect its cause. Although it tells the viewer, in general terms, what is happening in the story, it does not provide any specific information for those that are actually creating the film. What does the smoke look like? What does the character look like? Is that character frantic and running up the mountain? What time of day is it? How far is the mountain? What type of camera shots should be used? Therefore, it is important to expand this narrative into a format that will provide the amount of detail needed to start production.

Story Beats

The first step in transforming the premise into a script is to develop the *story beats*. These are the individual actions that must occur in order for the story to be told. Think of these as the basic building blocks for each scene. The story beats should be quick bullet point sentences that get quickly to the heart of the action. Therefore, the premise sentence "the hero, after seeing a distant plume of smoke, decides to climb to the top of the mountain to inspect its cause," would be transformed into the following story beats:

- The hero, huddled within his crude shelter, lifts his head quickly.
- The hero emerges from the shelter looking in all directions.
- Scanning the horizon, the hero notices a giant plume of smoke rising from the top of the tallest mountain to the north.
- The hero rushes into his shelter and grabs a weapon.
- The hero walks quickly away from his shelter.
- The hero leaves the open area of forest and into the deep brush toward the mountain.

Creating the story beats is beneficial for two reasons. First, it will give you the opportunity to analyze your story in its most basic of forms. Each beat should represent a specific action or event that helps to push the story forward. If the beat does nothing to help the story along, it is probably not worth the time and effort to put it in. For instance, if the story beat, "The hero saw a large bird in the air and stopped to hear it sing," was added, it should have a very specific reason for being in there. Although it might be a very cool-looking bird whose song is beautiful, if it does not help the story it should be removed. By contrast, if the bird ended up showing him the way to the top of the mountain, it certainly would be a justified story beat.

Second, creating story beats will help you translate your narrative story into a visual story. Therefore, your story beats should start to represent the individual scenes and shots of your film.

Outline

The next step of the process is to expand on each story beat by creating an *outline*. The outline will use the prose style of the concept/premise but with all of the story beats. The purpose is to create detailed descriptions for everything that appears in each scene, including characters, actions, and sets.

THE SCRIPTING PROCESS

The last stage in finalizing your story is to create the script. Building on the concept, story beats, and outline, the script has a very particular format that includes slug lines, visual descriptions, and dialogue. This format will add another layer of detail, including the dialogue for the actors/characters and specific instructions about sound, lighting, and camera work, in turn, allowing it to be used by everyone involved in the filmmaking process. It is also important to note that a script is typically written in both the third person and in the present tense.

ACT I

EXT. BARREN GRASSY LANDSCAPE – DAWN
ESTABLIGHING shot of vast grassy landscape. A flickering light from a fire is seen emitting from a small man-made structure located under a lone tree in the distance.

INT. MUD HUT - CONT.
CU-A small rabbit-like creature being cooked on an open flame. <CRACKLE, HISS, POP>

PAN UP TO REVEAL HUMAN – A large human creature with Neanderthal features is squatting over the fire poking the rabbit with a stick. An orange/red light from the sunrise begins to illuminate the inside of the crude mud hut.

HUMAN
< Frustrated sigh >

CU - Humans face - It is obvious that the meat from the rabbit will do little to curb the human's appetite. He continues to poke the rabbit which is starting to char.

EXT. BARREN WOODY LANDSCAPE – DAWN
REESTABLIGHING shot of vast woody landscape. A dark cave opening is seen protruding from the side of a steep hill.

CU-A large deer-like creature is lying lifeless at the edge of the cave.

PAN UP TO REVEAL CAT – A Cat-like creature is squatting over the fresh kill. An orange/red light from the sunrise begins to illuminate the inside of the cave.

MS - The Cat begins to tear into the carcass shredding it into bite-size pieces. The cat eats the raw flesh reluctantly.

CAT
< Frustrated sigh>

ECU CAT'S EYES – <BANG!> A huge earth shaking sound is heard. The Cat's eyes widen as as the sounds reverberates through the mud hut.

INT. MUD HUT – CONT.
QUICK CUT - CU – HUMAN'S HANDS – The human is tearing a piece of the charred rabbit. <BANG>

ECU – HUMAN'S EYES – His eyes quick widen as the same sound is heard but with a much different pitch implying that it is being heard from a different location.

visual |2–10|

Typical Script Format

Slug Lines

A *slug line* is a short descriptive headline that gives the reader the most basic information about the scene. Written in all capital letters, the slug line should convey details about whether the action takes place inside (INT – Interior) or outside (EXT – Exterior), specifics about the location, and the time of day. The following are two examples of a slug line:

- INT. CRUDE TENT-LIKE STRUCTURE - DUSK
- EXT. FORREST - NIGHT

visual |2–11|

Slug Line Example

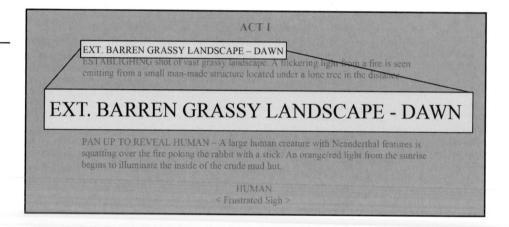

Visual Description

The *visual description* is very similar to prose that was written in the outline; however, it is edited to contain only the information the pertinent to that scene. Again, it should be as detailed as possible describing the characters, their actions, camera direction, lighting, and transitions.

visual |2–12|

Visual Description
Example

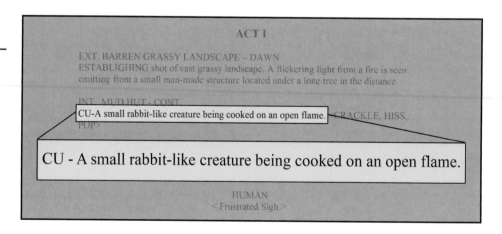

Audio Description

The *audio description* should work hand in hand with the visual descriptions and should be in the same prose format. However, the audio descriptions should include information about all the sounds that will appear in that scene, including ambient sounds, sound effects, musical score, and the character's dialogue. However, it can be tricky to use dialogue effectively, so it should be used sparingly in student animated films.

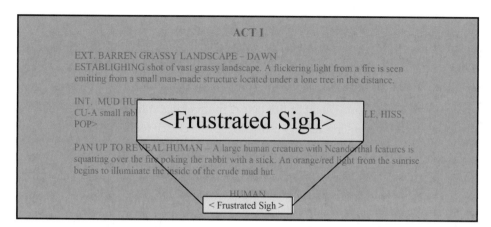

visual |2–13|

Audio Description
Example

COMMON STUDENT MISTAKES

I have been exposed to student films on a consistent basis for the last thirteen years, and some obvious patterns have emerged when it comes to the types of mistakes that are made. In fact, I made most of them myself while producing my first two student films as an animation undergrad. Fortunately, I was able to see the error of my ways and avoid these pitfalls when working on my graduate degree films. However, I'm convinced that these common mistakes can be avoided the first time out if you make a conscious decision to stay clear of the following:

- The Fight Scene
- Too Many Characters and Sets
- Telling versus Showing
- No Reason to be Animation

The Fight Scene

I'm always surprised how many times this particular scenario comes up. I think this is a result of the videogame culture in which we live, but students are drawn to creating really intricate fight scenes. The problem, of course, is that there rarely is a story attached to this fight scene. Therefore, the audience has no attachment to the characters involved and will get bored very quickly.

Too Many Characters and Sets

I think it is natural for a first-time filmmaker to think in terms of epic proportions. Although the enthusiasm and creativity is commended, the time constraints are overwhelming and will leave you with an unfinished film at the end of the semester. I always suggest that a maximum of two characters with two sets be used in a student film. This will allow you the time to create nice-looking models and believable character animation, which, in the long run, it is what you want your film and demo reel to achieve.

Telling versus Showing

Actions speak louder than words. I really cannot state it any better than that. Although dialogue is a critical component to live-action filmmaking, it usually is a downfall for most student films. Students tend to use dialogue as a crutch to accomplish one of two things: either they want to add backstory to the plot or they simply want to have a character say something instead of showing or animating it. For instance, a student might have a character tell another character that they went to store to buy some eggs instead of actually showing the character leaving the house, walking down the block, into the store, and purchasing the eggs. Although it is tempting to try to save time and energy by telling the viewer what is happening instead of showing it, the latter is much more visually compelling. A good rule of thumb is, if it is not important enough to animate the action, it is probably not important enough to be in the film anyway, and should be cut.

No Reason to be Animation

There are many students who develop scripts that could easily be shot with live-action film. Although it is technically impressive for students who are able to mimic reality with animation, there should be a reason for the film to be animated. The beauty of creating animated films is, in my opinion that anything is possible because you are not tied to real-life limitations. For instance, it would be impossible to film a *Road Runner* cartoon in live action. Therefore, I believe that if you can shoot it with live actors, then it probably shouldn't be animated.

ART DIRECTION—THE LOOK 'N' FEEL

With script in hand, it is now time to turn your attention to the *art direction* of your film. You have spent a great deal of time crafting a story that not only follows the rules of visual storytelling but also is achievable within the student filmmaker window of time. However, the film's art direction or *look 'n' feel* probably exists mostly in your head at this point. Although I am sure that you have a general idea of how you want things to appear, it is important to start considering all of the design elements within the film; from high-level decisions such as style and color palate to low-level specifics such as character and set design.

Look 'n' Feel Example of a Character

Style – Realism versus Cartoony

One of the first decisions that you will need to make with regard to the art direction of your film is the overall style. In politics, you have Democrats and Republicans; in animation, you have *realism* and *cartoony*. However, as with politics, the vast majority of filmmakers do not conform to the extremes but lie somewhere in between. Certainly, you will lean toward one side or the other, but you will draw on both to develop your own personal style.

Since the advent of *3D animation*, there have been groups of artists who strive to create *hyperrealistic* work (see Visual 2–2). The software manufacturers have been instrumental in this, as they continue to add features and functionality that help the artists mimic reality from modeling, animation, lighting, and rendering standpoints. Entire animation subgenres have developed around those who push the realistic envelope; paving the way for the wildly successful *special effects* and *visualization* industries.

In contrast, the cartoony style has been around since the beginning of time—well, at least since animation time. Certainly, this style doesn't need much explanation. From Walt Disney to Hayao Miyazaki, the cartoony style has a permanent place in the world of animation filmmaking.

A Cartoony Style

There were thoughts in the early 1990s that the 3D realism movement might kill the cartoony style altogether, but it just did not happen. In fact, the few attempts to make feature films hyperrealistic were a colossal disaster. The 2001 feature film *Final Fantasy: The Spirits Within* lost roughly $120 million and put Square Pictures out of business. Since then, 3D animation studios have figured out the right balance of realism and cartoony. Pixar, for example, leads the way with a unique realistic/cartoony style and sensibility that has become the benchmark for the animated feature film.

A Blended Style

CHARACTER DESIGN

Because stories are all about *character development*, it is extremely important to put serious thought and energy into the *character design*. This will, to all intents and purposes, define the overall style of your film. How you choose to represent the characters will translate into the set design, props, lighting, and colors.

Hero Face Design

Certainly, this is one of the most exciting parts of the film production process and often is seen as intuitive to many artists. In fact, there is a good chance that you have already created many character design sketches before the script was finished. Although this is not necessarily a bad thing, it is important to stick to the major rule of character design; let the form follow the function. It is vitally important that the story dictates how the character looks and acts.

Often, students will work in reverse, creating a story around a particular character design that they think is cool. It is natural for filmmakers, as visual artists, to brainstorm in terms of characters when developing an animation. However, developing the character before the story severely limits the creative process. For instance, the hero character in Visual 2–18 was developed directly from the script, including his weapon, clothing, posture, and cranium size.

Therefore, everything about the character has a reason for existing. His sword, for example, is crudely made of stone. Certainly, there are countless other types of materials or weapons that could have been explored, but this was the one that seemed to fit his situation the best. Knowing what we know about the character form the story, it was reasonable to assume he had the resources to construct this type of weapon. On the contrary, if we developed this character before the story, we might have given him a shiny, precisely cut metal sword. This might look great in the preliminary sketches, but it would seem forced or nonsensical when seen within the context of the animation.

Hero Body Design

Hero Weapon Design

Model Sheets

Once you have created the preliminary sketches, it will make sense to create *model sheets* for all of your characters. A model sheet, quite simply, is a character road map for the production team. It gives vital information about each character including design, proportions, construction, expression, and posture. This is a great opportunity to work out the kinks of your characters before you get into the timely production process. For instance, a simple thing such as the hero's proportions as compared to the villain's might turn out to be a big deal down the road. In this particular case, the script calls for the hero to deliver a deathly blow to the head of the villain at the end of Act II. However, it is critical to make sure that the hero actually can reach the head of the large villain with his sword. By creating model sheets of the two characters, you will be able to tell right away if this can be done and make adjustments accordingly.

Model Sheet for Hero
Character

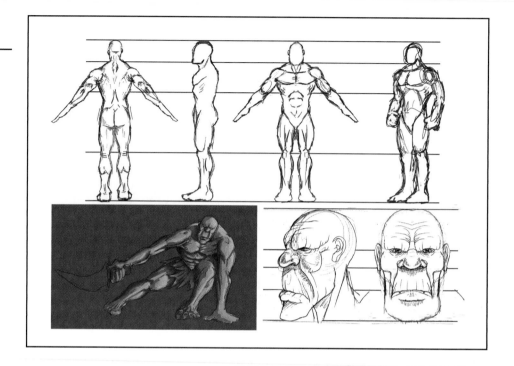

Set and Location Design

| NOTE |

A quick and easy search tool is available on the Yahoo!® homepage. Instead of searching under the default Web category, located directly above the empty search field, switch over to the images option. A quick images search for Stonehenge came up with over sixty-four thousand images. This should be more than enough imagery for reference and inspiration.

As with character design, the set and location design should follow the same basic principle—that is, form follows function. When developing the look 'n' feel for the sets and locations for your film, it helps to do some research. The Internet has made design research, and research in general, a much easier process. My first suggestion is to gather some inspirational imagery of places that are similar or that have similar elements to ones you envision for your film. For instance, Stonehenge was a big inspiration for the rock formation that the villain occupied on the top of the mountain.

visual |2–21|

Set Design Concept Sketch

Typically, the final sets and locations end up being a conglomeration of a bunch of different elements I find during the research process. Although I might use Stonehenge or other ancient formations as models to develop the look of the rocks, I might choose to draw from a completely different environment when developing the landscapes. In this particular case, the environment was based on imagery from Scotland. Although it is not that different from the British countryside where Stonehenge can be found, the Scottish terrain is more dramatic, with rolling hills and cliffs.

visual |2–22|

Set Design Color Concept

Also, it is important to note that the imagery that you gather during the research is not only fantastic for the high-level development but is a great resource for the tiny details that might otherwise go unnoticed. In this particular case, the Stonehenge imagery revealed a particular type of moss that seems to grow only on these ancient rocks in this particular climate. Including intricate details helps to enhance the overall believability of the sets and locations, even though they do not exist as such in the real world.

visual |2–23|

Set Design - Dwelling Concept

STORYBOARDING BASICS

Storyboarding was developed by *storymen* at the Walt Disney studios in the early 1930s. The storymen, who were responsible for the early Disney shorts and feature films, realized that they could save both time and energy if they drew out the key frames from the film to see if it worked visually. Storyboards can be as elaborate as full-color works of art or as simple as line drawings, but the purpose remains the same—to give the director and cinematographer a chance to make changes and edits to the story, script, camera angles, lighting, and sets, before the costly animation production process began.

visual |2–24|

Storyboard Example

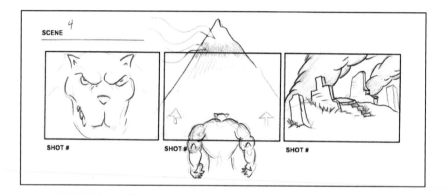

For instance, it is very easy to experiment with many different camera angles for a particular shot in your film while in the storyboarding phase. However, if you go straight to production, you might have to shoot it, watch it, and then reshoot the shot correctly. This could add time or expense on to your production, which easily could have been avoided with storyboards. However, storyboards also are used after the preproduction stage; serving as a valuable road map for everyone involved in the filmmaking process.

Used solely for animation production in the 1930s, the Hollywood studios caught wind of the effectiveness of storyboarding and started using them for live-action films in the 1940s. Today, storyboarding is used in almost every visual medium, including film, game, and Web design. In fact, the storyboarding process is now such an integral part of the production process that studios have hired specific storyboard artists, whose main responsibility is to translate the script into visuals.

visual |2–25|

Storyboard Example

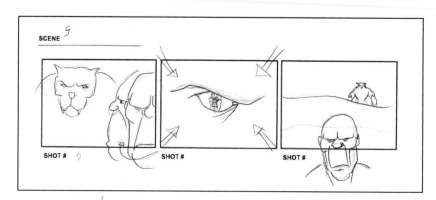

STORYBOARD CONTENT

Whether you are in a high-end studio or producing your own student film, the content within a storyboard should be quite similar. Simply put, your storyboards should include visual and textual information. Both types are needed in order to cover all of the different aspects of the filmmaking process, including not only what is happening in front of the camera but behind the scenes as well.

Visual Information

The *visual information* is, not surprisingly, the heart and soul of the storyboard. The main function of the visual information is to represent in as best a way as possible what will appear in front of the camera or what a final frame of the film will look like.

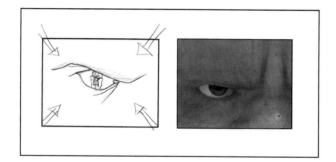

visual |2–26|

Example of Storyboard and Final Frame

As mentioned earlier, this information will help the director and the cinematographer to make easy, cost-effective decisions up front about the look of the shots before production begins. However, there are other types of visual information that should be included in your storyboards. For instance, there often are overhead schematic views of the shot to help relay information about the overall layout of the scene. Typically, it will include important information that is not seen by the camera in a particular shot but will have an effect on that shot or in a future shot. Some examples might include a *lighting setup*, a *camera rig,* or a movement within a *shot* or a character or object that is *off-screen* but will soon make an appearance of some sort.

A classic scenario in which an overhead schematic within the storyboard would be helpful is a scene where a car accident occurs. The main shot may be from an unsuspecting driver's point of view, which may seem uneventful at first, but a car is about to come out from a side street and cause a crash. The *overhead schematic* will clue the director in as to the location of the second car, which is not within the camera's view, and the point at which it will appear in the scene.

Overhead Schematic of
Battle Scene

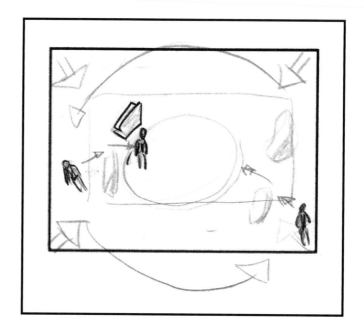

Textual Information

Textual information on a storyboard is as important to the director and crew as the visual information. It typically has a description of the action that is taking place in the scene. This will help to put the particular board into some sort of context within the story. Because it would not be prudent to create a storyboard for each little action and event, inevitably there will be some details that will need to be explained via text. Certainly, a great portion of the textual description will come directly from the script, including scene description and the dialogue. However, there are other items that you will want to include, such as the title of the film, the scene name, shot number, and audio and SFX information.

STORYBOARDING PROCESS

Storyboarding, much like any other part of the filmmaking process, is an art form. In fact, the larger studios and production houses hire storyboard artists who do nothing but storyboard. However, small to medium-sized studios often have the animators and CG artists create their own storyboards for whichever scene/shot they happen to be working on. Therefore, it is critical that, as a student filmmaker, you understand the proper process and techniques. Typically, storyboards are created using a three-step process, which will allow for maximum development and editing opportunities: thumbs, roughs, and finals. The process is similar to sculpting with clay, in that you start out with the rough shapes and work them up into the final piece.

Thumbs

The first step in the storyboarding phase is to create the *thumbs*, or *thumbnail sketches*, of all of your shots. A thumb is a very quick, ten-second drawing of the shot. The idea behind the thumbnail sketch is to communicate the most basic composition and layout for the frame. It should feel more like a brainstorming session than a drawing exercise.

The goal is to be able to quickly draw the entire storyboard so that you can get a basic feel for the flow of the film. It should become apparent if there are some gaping holes in telling the story or that some portions are too long or too short. Because thumbs take so little time to draw, you can easily create multiple versions of the same shot or series of shots to compare and contrast their effectiveness. If you are spending a lot of time on your thumbs, you are missing the point of the exercise. To revisit the clay sculpting analogy, this is where you are working with chucks of clay trying to create the basic size and shape of your piece without being concerned with details.

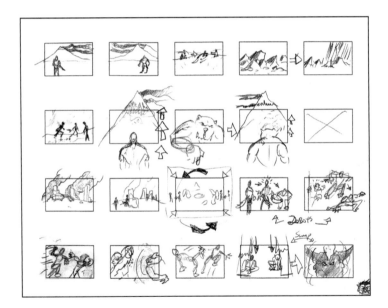

visual |2–28|

Thumbnail Sketches

Insider Info

One of the most popular questions asked by student filmmakers with regard to storyboarding is always about how many storyboards they should draw for each shot/scene. The most truthful, yet astonishingly unhelpful, answer to that question is, as many as it takes. However, the best place to start is with the story beats that you created during the scriptwriting phase. These beats will give you the minimum number of boards that you will have to create. It is important to note, however, that most beats will require more than one board to communicate the concept. It always helps to show the boards to someone that hasn't seen or heard about it before. If it makes sense to them, then you are on the right track.

Roughs

Once you are satisfied with the thumbs and the overall flow of your boards, it is time to start to work out the details of each shot. The *roughs* stage of storyboarding process is where you translate the small thumbnail sketches into larger, more detailed, frames that are closer or identical to the final size. Although you want to capture all of the pertinent visual information in the frame, do not be concerned with them looking like finished works of art. The roughs should be created using a pencil so that you may erase or add details on the fly. If done correctly, the roughs should be able to communicate, with enough detail and clarity, the storyline, the action, and the sound. In fact, someone completely unfamiliar with the project should be able to explain the entire film after only seeing the roughs.

visual |2–29|

Roughs

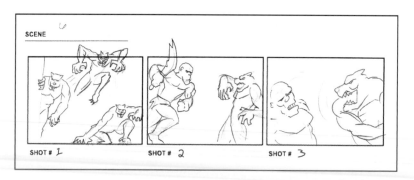

Finals – Ink and Color

After the director reviews the roughs, the artist will put the finishing touches on the storyboards. This final stage of the process involves cleaning up the drawings and adding some of the finer details that may have been overlooked until this point; including light direction, shadow placement, facial expressions, and body language. Typically, the artist will *ink-in*, either traditionally or digitally, the pencil roughs, as well as adding some important color information where necessary. Once complete, these storyboards will serve as the blueprint for the production of the film.

visual |2–30|

Final Storyboard Panel

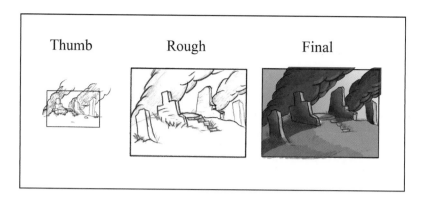

From Thumbs to Finals

STORYBOARD TEMPLATES

Storyboards are designed to communicate the critical visual and textual information of the film to the director and crew. Therefore, most artists will create a *template* for the storyboards in order to keep that important information organized. Although there is no absolute industry standard for the storyboard template, most contain the same basic information. Here is a list of the information that you should include when creating your own template:

- Studio Name
- Film Name
- Sequence Number
- Scene Number
- Shot Number
- Frame Number
- Time Length
- Visual Panel Drawing (Camera's View)
- Visual Schematic Drawing (Top/Side View)
- Textual Visual Description
- Textual Audio Description

Studio _____
Film Title _____
Sequence # _____
Scene # _____
Shot # _____
Frame # _____
Time Length

: :
mins : secs : frames

Visual Description

Audio Description

visual |2–32|

Template Example

SYMBOLS AND ICONS

Storyboards are a static medium trying to communicate a moving art form. Therefore, symbols and icons are often used within the visuals of the storyboards to communicate action or direction for the crew. For instance, arrows are used frequently to represent movement of characters, objects, or cameras within the shot.

Typically, if an arrow appears within the frame, it is implying physical movement of a character or object in the scene. If an arrow appears outside the frame, it is referring to a camera movement.

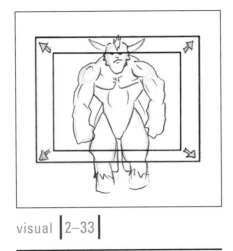

visual |2–33|

Arrows Used for Camera Movement – Zoom Out

visual |2–34|

Arrows used for Character/Object Movement

Symbols and *icons* also are used frequently within schematic views to portray objects that are both seen and unseen by the camera. Remember, the purpose of a schematic view is to give the director and crew some additional information about the shot that cannot necessarily be derived from the camera's view. A classic example is of a camera move within a single shot. An overhead schematic would help the cine-matographer to understand the camera's placement at the beginning and end of the shot. In this case, there are three ions that are used: the camera, the character, and the movement arrow.

visual |2–35|

Common Storyboard Icons

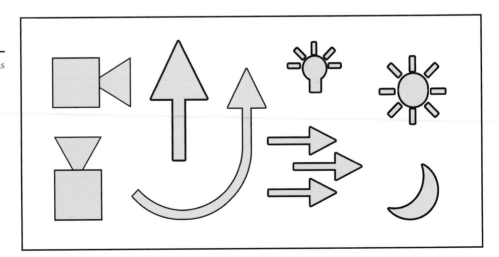

STORY REELS AND ANIMATICS

An *animatic*, also known as a *story reel*, typically is created once the storyboards are complete to get a sense of timing and flow for the animation. An animatic is a movie file that is created by matching the individual storyboard frames along with the film's soundtrack. Although there is technically no movement or animation, the animatic allows the director to see the shots in real time, much as they will appear in the final film. It is also a great resource for the director to see how the shots work on their own and as a whole. It becomes obvious which shots need to be longer, shorter, or cut all together, and because full production has yet to begin, the director can still make easy, cost-effective edits and additions.

SUMMARY

Filmmaking, or visual storytelling, is the art of stringing images together to communicate a story. The story is the center, or sun, of the filmmaking universe around which all of the many aesthetic production decisions, or planets, revolve. Therefore, it is critical that a solid script, which must include a beginning, middle, and end, be created before anything else. In keeping with the form follows function theory, the script will serve as the blueprint for all of the design elements that will be created; including the overall style, characters, sets, props, camera moves, and edits.

Although the preproduction process can seem rather daunting to a student filmmaker, it is designed to save work rather than to add to it. In fact, visualizing your film by creating storyboards and animatics is especially important for student filmmakers because their production timeline is extremely short. Any edits, changes, or additions that can be made to the film before getting into the production process will help to ensure that your time is well spent toward creating an amazing film with outstanding digital cinematography.

in review

1. Explain the concept of Visual Storytelling.

2. What is the spark in terms of idea generation?

3. What is the student-filmmaker equation and how does it relate to concept development?

4. Explain the three-act structure in terms of visual storytelling.

5. Describe the twelve stages of the hero's journey?

6. What is a story beat?

7. Explain the structure of a script.

8. How does form follows function relate to filmmaking preproduction?

9. What are the three stages of the storyboarding process?

10. What types of information should appear on storyboard?

11. Describe the types of symbols and icons that are most often used in storyboarding.

12. What is an animatic and how does it benefit the filmmaking process?

exercises

1. Find three examples of award-winning student films from the list of animation schools within this chapter. What similarities do you notice about these films with regard to:

   a. Overall length of the film

   b. Total number of characters and sets

   c. Story structure

2. Using Disney's *The Lion King* or Pixar's *Finding Nemo:*

   a. Describe the beginning, middle, and end of the story using a total of three sentences (one sentence per part)

   b. Identify and describe all Twelve Stages of the Hero's Journey

   c. Identify the common character archetypes within the film

3. Create two storyboard templates using Photoshop or Illustrator: one landscape and one portrait orientation. Make sure to include areas for all the different types of information needed.

4. Create a model sheet for an original character that is not currently tied with a particular story or script. Make sure to include turnarounds, measurements, action poses, and face details. Without changing the look of the character, revise the model sheet, including the drawing style, actions poses, costumes, and props, to reflect the following changes to the story:

   a. The character is the hero in an Action-Adventure film

   b. The character is the villain in a Horror film

   c. The character is a mentor in a Science Fiction film

5. Find an example of a car commercial, either on television or online, in which there are exterior and interior shots of the car traveling at a high speeds. Using the templates that you created in the third exercise, create storyboards for this commercial as if it has not been produced. However, you must include both the camera's view and an overhead schematic view for each shot. Be as detailed as possible when describing the set/locations and the camera moves.

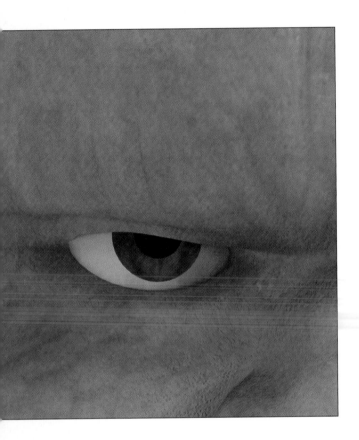

CHAPTER 3

objectives

- Understand the basic components and functionality of the camera
- Explore different camera setups
- Learn about the role of the camera as it applies to filmmaking
- Understand the makeup of a shot, including point of view, angles, and framing
- Explore a variety of camera moves and how they are used most effectively
- Discover the importance of continuity in directing

introduction

The basic building block of all filmmaking is the camera. Although its importance is undeniable in traditional filmmaking, it is arguably the most overlooked aspect in the creation of digital animation. Today's high-end 3D software packages push to provide the digital filmmaker with all of the camera options that a live-action director has, but in animation, the camera is often ignored or misused.

This chapter will give the digital animator an overview of the camera from a traditional filmmaking perspective. It will provide information to help you transform the camera from a passive means-to-an-end object into an active character that can add depth and beauty to your films.

DIRECTING THE CAMERA

OVERVIEW OF THE CAMERA – LIGHT, LENS, AND FILM

A director must master the tools of the craft before reaching creative potential. Of all the tools on a director's tool belt, none is more important than the *camera*. A great director not only uses one, but also understands its inner workings. The goal is the same whether you are a painter with a brush, a sculptor with a chisel, or a director with a camera; master the tools so that they become transparent to your creative process. In other words, a director should be so comfortable with the camera that the quality of the image becomes the most important thing.

Although we are most concerned with the motion picture/film camera for the purposes of understanding digital cinematography and directing, it is critical that we start with the basics of the still camera or *photography*. That is not to say that the process of still and motion photography is identical, they certainly have their own intricacies. However, the core principles of capturing an image, or many sequential images, on film are the same.

Let's start with the word photography itself. It is derived from two Greek words, meaning writing with light. Although photography, and the camera, have undergone some significant technological advances in the last 200-plus years since the invention of the *camera obscura*, the same three basic elements are still required: *light*, a *lens*, and *film*.

visual |3–1|

The Camera Obscura

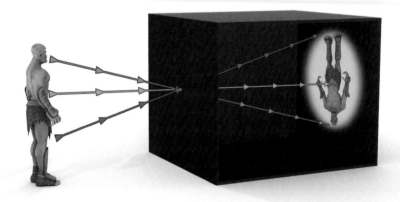

The Camera Obscura

The camera obscura, which is Latin for dark room, is widely known as the predecessor to the modern camera. As early as the fifth century BC, it was understood that light travels in straight lines. Therefore, when light passes through a small opening into a dark room, it forms a reversed image of what is outside the room. By the early seventeenth century, the camera obscura had become a self-contained box with a lens and mirror system that allowed for portability and image correction. The early 1800s would bring a version that incorporated light responsive metals that could capture that image; the birth of film and the modern camera (Leggat).

Whether it is a cheap disposable drugstore camera, a high-end photojournalist's camera, or a motion-picture camera, all cameras utilize light, a lens, and film to capture an image – that is, writing with light. The light, which can be anything from available sunlight to the flash on your camera, passes through a lens within the camera's body. The lens focuses the light onto the film, which exposes the image. Visual 3–2 helps to explain this process.

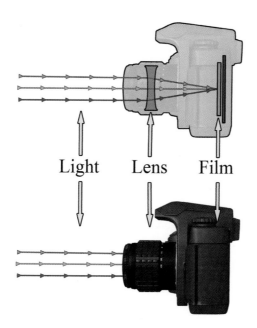

Light   Lens   Film

visual |3–2|

The Basic Camera – Light, Lens and Film

Beyond the light, lens, and film, there are many more components to a modern camera that aid in this basic process. As you will learn in this chapter, there are many options for a director to explore. In fact, understanding these options is what separates the good director from the bad and ultimately defines well-executed digital cinematography.

THE APERATURE

The first of the three basic components to photography is light. We will explore light in much greater detail in Chapters 5, 6, and 7, but it is important to discuss it in general terms now.

The basic equation is quite simple. No light equals no visuals. Light needs to emit from or bounce off an object before the human eye can translate the data to your brain into an image. The same holds true for the camera. Unless there is light that can be focused through the lens and, in turn, exposes the film, there will be no image created.

The amount of light available in the scene that you are attempting to photograph is one of the major factors that will determine the *exposure* and overall quality of the image. Therefore, one of the most important features in a camera is the *aperture*.

| NOTE |

We are not going to spend much time exploring film and the process of exposure. The reality is that film is quickly going the way of the vinyl record and is being replaced by its digital counterpart. However, the principles are exactly the same. Instead of exposing film, digital cameras expose 1s and 0s, or digital files. In fact, from a digital animator's standpoint, the virtual 3D camera will act in the same fashion as a digital camera; this process is referred to as *rendering*.

The aperture, also referred to as the iris or diaphragm, is an adjustable opening that controls the amount of light that is able to pass through the lens. It works in much the same way as the iris of the human eye.

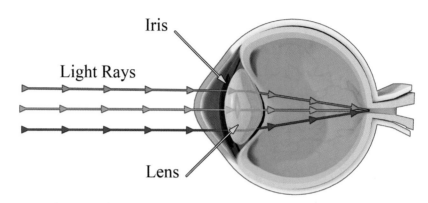

The aperture is a series of radiating metal blades that forms a circular opening that can be adjusted to allow more or less light into the lens depending on the particular scenario. For instance, if you are shooting in a low-light situation, for example, outdoors at dusk, you can widen the aperture to allow more light to enter the lens. However, if you are shooting in a high-light situation, for example, facing the sun at noon, you would want decrease the aperture opening, thereby eliminating the excess light.

F-Stops

The apertures circular opening or diameter is measured in millimeters and referred to as *F-stops* on the camera. The F-stops can be easily found on the outside ring of the particular lens you are shooting with. The numbers generally range from f/1.4 through f/22 in a series of nine steps or stops (f/1.4, f/2.0, f/2.8, f/4, f/5.6, f/8, f/11, f/16, and f/22). The numbers work inversely with the amount of opening in the aperture. In other words, the smaller the F-stop number is the wider the opening and, in turn, more light is allowed to enter into the lens. Visual 3–4 illustrates the aperture range of opening with corresponding F-stops.

Much like the other components of the camera, the aperture not only serves a functional purpose but also is the vehicle for creativity. From a functional standpoint, the director needs to be able to control the light entering into the camera to avoid complete darkness or a complete washout. However, what lies somewhere in between these two extremes are the director's vision and creativity. Their understanding and utilization of the aperture is the first step toward determining the look and feel of the imagery.

THE LENS

We will now focus our attention on the lens as we continue to follow the path of light through the camera. The lens captures the light that has been allowed to pass through the aperture and focuses it onto the light-responsive image plane. Created from glass or industrial strength plastic, the lens, or series of lenses, absorbs and focuses the light rays on the *image plane*. The light rays expose the film, creating a *negative*. In turn, when the film is developed, a *positive* is created, and the image will appear as it did in reality. Although this process sounds complicated, the technology behind it is centuries old. Simply, the image is achieved by the shape of the lens.

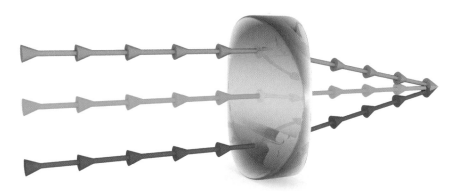

visual |3–5|

Cross-Section of a Typical Camera Lens with Light Rays Passing Through

Angle of View and Focal Lengths

Camera lenses are categorized, generically, by their *angle of view* and, specifically, by their focal length. Even if you are a novice photographer, I'm confident that you've heard the terms *wide-angle* and *telephoto* in reference to camera lenses. These generic terms describe a group of lenses that have similar angles of view. The angle of view is the amount of image that the particular lens can capture. For instance, a wide-angle or *fish-eye* lens has a large angle of view and therefore can capture more of the area in front of the camera. In contrast, a telephoto lens has a much smaller angle of view

visual |3–6|

The Focal Length is Measured, in Millimeters, from the Lens to the Image Plane

Focal Length
35mm

and is intended to focus in on much smaller objects or scenes. These are the extremes, and there are more common, or normal, lenses that fall in between the two.

Specifically, camera lenses are referred to by their focal length. The focal length of a camera lens is the distance, in millimeters, from the lens to the light-sensitive image plane in a camera.

It is this distance that determines the angle of view. Much like the aperture and F-stop, the focal length and angle of view have an inverse relationship. In other words, the smaller the focal length of a particular lens the greater the angle of view. The range of camera lenses will run between a *20mm*, or wide-angle, and *200mm*, or telephoto. Visual 3–7 illustrates the range and relationship between a lens focal length and angle of view.

visual |3–7|

The Range of Focal Length's and Resulting Angle of View

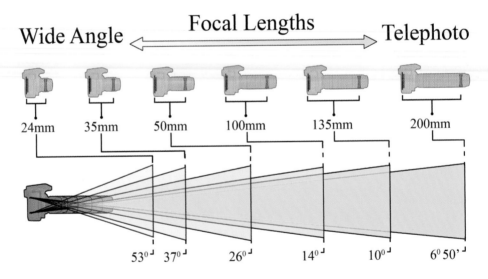

Wide Angle ← **Focal Lengths** → **Telephoto**

24mm   35mm   50mm   100mm   135mm   200mm

53°   37°   26°   14°   10°   6° 50'

| NOTE |

Because the 35mm lens has a wider angle of view than the human eye, the images taken with it tend to feel stretched. This is why you often hear that the camera add 10 pounds to the person being filmed.

The most common focal length on the market is the *35mm*. It is important to note, however, that the 50mm lens is actually the lens that comes closest to what the human eye perceives. Therefore, the 35mm, although the most common, creates an image that appears wider than that which you see with the naked eye. Visual 3–8 illustrates the different image results between focal lengths. Everything in the scene remains the same, including the aperture, or F-stop, and distance to the center of interest, except for the lens focal length.

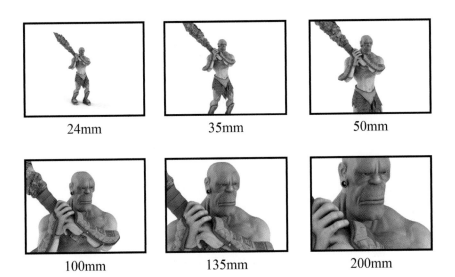

24mm   35mm   50mm

100mm   135mm   200mm

visual |3–8|

This demonstrates the effect the Focal Length has on the Final Image. The Aperture (F-Stop) and distance to the center of interest is the same in each image.

DEPTH OF FIELD

Depth of field is one of the most powerful optical tools for a director. However, it is not a component of the camera that can be turned, pushed, or clicked on. It is an effect that occurs naturally and is controlled by manipulating the components that we discussed earlier in the chapter.

But what the heck is it? Depth of field, or *DOF*, refers to the total amount of the photographed/filmed image that remains in focus. Something that is in focus appears sharp and clear. In contrast, something that is out of focus appears soft and blurry.

Typically, within every shot there is a center of interest that the director wants in absolute focus. The depth of field is the total amount of space or distance in front of and behind that center of interest that remains in focus. It is important to note that the transition from sharp to blurry, or from within the depth of field area to outside, is not harsh. Objects that are closer to outside edge of the depth of field will appear more blurry than those that are closer to the center of interest. Visual 3–9 illustrates the concept of depth of field.

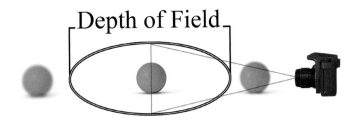

Depth of Field

visual |3–9|

Depth of Field

The use of depth of field can be a very powerful tool when making films. The director might create a very shallow DOF to ensure that the viewing audience is concentrating on something very specific. For instance, if you are filming an action film and the star detective is pointing a gun at the criminal, the director, with the use of depth of field, can keep his trigger finger in focus while the rest of the character is blurry. This would force the audience to focus on this very specific action and, in turn, heighten the overall intensity and drama of the scene.

visual |3–10|

Example of Shot Utilizing
a Shallow Depth of Field

In contrast, the larger or wider depth of field will keep more of the scene in focus. Typically, a director will use this type of DOF when there are events happening simultaneously that the audience must see. For instance, you might have two people engaged in conversation on a sidewalk while a car accident happens in the background. A large depth of field will ensure that the audience will see both situations unfold.

visual |3–11|

Example of a Shot
Utilizing a Large Depth
of Field

Adjusting the DOF

The Depth of Field is an optical phenomenon and cannot be controlled with one specific component of the camera. In fact, to accurately control the DOF within a given shot, the director must understand multiple functions/elements of the camera. The three major factors in calculating depth of field are the aperture setting, the focal length, and the distance from the camera to the center of interest. All three of these settings will affect the DOF dramatically. Notice in Visual 3–12 that as you increase either the F-stop or the distance to the center of interest, the overall depth of field will increase. In contrast, you must lower the aperture or the lens focal length to increase the DOF.

Depth of Field

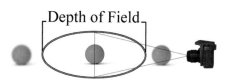

Larger F-Stop = Larger Depth of Field

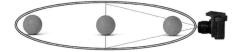

Larger Camera Distance = Larger Depth of Field

visual |3–12|

Depth of Field
Calculations

To further illustrate this point, Visual 3–13 uses the exact same image parameters, including the focal length and distance to the center of interest, and adjusts only the F-stop. You will notice that the depth of field and image brightness changes dramatically.

F-Stop's Effect on Depth of Field

Smaller F-Stop ⟵⟶ Larger F-Stop

visual |3–13|

The F-Stop's Effect
on DOF

From a workflow standpoint, it is very rare that a director will begin planning a shot around a desired depth of field and adjust the other parameters accordingly. It is advised that you start with one of the other parameters and adjust for the DOF around that. For instance, if you are shooting a scene at dusk, you should probably choose the aperture that works best with the available light. From there, you can choose the lens and distance that will create the desired DOF.

THE SHUTTER AND SHUTTER SPEEDS

The *shutter* is the last barrier that light must pass through before an image is created. Typically located directly in front of the image plane, the shutter quickly opens and closes, allowing light to hit the light-sensitive image plane.

visual |3–14|

The Camera Shutter

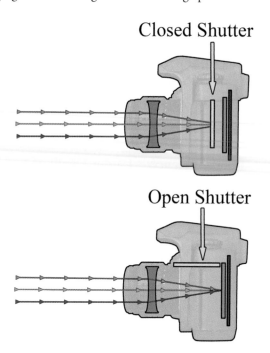

However, the key to the shutter's use is the amount of time that it remains open, exposing the film. That amount of time, or *shutter speed*, is measured in fractions of a second. Typical shutter speeds range from as long as one full second to as little as 1/2000th of a second. Changing the shutter speed effects two things as far as the image is concerned. First, much like the aperture or F-stop, it will affect the amount of light allowed to reach the image plane. Therefore, it is another device that can help the director to adjust the image output appropriately depending upon the available light in a scene. Second, it plays a crucial role in the camera's ability to capture action or motion. It is important to understand that when the shutter is open, it is capturing whatever is in front of the camera. If the object/person that you are shooting is perfectly still, you can keep the shutter open for a great deal of time. However, if the center of interest is in motion, a slow shutter speed will produce a blurred image, known as motion blur. For instance, if you are trying to photograph an Olympic sprinter, and you are using a slower shutter speed, one-half second, for example, there is a high likelihood that within that one-half second the sprinter will be in a dramatically different location at the end of the image capture then he/she was at the beginning. If the sprinter's arm moves three inches during that time, the image will keep exposing the film with every minute movement, creating an overlapping, blurry effect. This is not a lens focus issue; it is a speed issue. If you use a fast shutter speed, 1/2000th of a second, the film will be exposed for an extremely short amount of time. Therefore, the movement that the sprinter could generate in 1/2000th of a second is so minuscule that the image would appear sharp.

Slow Shutter Speed

Fast Shutter Speed

visual | 3–15 |

Two Images Capturing the Same Fast-Moving Object with Different Shutter Speeds

DIRECTING THE FILM CAMERA

Now that we have laid the solid foundation of camera fundamentals and photography principles, it is time to build the framework for directing the moving image. Without trying to oversimplify it, the major difference between the still camera and the film camera is that the film camera is capturing numerous still images in constant rapid succession. This is the basic building block for all film and animation. You are capturing, filming, or rendering a series of still images and then plying them back at a fast rate. This rate, know as *frames per second (FPS)*, typically ranges from 12 FPS up to 60 FPS depending on what medium and technique you are using. In traditional filmmaking, the camera is capturing or filming at twenty-four frames per second, which is exactly how fast the projector runs when it plays it back for you in the movie theater. However, video, TV, and digital 3D animation work at thirty frames per second.

Insider Info

The ability for the human eye to perceive a series of stills being played in rapid succession, twenty-four frames per second (FPS), for example, as continuous movement is know as *persistence of vision*. Persistence of vision is the phenomenon that occurs between the eye's retina and the brain in which an image is held for a brief moment longer than it actually appears in reality. This afterimage then blends with the next image that appears, creating a smooth transition. In fact, that is why most film, video, and animation is shot at 24–30 FPS. However, persistence of vision does have its FPS limitations. For example, 12 FPS is the lowest setting that can create smooth motion. Anything below 12 breaks down the persistence of vision and seems choppy to the viewer. Furthermore, traditional animation, including hand-drawn, cell, and clay, is often shot on two's to save time and money or labor. Although it is still played back at a normal FPS, the animators will shoot two frames for every one pose, creating what is actually a 12 FPS film. In contrast, there are higher-end cameras and projectors, *IMAX* format, for example, which shoot as high as 60 frames per second. Filmmakers believe that this FPS will create a higher sense of reality and motion or the viewer. The industry agrees that there is slight improvement from 30 FPS to 60 FPS in the smoothness of movement. However, a POV/FPS ceiling exists with no discernable visual improvement beyond 60 FPS.

Although the basic principles and functionality the camera apply to both still and motion photography, how you apply and utilize those principles differs dramatically when capturing a single image versus a movie. Because the motion picture camera captures both space and time, it creates countless camera options for the director. However, much like still photography, there are standards and conventions that will help the beginning filmmaker to make smart decisions along the way.

ANATOMY OF THE SHOT

The most basic building block of a film is one *frame*. When you combine a group of frames together, you create a *shot*. A group of shots create a *scene* and, finally, a group of scenes create a *film*. These building blocks of film can be easily compared to the building blocks of language. For instance, the frame can be considered a word and the shot a sentence. A sentence, or shot, is a combination of words, or frames, that follow some basic rules of grammar, or directing, the purpose of which is to communicate an idea. It is typically juxtaposed with other sentences, or shots, to create paragraphs, or scenes; all combined to serve the greater good of the story, or film.

Now that we understand its purpose, what defines a well-executed shot? Technically, a shot can be almost any length of time but it must be continuous from a camera's standpoint. In other words, a shot can be two seconds or twenty minutes, but it has to be the same camera throughout. The camera can be moved as much as you would like while filming the shot, but as soon as you cut to a different angle or another camera, the shot is over.

The director must balance the big picture of the film's purpose and message with the smaller details of the individual shots. Some of the most basic questions that the director must answer when planning out a particular shot are:

- What is the purpose of this shot?
- What shots precede and follow this shot?
- What is the pacing of this shot?
- Who or what is in the shot?
- Where and when is this shot taking place?

The answers to these questions will help determine the role that the camera will play in the shot including its type, point of view, position, height, angle, framing, movement, focus, and effects. The camera should not determine the shot; the shot should determine the camera.

BASIC CAMERA SETUPS

There are two basic options for the director when thinking about setting up the camera for a shot. Depending on what actions or events are happening in the shot, the camera is either going to be stationary throughout the shot or moving. The stationary camera setup is typically referred to as a *lock-off* because the camera is locked down to keep it from moving. Setup can be very boring or confusing for the viewer if not used in right way. For instance, if you are shooting a fight scene in an action movie and you set up a lock-off camera, one of two things will happen. First, you would have to move the camera far enough back in order to capture all of the action within the fight scene. Forcing the viewer to watch the entire shot from the same angle, height, and distance might turn an exciting fight scene into a yawn fest.

Film Grammar

Letter		Frame
⇩	⟺	⇩
Word		Shot
⇩	⟺	⇩
Sentence		Scene
⇩	⟺	⇩
Paragraph		Sequence
⇩	⟺	⇩
Story		Film

visual |3–16|

Film Components Compared to Language Components

visual |3–17|

An Action Sequence Shot with a Lock-Off at a Far Distance

The other option is to move the camera closer to the action. Although this might be more interesting in certain parts of the shot, you inevitably will have parts where the action is out of the camera's viewing plane. This can create confusion and displeasure for the viewer.

visual |3–18|

An Action Sequence Shot
with a Lock-Off at a Close
Distance

However, that's not say that lock-offs shouldn't be used in the filmmaking process. In fact, there are plenty of good reasons to use a lock-off throughout your film. First, it would be too much for the viewer to watch an entire film with a moving camera. Second, it can create a sense of stability and control for your film by letting the actors/action speak for itself. A lock-off can be used effectively to capture shots with small, yet important, bits of action. For instance, in an action shot, you might want to show the hero character squeezing his weapon tightly just before he is about to strike. This action of him gripping the weapon would be very tough to pick up with a moving camera.

visual |3–19|

Lock-Off Shot Used to
Highlight a Small but
Important Action –
Reaching for the Villain

The other basic option for the director is the moving camera. This movement is achieved by physically moving the camera's position in space, using the lens to zoom in or out, or both. It goes without saying how important well-executed camera moves can be to a film. Again, a film with only lock-offs would create an extremely boring/confusing result. The *camera move* should never dictate the action in a shot, but the action can definitely dictate the move. Simply put, the camera can capture an action with motion in way that allows for greater visual continuity for the viewer. It allows the director to document a complete action. For instance, if the shot is of a hero pulling out a sword, cocking it back and striking the villain, a movable camera would allow you to capture in one continuous shot without having to back up far away from the scene or chop it into smaller shots.

However, there is certainly can be a downside to the camera in motion – or, should I say, the camera in too much motion. I think it can be tempting for directors to become enamored with the camera move itself and lose sight of the purpose of the shot. For instance, if you are shooting a dialogue between two people and there is not a critical action, event, or revelation that happens, you might want to hold off on the extreme camera moves. In other words, if one character asks the other if they have a quarter for the vending machine, and you do a dramatic zoom up to the character's mouth as he says "sure," at best this will annoy the viewer and at worst this will dilute all the other dramatic moments/camera moves you have in the film.

In reality, the best directors use a blend of lock-offs and camera moves throughout their films, making choices depending on what they are trying to accomplish in the shot or scene.

CAMERA PERSPECTIVE

One of the first decisions that a director has to make when planning out a shot is the *perspective* of the camera. Although there are many options for camera placement, the camera will either be capturing the action from an *objective* or a *subjective* perspective. In other words, the camera will either be a passive object that is simply just there to record the events that are unfolding (the objective), or an active participant in the action (the subjective).

Objective Viewpoint

A camera with an objective viewpoint does not participate in the action or events that take place in the shot. Its role is to simply record the events and keep out of the way. In fact, the camera should not even be visible to those in the shot. If the characters in the scene were aware of the camera, it could change or alter their behaviors to the point where it could affect the outcome of the shot. A real-life example of an objective, non-participant viewpoint is a hidden security camera. The camera is there to capture the events and, assuming that it is not visible and that there are no warning signs, it will not affect the behavior of those in the shot. It is intended to allow the viewer to make all judgments and inferences based upon only what is taking place. Visual 3–20 illustrates a typical objective viewpoint within the action movie fight scene. The camera is capturing the action as is and the audience assumes that the characters are unaware of its presence.

visual 3–20

Fight Scene Shot with an Objective Viewpoint

Subjective Viewpoint

Although the objective camera is, by far, the most commonly used camera viewpoint in film, it doesn't mean that it is the most effective. When a director chooses a subjective or participant viewpoint, the camera can become linked with a particular character, allowing the viewers to see things from their standpoint. This provides a somewhat skewed outlook on the actions/events, and it also brings the audience closer into the character's mind and, therefore, into the scene. For instance, you might want to choose a subjective viewpoint for the hero of your film. It will create a bond between the audience and the hero that will heighten the danger, suspense, horror, love, and passion. Often, you will see a subjective viewpoint camera shot as if the viewer is looking at the scene through the character's eyes. This shot is illustrated in Visual 3–21.

visual |3–21|

Fight Scene Shot with a
Subjective Viewpoint

CAMERA ANGLES

Determining a shot's *camera angle* can be one of the director's most rewarding tasks in the filmmaking process. Creating dynamic camera angles can certainly make a shot more interesting or visually pleasing. However, a well-executed camera angle can take on greater meaning by becoming a focusing agent and a psychological manipulation tool. By combining age-old storytelling conventions with modern-day technology, an adjustment to the camera's angle can completely change the way the audience views the shot.

High-Angle

A *high-angle shot* is created when the camera is placed above the center of interest and angled downward to capture the action. This type of camera angle can not only be visually pleasing but also can be used to create a sense of hierarchy within the shot. In particular, shooting at a high angle gives a sense to the viewer that the character in the shot is physically, mentally, or emotionally inferior. This shot is typically used when the hero is about to overcome the villain.

visual |3–22|

High-Angle Shot

Visual 3–22 is a high-angle shot of our villain, and it creates a sense that he is at a significant disadvantage, which could lead to disgust or even pity.

Low-Angle

The *low-angle shot* is created when the camera is placed significantly lower than the center of interest. Often referred to as the worm's-eye shot, this angle is used to create a sense of hierarchy within the shot as well as an unsettling feeling for the viewer. This shot could be used to shoot a parent who is scolding their small child for getting into trouble, or, in the case of Visual 3–23, after the villain has been overtaken by the hero.

Bird's Eye

A *bird's-eye shot* is created when the camera is placed significantly above the center of interest and angled downward to capture the action. This type of camera angle is used to create an overview shot of the action, giving the viewer a greater sense of the environment. It doesn't have a hierological impact on the character/s in the scene because the viewer assumes that this view is not from anyone directly involved with the action. This shot is typically used for aesthetic and informational purposes.

Point of View

The *point of view shot*, or POV, is created by mimicking the eyesight of one of the characters in your film. The intent of the shot is to make the viewer think that they are seeing exactly what that particular character is seeing. The POV shot is not a specific angle but, rather, any angle that indicates the direction in which the character is looking. It has the same effect as placing a small camera in between the eyes of your character. This shot typically is reserved for the hero in the film, but it may be used sparingly with other characters to make a specific statement or elicit a certain emotion.

Over-the-Shoulder

The *over-the-shoulder shot* is created by, no surprises here, placing the camera over the shoulder of a character in your scene. It is the sister shot of the POV, with the intent of placing the viewer directly into the scene. The viewer can feel a connection to the character and can feel involved in the action. The over-the-shoulder shot is an excellent choice when filming a conversation between two or more characters.

visual |3–26|

Over-the-Shoulder Shot

Canted

The *canted shot,* also known as the dutch angle, is created by tilting the camera to one side, creating a skewed or oblique horizon line. This shot is used to illicit an off-balanced feeling from the viewer, and leads to an increased sense of unease or danger. It is typically used most effectively in suspense, thriller, and horror films. A classic example of the canted shot is in 1985's *Back to the Future,*

visual |3–27|

Canted Shot

when Michael J. Fox's character, Marty McFly, dresses up as a space alien to try to scare Crispin Glover's character, George McFly, into asking Marty's would-be mother to the Enchantment under the Sea Dance.

FRAMING

Framing is the process whereby the director can control the visuals from both an aesthetic and informational standpoint. Much like a painter, the director must consider the each individual frame as a unique work of art, and should pay close attention to balance, weight, contrast, positive/negative space, color, and light. A lot of that work lies outside the camera's influence, including storyboarding, set design, and lighting; however, the camera's obligation is to capture the shot at just the right angle and distance. As with most other visual arts, camera framing is as much about what is not seen as it is about what is.

Beyond the aesthetic, camera framing has a direct influence on the amount of visual information that is delivered to the viewer. Technically, this framing process is the

Camera Framing

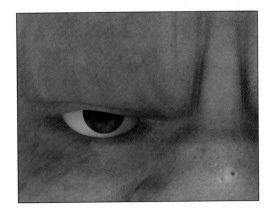

direct result of the camera's physical position in space and/or the type of lens that is being used. By determining how much is seen, the director controls the flow of information to the audience, thereby controlling the overall narrative.

As we have discussed, filmmaking is visual storytelling. Much like its textual counterparts, for example, novels, short stories, and poems,

filmmaking has guidelines and conventions to follow. Most stories by Western civilizations are told utilizing a far to near approach, with regard to how the information is delivered to the viewer. In other words, these stories start with more general, far-reaching information, or a long shot, and work their way into the fine details, a close-up shot, of the story and characters. We are familiar and comfortable with this approach and, to a certain degree, we expect it. Therefore, camera framing can help the director to control the visual information flow of the film, and timing is the key behind building suspense, drama, excitement, and humor.

Long Shot

A *long shot*, also known as a wide shot, is created when the camera is placed far away from the center of interest or by using a wide-angle lens. This type of shot is used to capture as much of the scene as possible to reveal some of the most basic, big-picture information to the viewer. For instance, if your scene revolves around two characters having a conversation in a car on their way to work, a long shot of a freeway with heavy traffic will provide critical background information to the audience.

Establishing Shot

The *establishing shot* is visually identical to the long shot. However, it is used specifically at the beginning of a scene/sequence to help set the stage for the other shots. In Visual 3–29, the establishing shot it used to give the viewer an overview of the environment where the battle scene is going to take place.

Establishing Shot of the Battle Scene

Extreme Long Shot

An *extreme long shot* has the same purpose as the long shot but it is taken a bit farther back. A classic example would be the opening credits of *Star Wars*.

Full Shot

The *full shot* is created by faming the center of interest completely in the field of view. In other words, the character should fully fill up the frame but not be cut off in any way. The full shot can be considered an establishing shot, not of the scene or environment, but specifically of the character. It is intended to give the viewer a good look at the physical traits of the character, helping to set up the shots/scenes that follow.

visual |3–30|

Full Shot of the Hero

Medium Shot

The *medium shot* is created by framing the top half of your character within the viewing plane. This shot starts to cross the line from the general to the specific or from the impersonal to the intimate. The viewer is now privy to some of the finer details of the character's personality, physical traits, and body language. This shot is often used when shooting a character that is speaking or engaged in a conversation.

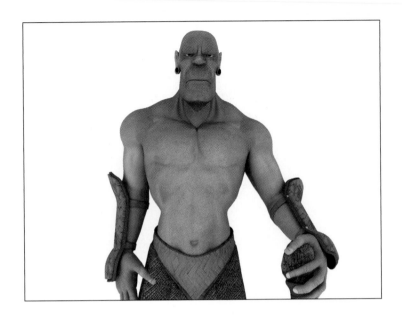

Close-Up Shot

The *close-up shot* is created by bringing the camera very close, or zooming into the center of interest. It is intended to provide focus and divulge details that even the naked eye might not pick up. The emotional impact on the viewer can be very powerful, and it is typically used to highlight a critical turning point in the film.

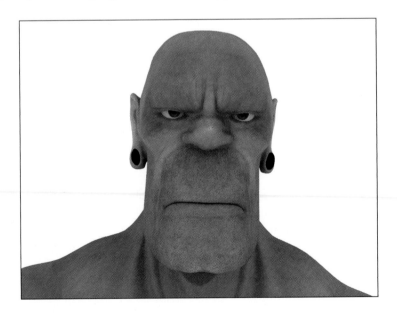

Extreme Close-Up Shot

An *extreme close-up shot* has the same effect as the close-up shot, but it is taken a bit closer in. The camera is pushed/zoomed in even further to reveal a minute detail within the scene. Visual 3–33 is an extreme close-up of the hero's eyes just before he attacks, capturing a tiny squint that encapsulates his distaste for the enemy.

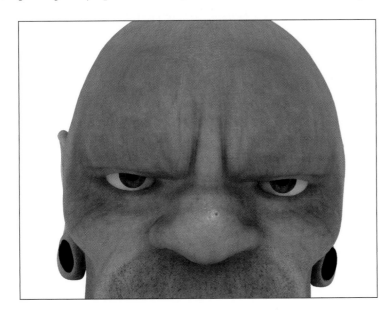

visual |3–33|

Extreme Close-Up of the
Hero's Eyes

Insert Shot

An *insert shot* is created when the director inserts a close-up shot in between two medium or long shots. Visually, the insert shot and the close-up shot are identical. However, from a continuity and storytelling aspect, the insert shot is inserted to quickly highlight a point that is being made with the wider shots. For instance, if you are shooting a scene in which the main character is sleeping in bed and the alarm goes off, an insert shot of the numbers on the alarm clock might work well. Visual 3–34 demonstrates its use within our battle scene scenario. The insert shot of the hero's weapon not only draws the viewer's attention to it but also foreshadows its use against the villain.

visual |3–34|

Insert Shot

Cut-Away Shot

The *cut-away shot* is the opposite of the insert shot. Instead of digging deeper into the same scene/action, it steps away completely to another character or event. The goal of the cut-away shot is to give the viewer a broader understanding of the storyline and action, which will bring greater meaning to the individual shots. For instance, you might have a scenario in which a child is playing with a ball on a busy city sidewalk. A cut-away

shot of a huge truck barreling down the street a couple of blocks away would not only give the viewer a greater sense of the environment but also would foreshadow an unfortunate event that might link the two together. This shot helps to bring clarity and drama. In Visual 3–35, we see a cut-away shot of our villain, who is peering at our unknowing hero from behind a rock.

Framing Heights and Abbreviations

Framing heights are a way to quantify the visual and spatial differences between the most common camera shots. These heights are relative to the size of the particular character that is being filmed. For instance, a close-up shot of an ant is quite different than a close-up shot of an elephant. Visual 3–36 illustrates the framing heights and their corresponding industry abbreviations.

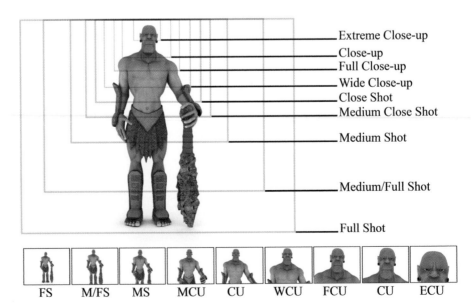

Extreme Close-up
Close-up
Full Close-up
Wide Close-up
Close Shot
Medium Close Shot
Medium Shot
Medium/Full Shot
Full Shot

FS   M/FS   MS   MCU   CU   WCU   FCU   CU   ECU

CAMERA MOVES

Filmmaking is the art of capturing space and time. Therefore, the director is not locked into only one camera position, framing, or angle for each shot. Camera moves fall into one of three different categories:

1. Physical Moves

2. Zooms

3. Combos

Physical Moves

Physical camera moves are created by adjusting the position of the camera within the duration of a shot. The movement of the camera can be very quick and extreme, slow and almost unnoticeable, or anything in between. Live-action filmmakers have developed highly sophisticated equipment to help the director achieve these eye-popping results.

Pan

A *camera pan* is created by keeping the camera stationary while it rotates on the horizontal, or left and right axis. The result is a sweeping visual effect that allows the viewer to see more of the scene. A smooth motion from the beginning to the end is ideal. A pan in combination with an establishing shot can be a great way to open up a scene.

Insider Info

When discussing camera moves, it is important to understand the power of *Parallax*. Parallax is an optical phenomenon that results when a camera is in motion. From the viewer's standpoint, it can appear that stationary objects are actually in motion and change position relative to other stationary objects in the scene. How far these stationary objects are from the camera will determine how fast or slow they appear to move. For instance, if a camera is following a character walking across a street, objects that are near to the character, such as street signs or parking meters, will appear to move very quickly, whereas other objects further away, such as buildings or mountains, will appear to move much more slowly. Parallax is not only a visual clue to the audience as to the relative distances between objects but also is a wonderful artistic tool to keep shots compelling.

visual |3–37|

Camera Pan

Camera Pan

Camera View   Top View

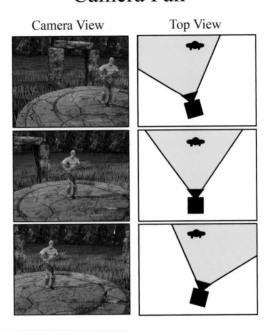

Tilt

The *tilt shot* is identical to the pan except that it rotates on the vertical, or the up and down axis. A tilt is a great choice to unveil a tall object to the audience and can add suspense to the shot. The viewer often associates this shot as a POV and, therefore, it can be used to show a size relationship between the viewer and the subject.

visual |3–38|

Camera Tilt

Camera Tilt

Camera View   Side View

Roll

Under the Cartesian coordinate system, the pan rotates the camera on the z-axis and the tilt on the x-axis, whereas the *camera roll* is rotated on the y-axis.

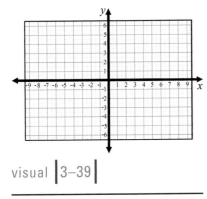

visual |3–39|

2D Coordinate System (X and Y axis)

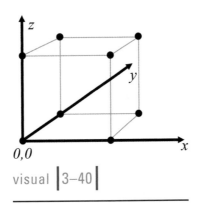

visual |3–40|

3D Coordinate System (X, Y, and Z Axis)

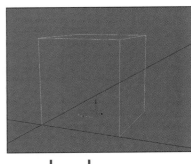

visual |3–41|

User Interface of a 3D Software Package

The roll provides a similar effect to audience as the canted shot. In fact, think of the roll as a move that starts from the normal upright position and rotates into the canted shot.

Tracking Shot

The track is created by physically moving, but not rotating, the camera on the horizontal axis to follow an action. The smooth movement is achieved by mounting the camera to a mobile platform called a truck or dolly. The *tracking shot* is often used to follow someone walking down the street or driving in a car.

Camera Roll

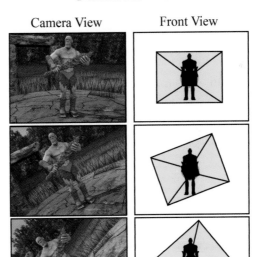

Camera View   Front View

visual |3–42|

Camera Roll

Insider Info

The Cartesian coordinate system was developed in the seventeenth century by the French mathematician René Descartes. The system, the backbone to geometry and calculus, is a tool to define points in space. Although it was originally designed in two dimensions (x and y Axis), the third (z) axis was added in the nineteenth century. Both the 2D and 3D versions of the Cartesian coordinate are used as the framework for most 3D animation software interfaces.

Tracking Shot

Camera Track

Dolly Shot

The *dolly shot* is similar to the tracking shot in that the camera is physically moved instead of rotated. In this case, the movement is either toward or away from the center of interest, and not side to side. In a live-action movie, this shot is controlled by the dolly grip, who is in charge of moving the dolly that the camera is mounted on. It can be used effectively to bring focus or attention to a specific character or object in the scene.

Dolly Shot

Camera Dolly

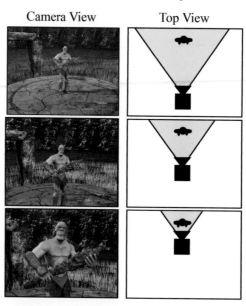

Handheld Shot

The *handheld shot* is created by picking up the camera and using your body to control its movement. It captures a very shaky an uneven image creating an uneasy for the viewer. It is typically associated with reality based or amateur films. A classic example of the handheld camera is the *Blair Witch Project*. The entire film was shot in this fashion.

The Steady Cam

A relatively new invention in the world of filmmaking, the *steady cam* provides the best of both worlds. The camera is mounted to an intricate stabilization system, which you can carry around as you shoot. This is an extremely popular and versatile shot; it allows the director the freedom that the handheld shot gives but with the smoothness of motion of the track or dolly.

Cranes and Booms

The camera *crane* and *boom* are moveable arms that a camera can be mounted on to create large sweeping movements, either side to side or up and down. These pieces of equipment were developed to reach heights and lengths that would be impossible to achieve otherwise. These shots contrast nicely with the more normal camera heights and moves, adding visual complexity, variety, and interest to the shot.

Zooms

The camera *zoom* is created by adjusting the focal length of the lens during a shot, allowing the view to change from a wide angle into a telephoto or vice versa. Although it has similar visual results to the dolly, the camera does not physically move. A typical zoom lens actually contains multiple lenses that move from front to back in order to achieve the particular zoom you are looking for.

Adjustable Zoom Lens

visual |3–45|

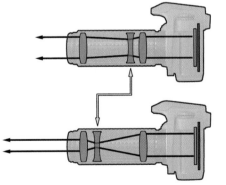

Diagram of a Zoom Lens

It is important to note that, unlike the dolly shot, the zoom works with the focal length, which, as you learned earlier in this chapter, changes the overall perspective of the shot. It is important for the director to consider the differences between the zoom and the dolly before shooting. Zooms can be a great focusing tool for the director; allowing for quick and easy results. Visual 3–46 illustrates the visual differences between the zoom and the dolly.

Camera Zoom vs. Dolly

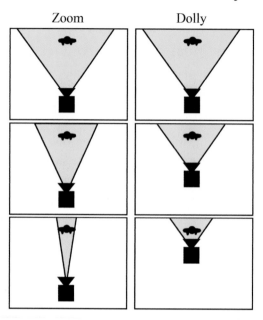

Zoom   Dolly

Combos

Camera moves, both physical and zooms, have great power and application for a film-maker. However, because dollys and zooms affect the image perspective in different ways, blending the two can create powerfully unique results.

Camera Zolly

Camera View   Top View

Zolly

The quintessential combo shot is the *zolly*. Also know as the dolly zoom, *Vertigo*, or Hitchcock shot, the zolly is created by combining a dolly-out with a zoom-in. It was first used by Alfred Hitchcock in his 1958 classic thriller *Vertigo*. If done correctly, the shot keeps the center of interest in the same position within the frame while the background's perspective changes dramatically. The result is a mind-bending effect often used for the physiological implications to the viewer. It has been used in a number of films since *Vertigo*, including *Jaws* and *Goodfellas*.

RACK FOCUS SHOT

The *rack focus shot*, also known as *pull focus*, is created by adjusting the depth of field (DOF) to change focus between objects/characters within the image. It is a great tool for the director to shift the viewer's attention at a specific time/pace. Although it seems like a camera trick, rack focus is remarkably close to how the human eye operates. For instance, as I sit here writing this chapter on my laptop, the words on the LCD monitor are in complete focus but the objects behind the computer are quite blurry. However, if I decide to shift focus on the pictures hanging on the wall fifteen feet beyond the LCD monitor, I need not change positions or angles; I just refocus my eyes. A rack focus shot simulates this effect for the viewer.

Rack Focus Shot

Camera View   Side (DOF) View

Rack Focus Shot

SUMMARY

At the center of the filmmaking universe is the camera: the portal through which a director's vision becomes reality. Often overlooked or misused by 3D animators, the digital director must understand the basic functionality of the camera and traditional live-action filmmaking conventions before setting-up their first virtual shot.

Successful directors can translate their intimate knowledge of both the inner workings and outer workings of the camera into stunning cinematography. As light passes through the camera on its way to expose the film, the director is presented with many options and features that, if mastered, can create limitless creative options. Furthermore, the well-directed camera brings an entirely new dimension to a film, enhancing the drama, action, or humor, and playing as important a role as the lead character.

in review

1. What are the three basic elements of photography?

2. What is the circular adjustable opening that controls the amount of light that is able to enter the lens?

3. What does stopping-up or increasing the F-stop on your lens achieve visually?

4. Camera lenses are categorized in which two ways?

5. Explain the concept of focal length.

6. Which focal length is closest to what the human eye sees and why?

7. Depth of field (DOF) is controlled by which three camera settings?

8. Explain the phenomenon of persistence of vision.

9. What are the two types of camera viewpoints?

10. From a framing standpoint, list five different types of shots.

11. What are the three types of camera moves?

12. Explain the difference between a dolly and a zoom.

exercises

1. Gain access to a still camera with manual F-stop/aperture controls:
   a. Under a normal lighting situation, adjust the F-stop to produce both an underexposed and overexposed image.
   b. Set up a scene in which you have three objects that are at varying distances from the camera: one near (within 5 feet), one at about 20 feet, and one far (50 feet or further).
      i. Starting with the lowest aperture setting, try to capture an image with only the closest object in focus.
      ii. Continue to adjust the F-stop to capture the middle and then farthest object in focus.
      iii. If you strung these three images together, they would serve as a storyboard for what type of camera shot?

2. Examine the first minute (not including credits) of any of Pixar's feature films. Quickly jot down the different types of shots that are used to introduce the movie. Do you notice a pattern?

3. Without looking at a real-life example, storyboard (five panels) what you think a zolly shot would look like. Use a single character as the center of interest with plenty of objects in the background for reference. After you have finished, take a look at a real zolly and explain what the differences between that and your storyboarded version.

CHAPTER 4

objectives

- Explore the transition from a real-world camera to a virtual camera
- Understand the common parameters within the 3D camera
- Understand the basics of camera framing and composition
- Learn the fundamentals of virtual camera blocking
- Recognize the axis of action within any shot
- Explore advanced 3D techniques with camera shake and motion tracking

introduction

Creating beautifully directed animated films requires not only a solid understanding of real-world or live-action camera but also how to translate that knowledge into a 3D environment. To fully unlock the power of today's high-end software packages, the director must respect the basic rules of filmmaking and be able to create, or recreate, shots that are typically associated with live action films convincingly. However, it is critical that the director can translate that knowledge into the *virtual camera*, understanding how to exploit its differences and similarities to the real-world camera.

This chapter will serve as the bridge to digital directing, and we will explore the most common parameters of virtual camera as they are seen in today's high-end 3D animation software packages. Building on the knowledge gained in the first three chapters, your skills will be put into practice as some of the more advanced camera and directing techniques are explored, including framing, blocking, and continuity.

INTRODUCTION TO THE VIRTUAL CAMERA

In many ways, software manufacturers have gone out of their way to make the virtual camera, within the most popular 3D animation packages, as close to a real camera as possible. That is, they have tried to give the digital director all of the same type of control, both internal and external, that a traditional filmmaker would have. In fact, the digital director has software options that are just not available with a physical camera.

With all of those choices, the virtual camera is an amazing tool that can create almost any shot that your imagination can conjure up. However, to take a page from the Spider-Man comics, "with great power comes great responsibility." Although it is tempting for beginning filmmakers to create fantastically impossible camera movements and zooms, more often than not, these end up hindering the film rather than helping it. There is a fine line between innovative and annoying when it comes to directing the virtual camera. Understanding this difference is the key to well-executed digital cinematography.

TRANSITION INTO THE 3D ENVIRONMENT

The camera within a 3D environment serves two main functions. The first is to serve as the eyes of the filmmaker. Because you are working within a virtual environment, and none of the objects/geometry is real, the camera is the only way by which anything can be seen. Therefore, when you first open up a 3D software package, typically you will see a four-camera layout. The Top, Side, Front, and Perspective views are the most commonly used.

visual |4–1|

Example of a Typical
Four-Camera Layout

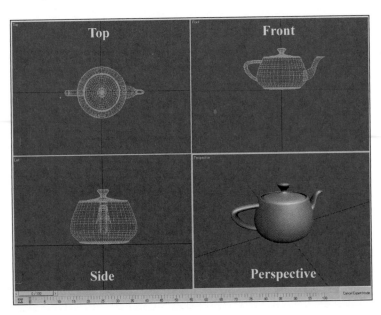

These four cameras, or *viewports* as they are often called, are designed to give the user a simultaneous look at the virtual set from different angles, or cameras. Because we don't have the opportunity to just get up and walk around the set, we have to use a variety of different cameras to monitor what is happening. Think of it as setting up multiple spy-cameras on a set that is two miles away. However, unlike a spy-camera, you can interactively move/zoom these cameras to any location on the set that you see fit.

The second function of the virtual camera, similar to its physical counterpart, is to record the specific frames that you would like to appear in the film.

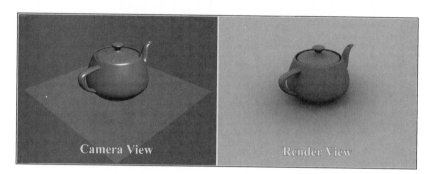

visual |4–2|

Example of the Camera View and the Rendered View

The camera is set up to reveal as much as or as little as the director sees fit. Therefore, these are the cameras that will be rendered after all of the modeling, animation, and lighting has taken place. Furthermore, these *rendering* cameras will dictate how much geometry, animation, and lighting is needed for each shot. In other words, just like a Hollywood production, you only need to be concerned with objects and characters that can be seen, referred to as on-camera. Anything that isn't seen, or off-camera, is a misuse of time to create or prepare.

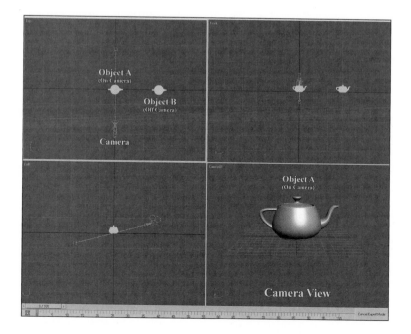

visual |4–3|

Example of Off-Camera Objects versus On-Camera Objects

Camera Representations and Icons

Within the 3D environment, the virtual camera is considered an object just like anything else. It is typically broken up into two very distinct components: the *base camera* and the *target* or *aim*. The base camera, which often looks like a movie camera, will hold all of the parameters in which you'll need to adjust as a director, for example lens type and focal length.

Examples of Common
Base Camera Icons

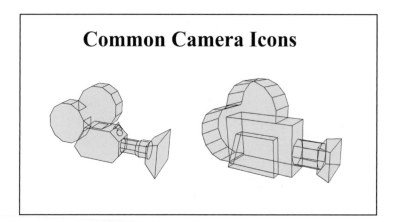

The camera target is just that: the target or direction in which the base camera is aiming. Although the target has no inherent parameters to adjust, it is often represented as a small box or sphere, which can easily be identified and adjusted.

Example of the
Camera Target

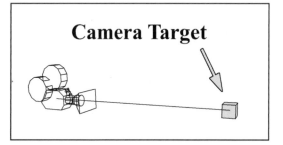

Because they are treated like objects, both the base camera and the target can be moved and animated together or independently. However, the camera is by default a *nonrenderable object* in the scene. That is to say, you can see it in all of the viewports, but it will not appear in the final render or frames in the film. This is one of the many great benefits of working within the virtual environment. The director can decide which objects can be rendered and which ones will not. In an environment in which ten cameras looking at the same scene is not uncommon, not having to worry if they will be seen by another camera is a great time-saver.

Orthographic Views

Of the four cameras that make up the standard *viewport configuration* (Top, Side, Front, and Perspective), three are *orthographic* views. Orthographic, or flat, view captures the scene without taking perspective into consideration. Objects of the same size will appear that way even if they are at different distances from the camera. Therefore, the orthographic cameras are great resources for the modeling and setup stages in the production process but, because of their flat look, are not often used as renderable cameras.

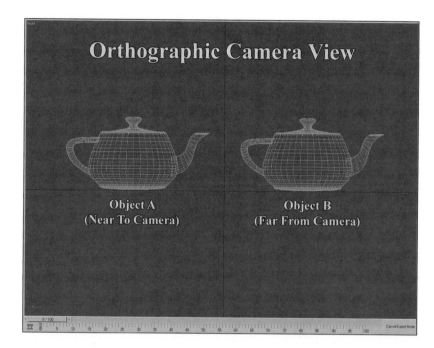

visual |4–6|

Orthographic View

Perspective Views

The perspective camera view mimics a real-world camera. Depending on how you adjust its parameters, it can be made to look like almost any type of camera on the market. These cameras are what you'll want to use to render your final shots, as they are the most flexible. Although there is often a single perspective camera when the program opens, you can create an unlimited amount of them and rename them whatever makes the most sense in your scene.

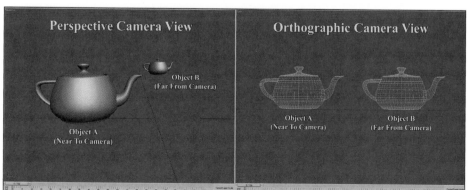

visual |4–7|

Examples of an Orthographic View and a Perspective View

COMMON PARAMETERS

Within all of the most popular 3D software packages, there are numerous options from which the user can tailor the virtual camera to the film's particular needs. Although these may vary slightly from package to package, a digital director can rely on the fact that all have these common parameters.

Camera Type

The first choice you will need to make when creating a new camera is the camera type. This decision should be based on the types of camera shots and moves that you plan to use. The most common camera type is one with both the base and the target/aim.

However, there is also an option to have a camera without the target or aim, which is often referred to as a *free camera*. This camera is typically reserved for very specific shots and camera moves where the target and base camera direction must be locked together.

Lenses

This next camera decision is based less on the movement possibilities and more on the actual look of the image. The *preset* for a new camera in most programs will be a lens with a focal length somewhere in the 35–45 mm range. That will give you a look that is typical in the filmmaking world and something that the average audience can identify.

Free Camera

An informed digital director will make camera lens/focal length decisions based on the needs of the shot. Keep in mind that the virtual camera is also the ultimate zoom lens. It can be set at any focal length, including those that are impossible to achieve with a real camera, or it can be animated to change throughout a particular shot.

As you will see in Visuals 4–10 to 4–12, the same object has been rendered with three different camera focal lengths. Although the geometry and lighting have not changed, the varying focal lengths elicit dramatically different feelings from the audience. Anything lower than a 50 mm focal length will produce a wide-angle affect with a great deal of separation between foreground and background. Anything higher than the 50 mm length will produce a telephoto effect that will flatten the image.

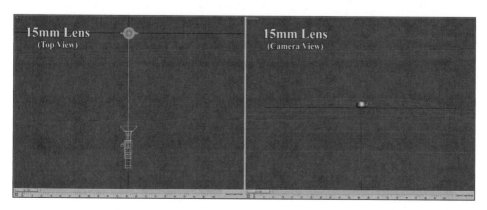

Example of 15 mm Lens
(Wide-Angle)

Example of 50 mm Lens
(Human Eye)

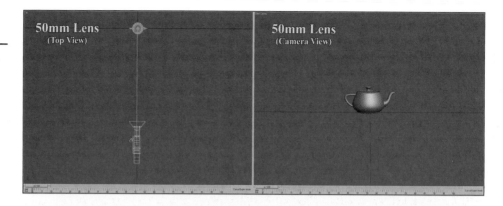

Example of 200 mm Lens
(Telephoto)

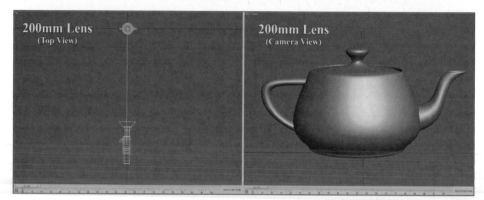

Cones and Clipping Planes

Camera cones and *clipping planes* are essential tools for the digital director when working in the virtual environment. The camera cone and clipping planes form the framework of the viewable area of the camera. In other words, only objects that fall inside the cone and clipping planes will be seen by the camera.

The camera cone is a conic shape that begins from the lens of the camera and grows outward. The shape or volume of the cone is determined by the focal length of the lens, and the larger the focal length the smaller the cone, overall volume, and viewable area. The camera cone will be much larger, and it will have more volume and a larger viewable area the smaller the focal length.

The camera cone is a critical tool for the director especially during the animation phase of the production. Although you can always look through the camera in one of the viewports, similar to looking through the camera in traditional filmmaking, being able to use the cone in the top, side, front and perspective viewports for reference allows for precise adjustments as to what is being seen and not seen in a particular shot. For instance, in Visual 4–15, you can see that the teapot is clearly not inside the camera

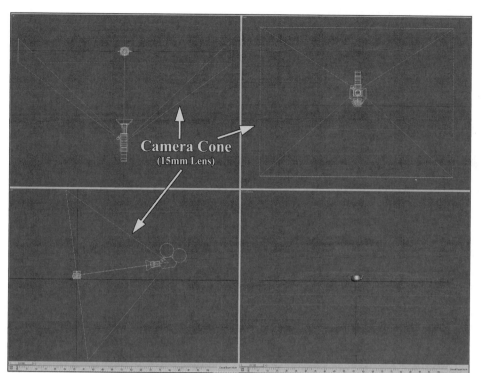

visual |4–13|

Example of the Camera
Cone from a 15 mm Lens

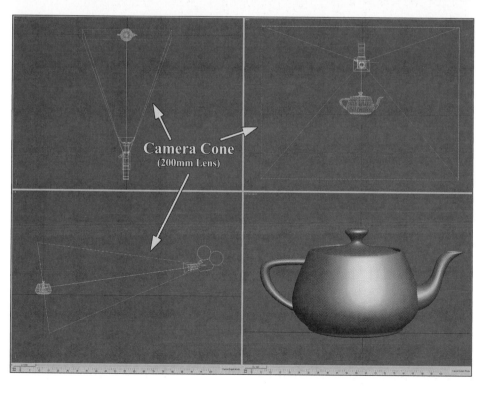

visual |4–14|

Example of the Camera
Cone from a 200 mm Lens

cone; consequently, will not be seen by the viewer. However, in the very next frame of the shot, Visual 4–16, the teapot is clearly within the camera cone and produces the render in Visual 4–17.

visual |4–15|

Example of Object
Outside the Camera Cone

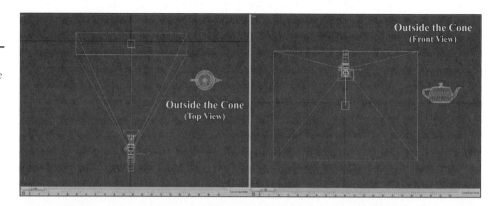

visual |4–16|

Example of Object Inside
the Camera Cone

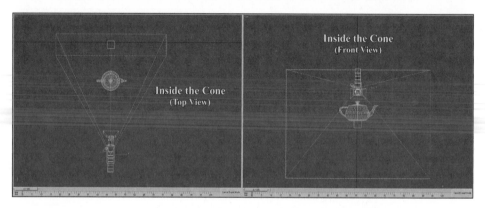

Working hand in hand with the cone to frame the viewable area of a camera are the clipping planes. Although the camera cone defines the width and height of the view space, the clipping planes determine the overall length. In particular, there are typically two clipping planes, near and far, for each camera that the director may adjust accordingly. The near clipping plane determines the exact distance from which the camera will start to see objects. In contrast, the far clipping plane will determine where the camera stops seeing objects. However, it is important to note that the clipping planes always follow the path of the camera cone.

visual |4–17|

Render of Visual 4–16

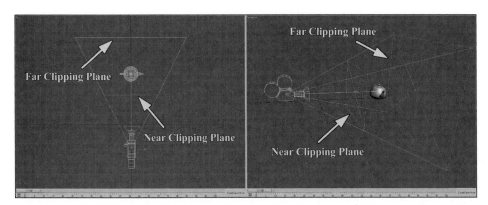

visual |4–18|

Example of Near and Far
Clipping Planes

Image Planes

Image planes are often used in combination with virtual cameras to easily create background imagery and/or reflections in the scene. Although they are visible as three-dimensional objects within the workspace, in fact they are two-dimensional, in that their relationship to the camera is fixed. In other words, the image plane, and whatever image color is applied to it, will always be parallel to the film plane in the camera and therefore will appear flat.

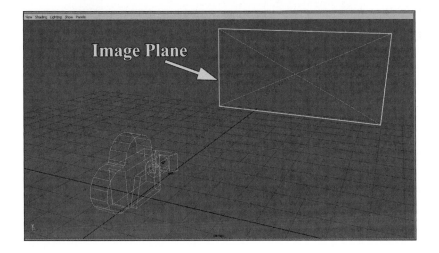

visual |4–19|

Example of an Image
Plane Assigned to
a Camera

From student films to Hollywood feature films, image planes are used to mimic background objects, landscapes, and environments that would otherwise be very time-consuming to create in 3D. Much like a movie sound stage or set, the image plane can be made to look like almost anything your shot requires. In fact, they are used so often in today's production environments that specific jobs have been carved out for artists who create the amazing imagery that is placed on the image planes. These artists, or digital matte painters as they are more commonly known, are much more akin to fine art painters than they are 3D artists. However, their role within 3D production is as critical as the modelers, lighters, and animators. Furthermore, the best digital matte painting examples are so realistic that you would not be able to tell that they are flat images.

Background Color

The default background color within most 3D packages is black. Any space within a given render that is not taken up by geometry will appear as a black void. Although that might work for a few small productions, chances are that you are going to want to adjust that color. In some 3D packages, that color is controlled through the camera settings directly, and in other packages, it is controlled through the environment settings.

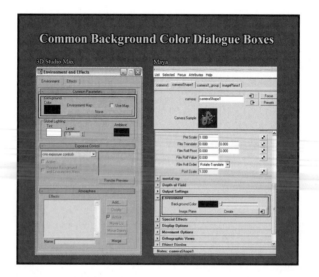

DEPTH OF FIELD REVISITED

Depth of field (DOF) is a powerful optical tool for both the live action and virtual director. It can be used for pure artistic expression, as a focusing agent for the viewer, but, more often than not, it is used as both. Although the live action director must carefully balance lens-types, focal lengths, and object distances in order to harness this, the virtual director has complete control over a camera's DOF. In fact, the virtual director has control beyond the limits of reality; making the DOF creation process a streamlined, artist-friendly endeavor.

By default, most 3D programs have DOF turned off. Therefore, all objects in your scene will appear to be in sharp focus independent of camera, lens, or distance. However, with a few clicks of your mouse, you can adjust any camera to mimic the real-world DOF effect.

Determining the Focal Point(s)

The beauty of working with DOF within the virtual environment is the ease of use and pinpoint precision you have over the effect. Irrespective of what camera lens-type you are using and object distances, you can achieve almost any DOF effect you can imagine. You will want to decide what object or series of objects within your scene you want to be in focus. These objects and, more important, their distance from the camera, will need to be designated as the camera's *focal point*.

Example of Virtual
DOF Shot

There are two different ways that you can designate the camera's focal point within a given shot or scene. The first and the most straightforward approach is to choose a particular object or set of objects in the scene as the focal point. Although this is not offered in every 3D package, it will allow the virtual director to pick what should be in focus at a particular frame in the film quickly. However, it is important to note that this approach is great for a shot that will either not change its DOF or will follow one particular moving object or group of objects.

If your shot calls for the DOF to switch focus from one object to another object within the same shot, you will want to use the camera target to designate a focal point. This approach requires a little more effort to make sure that the camera target is always in alignment with where you want the focal point in your shot. However, you can animate the camera target, much as you would any other object in your scene. Therefore, the camera DOF can move between objects over time, which would result in a nice rack focus effect.

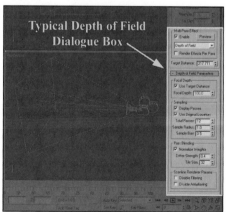

Typical DOF
Dialogue Box

Adjusting the Focal Parameters

Once the camera's focal point has been determined, you will need to adjust the focal parameters to obtain the desired level of DOF within the image. There are typically two things to consider when adjusting the magnitude of the DOF; the range of the overall focus and the intensity of the blur. The focal range or region scale will determine how shallow or not the DOF is within the shot. For instance, there will be a great difference in the focal range from a shot that is trying to focus on one cornflake in a bowl of cereal versus trying to focus on a tree within a forest. The larger the focal range, the larger the area surrounding the focal point that will appear sharply in focus. Conversely, the smaller the focal length the more shallow the DOF and smaller the area around the focal point the will appear in sharp focus.

The last parameter you will want to adjust when developing a DOF effect for a camera is the magnitude of focal loss. This will determine the intensity of the blur for those objects outside the DOF. A large focal loss will result in a sharply-focused focal point object with extremely blurry objects around it. The overall effect of a large focal loss is not only an extreme focusing agent but gives a sense of great depth within the shot even for those objects that are quite close.

A small focal loss within your focal parameters will result in a more subtle difference between those objects that are inside the DOF area versus those that are not. Depending on how blatant the virtual director wishes to be with the audience, the focal loss can be adjusted accordingly. Objects that appear in shots that utilize a small focal loss will appear to be closer than those that have a large focal loss.

visual |4–23|

Example of a Large Focal Loss

visual |4–24|

Example of a Small Focal Loss

CREATING BASIC 3D CAMERA MOVES

Unlike the live-action film camera, the 3D camera is not limited by time, space, or gravity, leaving limitless possibilities for the virtual filmmaker. The 3D camera is capable of mimicking almost any real-world camera move as well as many more that just simply would not be possible because of physical or financial limitations. Whether you are doing the simplest of dollies or an elaborate fly-through, there are two basic vehicles for creating the basic camera move in 3D.

Keyframed

The most common way to create a camera move within a 3D environment is with keyframes. The camera, and its position within 3D space, is treated like any other object in the scene. Therefore, you can place it anywhere in scene and create movement by setting at least two keyframes.

For example, to create a simple 3D camera truck, let's begin by placing a sphere in the scene at the origin (see Visual 4–25). Create a targeted camera in the top viewport and make sure that aim is pointed in the direction of the sphere. Pick the base camera, still in the top viewport, and make any adjustments you need as far as distance is concerned (see Visual 4–26). Next, change the perspective viewport to the new camera, typically named Camera 01, so that you can see exactly what the camera is seeing. You will probably notice that since you created the camera in the top viewport that it is probably lying flat on the ground plane. To adjust the camera height, pick the base camera leaving the camera target alone and using a side viewport and move the camera above the ground plane (see Visual 4–27). This will create a slightly more appealing downward view on the sphere.

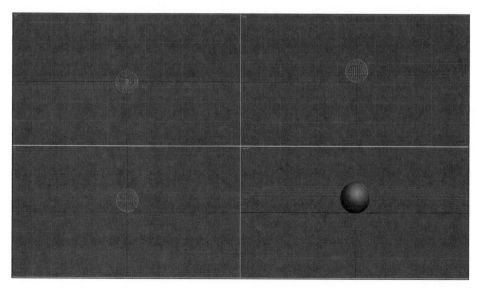

visual |4–25|

3D Camera Truck –
Object Placement

3D Camera Truck –
Camera Placement Top

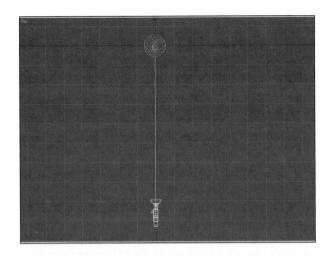

3D Camera Truck –
Camera Placement Side

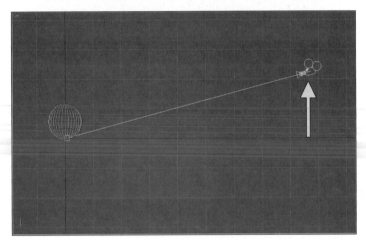

Once you feel as though the camera is an appropriate full-shot view, the complete sphere is in the frame, you can set your first keyframe at frame 0 on the timeline. Next we will want to move the timeslider up to frame 30 to prepare to set our next keyframe. Because this will only be a one-second camera move, this will be the last keyframe that we will need to set. Next, we can move the base camera to a position much closer to the sphere. We will also probably want to flatten out the camera's height a bit so that we are not looking directly down on the top of the sphere in Visual 4–29. Once it is in the appropriate position, set another keyframe at frame 30.

Animation Tangents

One of the more important settings to consider when creating keyframed camera movements are the *animation tangents*. Every keyframe that you set has an In Tangent and an Out Tangent. That refers to how the software package interpolates

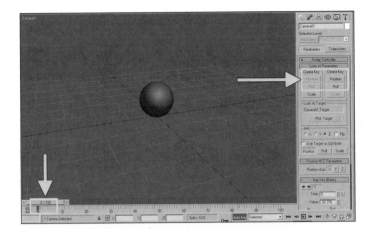

3D Camera Truck – First
Keyframe

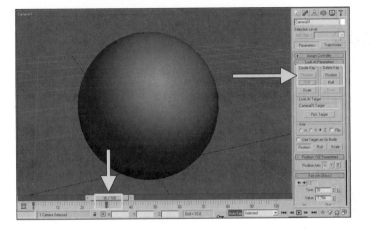

3D Camera Truck – Last
Keyframe

the movement from one keyframe to another. For instance, in the camera truck example, we set one keyframe at frame 0 and one at frame 30. However, there are many different ways that we can control how the camera gets from Point A to Point B. The most straightforward approach would be an even interpolation in which the movement is divided into equal steps depending on how many frames are between keyframes. However, that will result in a very unnatural and robotic movement. There might be scenarios where you might want this effect but, more often then not, you are going to want to create a more natural and realistic movement with your animations.

In general, you can create very realistic movements using some of the default tangent types within the 3D software such as smooth and flat. Objects tend to move a little slower at the beginning and end of each movement. This rule of thumb is especially true when it comes to camerawork.

Animation Keyframe Tangents

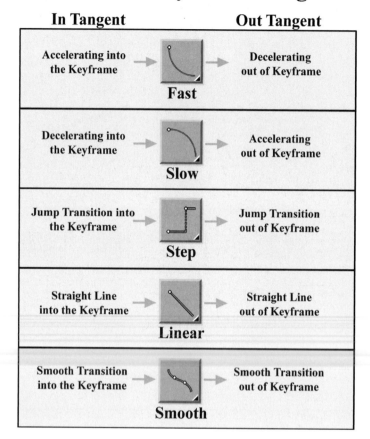

In Tangent		Out Tangent
Accelerating into the Keyframe	**Fast**	Decelerating out of Keyframe
Decelerating into the Keyframe	**Slow**	Accelerating out of Keyframe
Jump Transition into the Keyframe	**Step**	Jump Transition out of Keyframe
Straight Line into the Keyframe	**Linear**	Straight Line out of Keyframe
Smooth Transition into the Keyframe	**Smooth**	Smooth Transition out of Keyframe

Camera Paths

The other basic approach to creating camera movements within the virtual environment is with *camera paths*. Unlike the keyframed approach, the camera is attached to a fixed path within the scene. This technique is great for creating precise, robotic camera movements. Although the camera must stay on that path, the user can determine its position along the path for a particular point in time. Therefore, a camera movement can be created by keying in various pat positions at various frames along your timeline. For instance, one of the more common student demo reel pieces is a 360-degree camera rotation around a model. However, it is not very easy to create a seamless rotation utilizing the keyframe-only method. If you attach a camera to a circle spline, it becomes very easy to achieve the perfect rotation.

Camera paths are also commonly used in architectural visualizations to create virtual fly-throughs. Again, the camera path technique allows the director to easily set up a camera animation through the various environments without intersecting any walls and furniture.

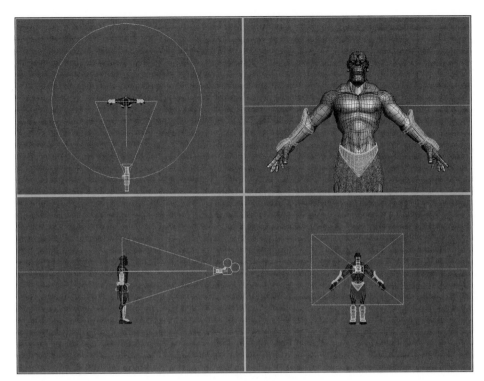

3D Camera Path Rotation

THE MEANING BEHIND THE MOVEMENT

Camera moves are an outstanding filmmaking tool, but there must be a significant motivating reason or purpose behind every one. *Empty moves*, or camera moves without purpose, can result in viewer distraction and annoyance. Therefore, it is important to explore some of the psychology behind the moving camera before setting a single keyframe.

Insider Info

Filmmaking is a time-based media in which the viewer experiences each frame, shot, and scene. That experience is completely controlled, in digital filmmaking, by the virtual director. Every camera move tries to mimic reality or to enhance reality for the audience. In other words, the director must make a conscious choice about how to translate the actions and events that transpire in the film through the camera to the audience. Will the camera play a passive role in the film, simply recording the events that unfold in front of it? Will the camera play an active role, not only recording the events but also enhancing the viewer experience, good or bad, by providing more or less visual details than would normally be available?

Passive Moves

Passive camera movements are designed to capture the action that is presented without passing judgment or bias along to the viewer. The viewer experience is that of a third-party nonparticipant, and, therefore, any camera movement that is involved is simply to capture that which would go unseen otherwise. For instance, if two characters are standing and talking at a specific location and then decide, in mid-conversation, to start walking to another location, a passive camera move could be used follow the action. The camera move plays a very specific role for the viewer, allowing the character's conversation to be uninterrupted visually.

Active Moves

Active camera movements go beyond what is necessary to add drama, suspense, intrigue, and creativity to the events that are taking place in the shot. The director decides that a particular camera move, although not absolutely necessary to capture the events, will enhance the viewing experience. For example, the zolly often was used by Alfred Hitchcock to give the viewer a sense of panic and confusion that the character on screen was feeling.

INTRODUCTION TO CAMERA STAGING AND BLOCKING

In the simplest forms, *staging* is the art of placing all of the characters and objects in the scene at the right place at the right time. *Blocking*, by contrast, is the art of placing the camera at the right place at the right time. The two are closely connected and is almost impossible to talk about one without the other.

Staging and blocking are the director's attempt to precisely plan each movement, character, object, or camera. The end result of a well-staged, well-blocked shot will be significantly compelling and engaging to the viewer. In fact, this is the downfall for most amateur animated films. There is so much concentration put on the modeling and animation that the camera-work becomes a utilitarian means to an end. In fact, if you ask most of those filmmakers why they put the camera where they did, they would not have an answer. The problem with that is that poor staging and blocking can actually turn the

visual |4–32|

Camera Blocking

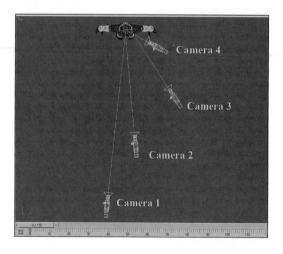

viewer's attention away from any of the modeling and animation in the film. There are some golden rules of thumb that will aid in the development of great staging and blocking. In fact, although blocking is critical in both live-action and digital filmmaking, it is so quick and easy to set up in the 3D world that it has become an integral part of the production process in most studios.

Image Composition

Much like a fine art painter, the virtual director must consider the overall composition of the image when working with the camera. Although paintings have a real-life boundary called a frame, the digital director has to work within certain frame/image requirements as well. Typically, these requirements are dictated by the delivery medium that can have varying aspect ratios, which is the display pixel width divided by the pixel height. For instance, if the animation is intended for television, the frame of the film will have to fit within the NTSC aspect ratio of 4:3, or 1.33:1, or 640 pixels × 480 pixels. Therefore, the director must work within those parameters when designing the camera placements/moves. Visual 4–33 illustrates some of the more common aspect ratios.

visual |4–33|

Common Aspect Ratios

Most 3D software programs allow you to customize the aspect ratio within the Render Settings dialogue box.

Once the aspect ratio or frame of the image has been determined, the director must understand how to use that available image area to the best interest of

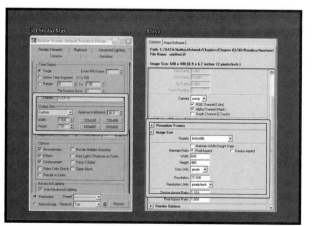

visual |4–34|

Render Dialogue Box –
Aspect Ratio Settings

the shot. Although there are endless possibilities for camera framing, there are some basic criteria for determining the best options for that particular shot.

Image Balance

When setting up a particular camera shot, it is extremely important to consider the overall balance of the image. Much like a real-life balance or scale, an image has weight that can be distributed in different manners. The easiest way to determine an image's balance is to divide it into halves, left and right and top and bottom. If the images are leaning too far to one side, your focus and attention will be leaning to one side of the image. This pulling of the viewer's attention is a result of an unbalanced composition that will lead to an unpleasant, uneasy, and stressful feeling from the viewer. Although there may be times that a director may want this exact feeling, the majority of shots will want some form of balance, symmetrical or asymmetrical.

visual | 4–35 |

Unbalanced Image

Symmentrical Balance

Symmetrical balance is achieved when the viewer's attention is diverted from the edges of the frame to focus on the center. Utilizing the grid we used to determine balance, a symmetrical image should have the same number of characters, objects, and colors, on one half as it does the other. It can either be the left and right half or the top and bottom and does not have to be both.

Symmetrical balance has the tendency to put the viewer at ease. However, it is often used as a comparison tool, as both a confrontational and nonconfrontational tool. In Visual 4–36, two characters are approaching the same object from different directions, which results in a symmetrically balanced image.

Symmetrically
Balanced Image

Asymmetrical Balance

An asymmetrically balanced image is similar to the symmetrical variety in that the weight of the image is even across the frame. However, unlike symmetrical balance, the *asymmetry* is formed when the image is not mirrored but balanced with different types of objects. For instance, in Visual 4–37, the hero is seen outside his hut. The hero is the dominant or main object filling up the right side of the screen, whereas the hut is serving as the weight for the left side.

visual |4–37|

Asymmetrically
Balanced Image

Rule of Thirds

The *Rule of Thirds* is a compositional guideline that stems from the Ancient Greek Golden Rectangle philosophy, which says that there is a mathematical equation for the proportions of beauty. Building on the balance grid that we just created, let's break down the image even further into nine equal parts. To achieve this break the image frame into three equal parts both horizontally and vertically.

visual |4–38|

Rule of Thirds Diagram

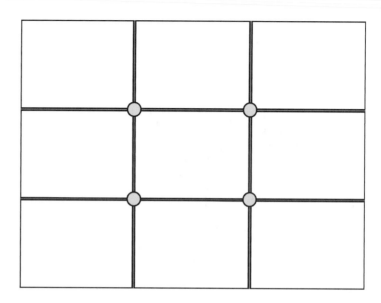

Points of Interest – Power Points

The four lines that you drew to create the nine equal parts of the frame have four extremely important intersecting points. These points are often referred to as the *Points of Interest,* or Power Points, as they pinpoint the areas in the frame that will generate the most interest from the viewer when aligned with the important features in your shot. For instance, both Visuals 4–39 and 4–40 are relatively the same shot. However, Visual 4–39 places the focus point in the center of the frame, whereas Visual 4–40 utilizes the Rule of Thirds to determine the composition. In particular, the horizon line has been aligned with the bottom horizontal guideline and the hut is placed slightly to the right of center over one of the Power Points.

visual |4–39|

Image Not Utilizing the Rule of Thirds

visual |4–40|

Image Utilizing the Rule of Thirds

Closed Framing

Closed framing is achieved when clear borders are formed around the edges of the image frame. These borders can be characters, objects, or props, but they must give the appearance that outside world is shut off from the viewer. More important, closed framing alludes to the audience that the shot is a self-contained world where no other information is needed to accomplish the shot's goal. For instance, in Visual 4–41, the hero is seen inside his hut. The doorway around the character forms a nice border, creating a closed frame for the viewer.

visual |4–41|

Example of a
Closed Frame

Open Framing

The opposite of the closed frame, the *open frame* leaves the borders of the image frame open. This typically used in outdoor shot where the audience is to believe that other important events are happening elsewhere at the same time. For instance, Visual 4–42 shows the hero character about to leave his safe home to climb the mountain, which is depicted in the background. The viewer is left wondering what the mountain has in store for the hero.

visual |4–42|

Example of an
Open Frame

CAMERA BLOCKING CONVENTIONS

These days, it seems everyone is inundated by professionally produced camerawork. Whether it is live-action films, animation, television, or the Internet, people are constantly seeing imagery via the camera. With this constant bombardment comes an innate ability to recognize basic camera techniques. The average person cannot articulate what these conventions are or why they work, but they can tell the difference between good and bad camerawork.

Although it is tempting for beginner filmmakers to ignore these conventions, especially within the 3D virtual environment, every director must understand that these building blocks are not only time-tested but form the foundation of the language of film. That's not to say that filmmakers shouldn't push the boundaries and develop a unique personal style. However, this foundational film language is ingrained in the general viewer's psyche and will serve as a launching platform for your own creative spin.

Most beginners will create films that involve characters of some shape and form. Although it is critical that there are not too many characters in your first few films, especially for the animators, there probably will be more than one. Therefore, it is critical to understand how to block out shots where the characters interact. Let's examine the three types of shots that, combined in any number of different ways, will create a baseline camera-blocking methodology.

Master Shot

The most encompassing of all three shots, the master is a wide-angle shot that captures all of the necessary action and events in the scene. In a typical character interaction setup, the *master shot* should be at a relatively equal distance from each person involved generating an intentional third-person, neutral feel for the viewer. Visual 4–43 shows a simple overhead diagram outlining a typical camera position for a master shot.

visual | 4–43 |

Master Shot Diagram

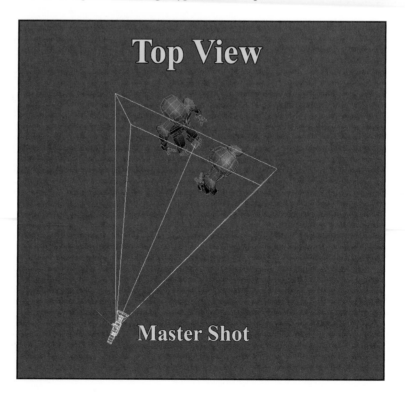

Live-action directors will often want to shoot the entire scene with this camera so that they have plenty of options when it comes to the editing process down the road. However, it is less important for the 3D animator because you can always perfectly recreate each acting performance. Therefore, if you need additional footage, it is easy to render.

Exterior Shots

Working inward, the next shot is the *exterior shot*. The purpose of this shot is to involve the viewer in the action, which will automatically heighten the drama and intensity. This shot will be an over-the-shoulder of one of the characters looking at another character or object. Visual 4–45 shows a simple overhead diagram outlining a typical camera position for an exterior shot.

visual |4–44|

Example of a Final Master Shot

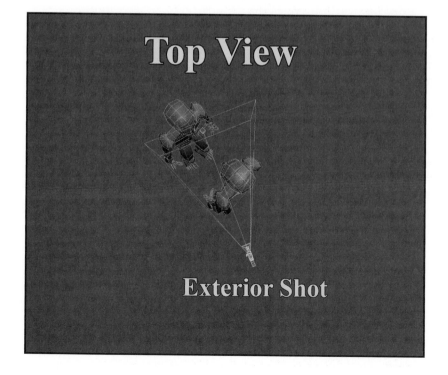

visual |4–45|

Exterior Shot Diagram

Example of a Final
Exterior Shot

Interior Shots

Interior shots are similar to a close-up or POV shot in that the character or object fills up the majority of the frame. This shot brings the audience into a dramatic and intimate place within the scene. The viewer becomes an active participant as they feel as if they are looking at the character themselves. Visual 4–47 shows a simple overhead diagram outlining a typical camera position for an interior shot.

Interior Shot Diagram

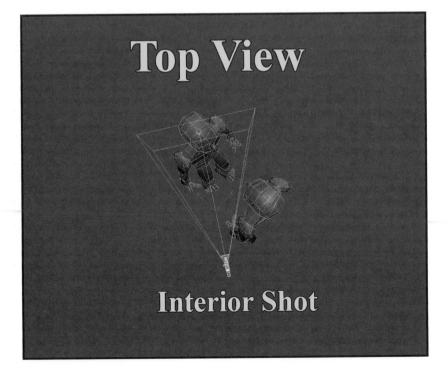

Example of a Final
Interior Shot

Putting it Together

A common progression for a character interaction scene is to start with a master shot and work the camera closer and closer to the characters. Inevitably, the action within the scene will build as well and the camerawork will help to reinforce that. Visual 4–49 shows how all three shots put together would look. Notice how the drama builds visually even when you do not know the reason for the interaction.

	Master	Exterior	Interior
Wire			
Render			

visual |4–49|

Example of All Three
Shots Put Together

CONTINUITY

Because cameras are extremely easy to create and duplicate in the 3D environment, there is no reason not to have a multicamera production. However, with the addition of every new camera in a scene comes increased opportunity for breaks in *visual continuity*. In other words, every time the view switches from one camera shot to another within the same scene, there must be overlapping visual cues to maintain the viewer's bearings. Otherwise, the continuity will be lost, confusion. As with most other aspects of the digital filmmaking process, there are some rules of thumb that can help even beginning directors to navigate the sometimes choppy continuity waters.

Axis of Action

The *axis of action*, also known as the line of action, is an invisible line that connects the main characters or objects in a scene. This axis of action can be really easy to determine in some shots and not so easy in others. You can have two characters having a conversation with each other. The invisible line is formed between the two characters' eye lines.

Axis of Action Example –
Two Characters

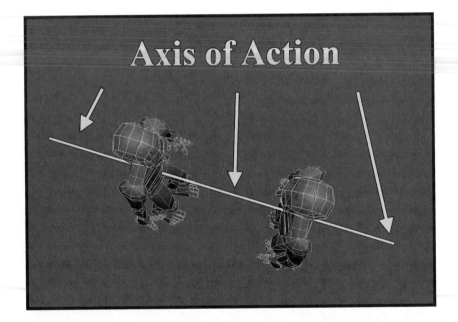

However, finding the axis of action when there are three or more characters can be tricky. In fact, there might be multiple lines of action within a given scene if two of the characters have a subconversation in the midst of larger conversation between three or more.

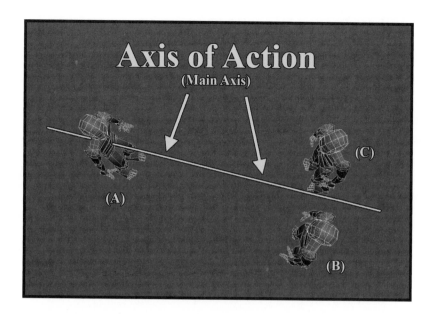

visual | 4–51 |

Axis of Action Example –
Three Characters
(Main Axis)

Pivot Shot

When blocking scenes with multiple lines of action, it is critical that a *pivot shot* is used as a transition. The pivot should be of the character or object that is common to the two different shots. For instance, character (B) in Visual 4–52 is the perfect pivot between the two lines of action. The character will serve as a visual compass for the viewer as you switch between shots, allowing for the overall continuity to be preserved.

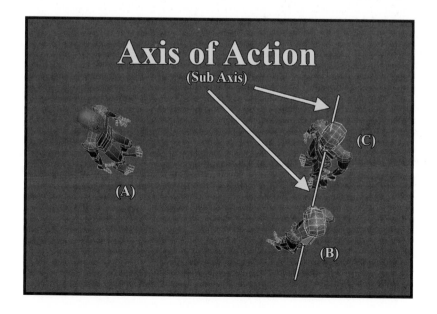

visual | 4–52 |

Axis of Action Example –
Three Characters
(Sub Axis)

180 Degree Rule

The *180 degree rule* works hand in hand with the axis of action to make sure that visual continuity is preserved. Depending on which side of the line the initial camera is positioned, all subsequent camera positions will have to remain on that side of the axis of action. Although this may seem somewhat limiting at first, you only have to break the rule once to see how annoying it can be to the viewer to break the visual continuity.

visual |4–53|

180° Rule Diagram

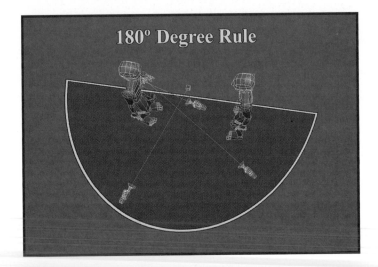

Although we didn't discuss the axis of action or the 180 degree rule at that point, the three shots used to create Visual 4–49 follow the rule. However, compare those images to the diagram in Visual 4–54 that intentionally breaks this rule. If this blocking were to be used, it would be unclear to the viewer if it the director cut between two different scenes.

visual |4–54|

180° Rule Broken

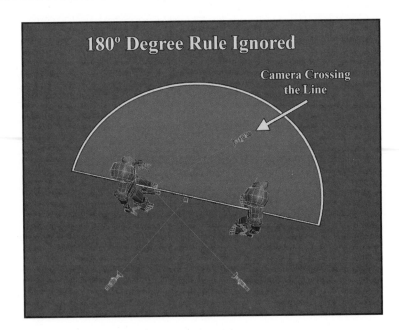

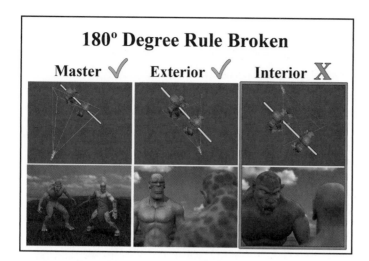

ADVANCED 3D CAMERA TECHNIQUES

Because of its unique ability to ignore the laws of physics, the 3D camera can make certain shots that would be very difficult to achieve with live-action a breeze.

Camera Shake and the Dynamically Driven Camera

Camera Shake is often referred to in negative terms when discussing the basics of filmmaking. At a high level, a camera that is shaking can be extremely annoying and discomforting to the average viewer. However, if the shake is done correctly, it can give the appearance of a hand-held camera or home-movie look. This particular look became very popular after the release of feature films such as *The Blair Witch Project* and *Pi* and has become even more familiar to the average viewer as a result of the recent popularity of reality television.

Beyond the purposeful camera shake, even hard-mounted live-action cameras have a very slight shake to them when they move. Although this shake may go unnoticed by most, it registers subconsciously as a cue to the viewer that this shot is from a live camera. These slight movements and shakes, however, are not the 3D camera's forte. The 3D camera is great at making extremely smooth or extremely robotic movements, which tend to give animations a very unreal feel. Although that may be desirable in certain circumstances, for the most part virtual directors want the camera to add to the story.

There are a couple of options to help add some of those human touches. The first is to hand keyframe some of the jitter, shake, and overlapping motion that ordinarily would appear in live-action filmmaking. To accomplish this, you should first keyframe the camera as you would normally and then go back to add the imperfections. Remember, the goal is to add just enough so that it is barely noticeable. In fact, if the viewer notices it at all, you have gone too far. You should be most concerned with the stops and starts of the camera moves as that is when most of the shakes and jitters happen.

Camera Shake Diagram

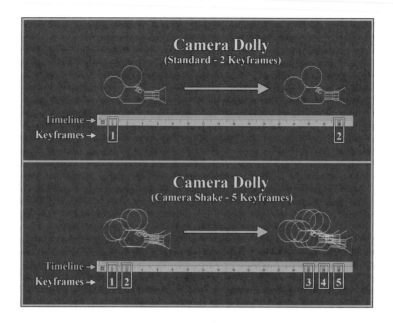

The other option, which is significantly more complex, is to create a dynamically driven camera. Most high-end 3D software packages have some form of dynamic simulation capabilities built in. *Dynamics,* as it is known, encompasses a suite of virtual tools that allows for the simulation of real-world physics onto 3D objects. Elements that are commonplace in the natural world such as gravity, wind, cloth, water, fire, hair, springs, and collisions, involve extremely complex mathematical computations to recreate in the 3D world. However, the software manufactures have developed amazingly intuitive tools to help bring these capabilities to the virtual director. For example, you can place gravity into a 3D scene and have objects fall to the ground as they would in real life. Also, you can create collision objects so that when that object falls to the earth it will react to the ground instead of just falling through it.

Visual 4–57 shows a sample diagram of how a dynamic camera might be set up.

Dynamic Camera
Example

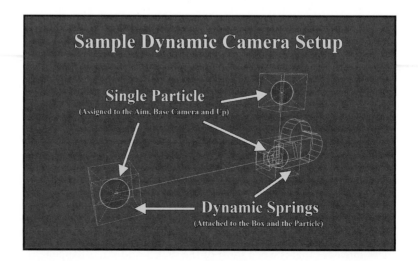

Match Moving and Camera Tracking

Match moving and *camera tracking* has become a huge part of the production process in the special effects industry. This is because so many special effects shots are created in the computer, and, more specifically, with 3D animation. In fact, there are entire movies that are now being shot with *Green Screen* technology so that they can fill in everything from the background to main characters in 3D. However, one of the major sticking points with this process has always been matching live-action moving cameras with those in the 3D packages. For instance, if you are shooting a truck shot on a live actor and need to create the background in 3D, the cameras have to match or the background will look like its moving out of sync with the actor. Therefore, match moving or camera tracking capabilities have been incorporated into most 3D packages to handle just these scenarios. The theory is quite simple: Import some footage into the virtual world and assign specific points in the 2D footage for the software to track over time and convert to 3D camera data.

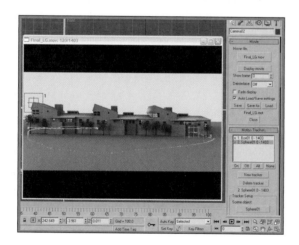

visual | 4–58 |

Example of a Match Move Interface

Although this is great for people in the special effects industry or for anyone trying to combine live-action and 3D footage, this also can be used to create more realistic camera moves in 3D similar to the results that you obtain with a dynamically driven camera. For instance, you could shoot some footage with a video camera that mimics what you would like to see in the 3D world, import it into the software package, run a match move on the footage, and use that camera for your virtual shot. Although you never intended to use that video footage in your film, it can give your camerawork a realistic look and feel.

artist SPOTLIGHT   *christopher cordingley*

Character Animator, Walt Disney Feature Animation

visual |4–59|

Headshot of Christopher Cordingley

Christopher Cordingley graduated from Ringling School of Art and Design in 2001 and has since served as a Character Animator for both Rhythm and Hues Studios and Disney Feature Animation. His short film, *After You,* was accepted into SIGGRAPH's Electronic Theater in 2003. He has given numerous lectures on computer animation within the United States and abroad. You may also see his work on his Web site at *http://www.cordingley.com*

Credits:
2004-Present
Meet the Robinsons – Character Animator
2003–2004
Garfield – Character Animator
2001
After You – All Aspects of Production including Animating, Story, Directing, Modeling, Rigging, and Lighting.

Artist Spotlight with Christopher Cordingley
Looking Back at the Making of His Award-Winning Student Film *After You*

Q. What were your main criteria when developing the story/script for *After You*?

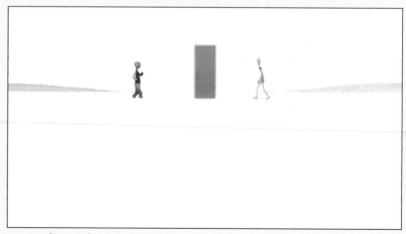

visual |4–60|

After You – Christopher Cordingley

A. I wanted to show some sort of interaction between two characters with contrasting personalities. I heard that was good demo reel material. I also wanted to keep things simple overall, but that's basically it. I remember growing frustrated about what I wanted to do even three years before I started working on my senior project. I had no idea what I wanted, so I jokingly mentioned to a friend that my animation will probably be just characters on a blank stage. It's funny that that actually happened.

Q. I stress to my students who are developing their senior film the 2-2-2 rule. Their films should be nor more than two characters, two sets, and two minutes in length. It seems as though *After You* fits right into that mold. Was this a conscious decision? If so, what were some of your other production limitations?

A. That's pretty close to the guidelines my teachers gave us, too. Although they wanted us to plan it out so that it was no longer than one minute, because often times the shots get longer when it comes to actually animating them. This was definitely a good guideline for me. And although mine ended up being about two and a half minutes, the fact that I had only two characters and one set let me spend more time working out the story. In total, I probably spent about seventy percent of my time on the story alone. I really needed that time. One other limitation we had, since we all shared the same resources as students, was that each frame could take no longer than ten minutes to render. I think mine ended up being about five minutes at the most.

Q. Since there was no dialogue in your animation, the story had to be delivered in other ways. While the acting played a huge role of course, how much of that story delivery do you think was the work of the camera?

A. One of my attempts to block out my animation involved showing everything in one shot and with no camera

visual |4–61|

After You – Christopher Cordingley

moves. This was partially due to a suggestion from a friend, and partially due to the fact that I had to show my progress on schedule and I simply wasn't ready to plan out individual shots yet. It was a little discouraging because I was no model student when it came to showing my progress. The story basically read in a single shot (sort of), but it was odd, hard to follow and boring. Camerawork helped simplify and clarify everything. It also helped support the feeling I was going for. Whether it was an up shot or a down shot of each character aided in their display of status. Composition and camera moves aided the emotional and dynamic impact of each shot. And simply the angle a shot was taken from helped those shots toward the end where I used the physical door or door frame for support.

Q. What was/is your overall philosophy when it comes to camerawork and blocking? How much do you pull from traditional, live-action film making?

A. I wanted my camerawork to support my animation. My goal after graduation was to get a job doing character animation, so I focused on that and heightened it with the camera. I think that all of my use of the camera came from traditional films. The principles I used work in both media simply because they are both pictures in motion. I can't reference anything specifically as inspiration, but I knew I was not doing anything new here as far as camera work. I think my overall philosophy is to support what's going on with the camera and not to add anything for the sake of adding it. That basically went for everything.

Q. As a filmmaker who uses animation, who are the film-makers and directors that you admire and why?

A. Working in the film industry I'm probably the worst when it comes to actually seeing them. However, one film-maker that sticks out right now is Stanley Kubrick because the simplicity of his compositions and his cam-erawork. One great thing about art is that we're free to simplify and exaggerate life so we can see it more clearly, and I think Stanley Kubrick did this really well. Especially during that shot in the *Shining* where the ax goes back and forth against the door and he moves the camera to follow it, emphasizing the threat.

Q. How much of a role in your ability to break in the industry at Rhythm and Hues do you think was a result of the suc-cess of *After You*?

A. Rhythm and Hues came to my school to do some recruit-ing. Among other examples of animation, I showed a work in progress of *After You*. I can't recall how much of it was complete at the time, but they must have liked something in there. I got a lot more attention after it was shown at SIGGRAPH in 2003. I was so lucky for that. Getting a job at Disney was entirely a result of *After You* and the promotion from SIGGRAPH.

Q. What suggestions would you make to student's who are about to create their first animated short with regards to idea-generation, production processes, and self-promotion?

visual |4–62|

After You – Christopher Cordingley

A. Being in school you're always under a deadline and are given a lot of instructions, but do it for yourself and be sure that you are emotionally attached and influenced by it. And do what *you* need to do in order to get it done. Show it to people and be open to critiques. Also, don't be afraid to change anything and everything in the early stages. As far as self-promotion, make a Web site and submit it to festivals. Most of the attention *After You* received came from my Web site or festivals. You'd be surprised who looks at your Web site over time.

Q. What are some of things that you learned during the making of *After You* that you think still help you in your day to day work as an animator for Disney?

A. It's nice to have an understanding of how everything fits together. I was responsible for everything in *After You* and having that experience helps me communicate with other departments at work. Also, while animating, under-standing how rigs are made directly helps me figure out what is the best way to approach certain motions and troubleshoot glitches. Making *After You,* I got a lot of practice listening to critiques about my work from other students and teachers. Being able to take constructive criticism is a huge part of working successfully at Disney.

Q. Finally, are there any other additional thoughts you'd like to share about *After You*?

A. It was a long and exhausting process. I got lost and confused half way into it and almost ditched the whole idea. The entire process was nerve racking and sporadic. I really want to do it again because it was amazing how much I learned, and it was rewarding beyond anything I imagined.

SUMMARY

The road to becoming an outstanding virtual director is a three-step process that involves understanding the inner workings of the live-action camera and lenses, becoming fluent in the language of filmmaking, and bridging that knowledge into the 3D environment. Although the gap between the live-action camera/filmmaking and the virtual world is quite small in some respects and enormous in others, the best directors recognize those differences and are able to exploit them to the benefit of their digital films. From the 180 degree rule to the dynamically driven camera, combining the essential filmmaking strategies with the latest software techniques can unleash the cutting-edge cinematography of your dreams.

in review

1. What is the difference between an on-camera and off-camera object?

2. What is the camera target and how does it relate to the base camera?

3. Explain the difference between a near and far clipping plane.

4. How will the camera cones of a 50 mm lens and a 200 mm lens compare?

5. What are the two most common ways to adjust the background color of a camera?

6. How does the creation of the Depth of Field (DOF) effect in a virtual camera differ from that in a real-world camera?

7. What are the two basic creation methods for virtual camera moves?

8. Explain the differences among master, exterior, and interior shots as it refers to camera blocking.

9. What is the 180 degree rule and how does it relate to the axis of action?

10. Explain the importance of continuity when developing a film's camerawork.

11. What is camera shake and is it a good thing?

12. Explain the process of camera tracking and it can be used effectively in digital filmmaking.

exercises

1. Place a character model into a new scene at the origin.

    a. Create a thirty-second 360° camera rotation around the character using the path animation technique.

    b. Repeat the same exercise, only using the keyframed technique with animation tangent adjustments. What do you notice about the two different techniques?

2. Obeying the 180 degree rule, block out a conversation between two married characters standing face to face. Not worrying about the specific dialogue at this point, create a one-minute sequence in which the female character is revealing, to the other character's delight, that she is pregnant. Make sure to utilize all three blocking shots: masters, exteriors, and interiors.

    a. Repeat the same sequence, but now block it as if the characters are not married. What changes to the timing and shot selection did you make?

3. Create a camera truck into a character using only two keyframes: beginning and end. What do you notice about this virtual camera move as compared to that in a live-action film?

    a. Gain access to a video camera and capture the real-world equivalent of what you already created in 3D. What do you notice about the difference between your virtual move and the real one?

    b. Revisit the virtual scene and add keyframes at the beginning and end to add some of the subtle natural camera shakes and overlapping action that you noticed in the video. Although the acting, objects, and lighting have not changed, did the overall shot quality improve? Why?

CHAPTER 5

objectives

- Understand the electromagnetic and visible spectrums
- Explore the components of white light
- Understand how light reacts and interacts with objects and the environment
- Learn about the six different characteristics of light
- Learn about color temperatures and the Kelvin scale
- Understand the principles of color theory

introduction

Today's digital cinematographer must have a deep understanding of light and color, as well as where it comes from, its real-world application in live-action filmmaking, and how to translate that knowledge into the 3D environment. Quality lighting can transform models into characters, illumination into atmosphere, and image sequences into films. Lights should play an active role in every scene by focusing attention, creating depth, and adding visual interest.

The journey to becoming a great lighter is a three-step process. This process begins with the exploration of the art and science behind light, traditional filmmaking theories and techniques, and finally, the translation of that knowledge into the 3D universe. The next three chapters will explain this process in greater detail. This chapter, in particular, will serve as your formal introduction to step one: exploring the creation, appearance, and interaction of light and color. This information will be the foundation for all of the practical lighting decisions you will need to make during the digital filmmaking process, including sources, interactions, and symbolism.

LET THERE BE LIGHT!

So much focus and attention is put into the modeling and animation portions of the digital filmmaking process that cinematography often falls through the cracks. *Lighting* is often thought of as an inherent ability that all artists have. Because we are constantly surrounded by, and observing the effects of light, there is a common misconception that lighting will just come naturally and therefore, it is left to the end of the project. That's not to say that lights aren't used during the production process, they are almost always present. However, they are typically used for a singular utilitarian purpose; to *illuminate* the objects and the scene so that the artist can more effectively model or animate.

Well-executed lighting brings a great deal more to the filmmaking table than visibility. An amazing *light setup* can make what would otherwise be considered mediocre models and animation look stunning. Great lighting can hide the flaws while accenting the assets.

So, without hesitation, let's jump right in and take the first step on the journey to becoming a better lighter by looking closely at the art and science behind light itself. Although this information has been difficult to gather into one concise, easy-to-understand format, this chapter will attempt to do just that. It is this foundational knowledge that will serve as the visual vocabulary that will allow you to discuss and analyze the core lighting theories and principles used in traditional or live-action films.

visual |5–1|

3D Visualization of a Kitchen

In fact, understanding physical or real-world lighting is, in many ways, very similar to the process used in the virtual environment. However, it is important that we do not get ahead of ourselves.

ELECTROMAGNETIC RADIATION

Let us start at the very beginning by answering the most basic of questions. What is light and where does it come from? Everyone understands that light can come from a natural source, the sun, as well as from a man-made one, a light bulb. However, most people do not fully understand how the two are related. The fact is, light is just a small portion of the total *electromagnetic radiation* being transmitted through the universe at any given moment. Electromagnetic radiation, which contains both electric and magnetic properties, is the key component that makes the transfer of energy possible.

Encompassing a wide spectrum of incarnations, electromagnetic radiation can be categorized into seven major categories: radio waves, microwaves, infrared radiation, *visible light*, ultraviolet radiation, X-rays, and gamma rays. Whether it is the radio waves that allow us to hear our favorite music, the microwaves that allow us to quickly heat up last night's leftovers or the light waves emanating from a spotlight, electromagnetic radiation is around us at all times (Millerson 19-23).

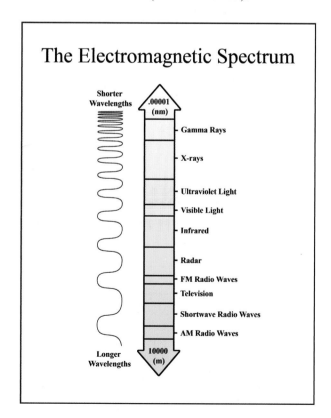

visual |5–2|

The Electromagnetic Spectrum

What is the difference between a radio wave and a gamma ray or a *light wave* and an X-ray? Remember, by definition, all forms of electromagnetic (EM) radiation contain both electric and magnetic components. These two components, or fields, oscillate perpendicular to one another allowing the wave to propagate or move through space.

visual |5–3|

___

Typical EM Radiation
Wave – Amplitude

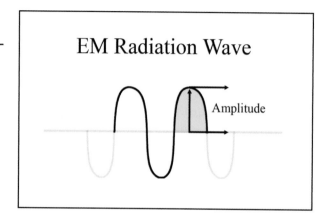

However, it is how the individual waves of EM radiation move through space that will define or differentiae them. The two main dimensions used to evaluate a wave are the *amplitude* and *frequency*. The amplitude is measured by the height of the wave and the frequency is measured by the length. It is important to note that the shorter the wavelength, the higher the frequency. In other words, the shorter the wavelength, the more times the wave will repeat itself as it propagates through space. Therefore, although amplitude certainly plays a role in the overall intensity of the waveform, it is the frequency that will determine if the EM radiation is a radio wave or a light wave.

visual |5–4|

___

Frequency Diagram

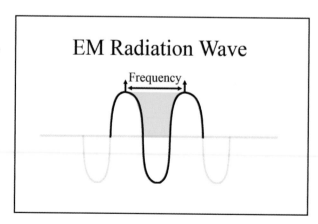

THE VISIBLE SPECTRUM

Now that we have a better understanding of the electromagnetic spectrum, let's focus on the portion that concerns us the most, the visible spectrum. Also known as visible light or simply light, the visible spectrum is the portion of the electromagnetic spectrum that the human eye can perceive. This portion of the spectrum, as you can see in Visual 5–5, is a very small piece of the overall EM pie.

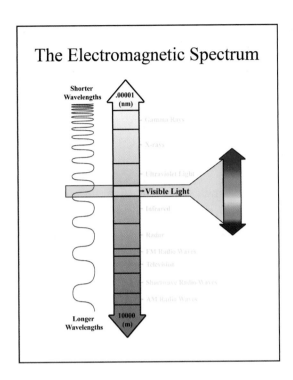

Visual 5–6 highlights the frequency range of visible light, which ranges from 400 nm (Shortest/Violet) to 700 nm (Longest/Red). More important, the chart demonstrates the critical correlation between light's *wavelength* and its perceived color. Consequently, any and all colors are created by the differences in frequencies of visible light.

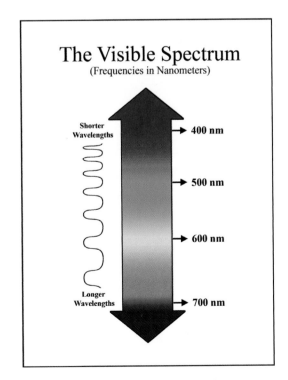

WHITE LIGHT

Until the mid-seventeenth century, the scientific community believed that the different colors of light were produced by combining *white light* with an unknown additive. In other words, white light was thought of as the base component to light. Somehow the color was added in, in the same way as color was added to acrylic paint. However, in 1666, *Sir Isaac Newton* performed an experiment that would not only change the popular beliefs of light and color but also would spark an entire field of study, called optics.

Newton was able to isolate a single ray of white light through a small opening in a window into a dark room. He then placed a *prism* into the direct line of the ray of light and noticed some remarkable results. The light entered into the prism as a single white beam but left as a series of rainbow-colored rays.

The prism had, in fact, *refracted* or broken the white light into its separate components based on their wavelength or frequency. These components are identical to the ones highlighted in the visual spectrum diagram in Visual 5–6. This led to the conclusion that white light, such as sunlight or the light from an *incandescent* light bulb, contains equal parts of all the various colors or wavelengths. In other words, white light is not the absence of color but rather, the combination of all colors. For this reason, you do not see white within the visible spectrum.

visual |5–7|

Visible Light Separation
from a Prism

Based on Newton's findings, we are able to conclude that colored light is the result of white light that has had specific portions of the spectrum blocked. For instance, a light will appear red if the shorter wavelengths, 650 nm and under, have been dispersed or scattered. There is no better example of this than a sunset over the ocean. Because the sun is at a much lower angle and father away during a sunset, only the longer wavelengths, which include yellows, oranges, and reds, are able to be seen. The shorter wavelengths are easily *scattered* by the atmospheric particles, the saltwater air in this case, and therefore are unseen.

visual |5–8|

Sunset Graphic

Blue & Red Wavelengths

Red

Blue

visual |5–9|

Blue Wavelength versus
Red Wavelength

INTERACTION WITH OBJECTS

Although it is extremely important to understand how light travels through space, it is really light's interaction with the objects around us that impact the digital filmmaker the most.

In fact, light on its own cannot be seen at all. Whether it is the illumination of a room from an incandescent light bulb or the atmospheric dust particles in the air forming sunbeams, the eye can only perceive the effects of light.

In most cases, white light from the sun or a light bulb will enter a scene and illuminate those objects and environment. However, most casual observers will think that the white light is simply illuminating the colored objects around. In other words, the objects contain the color and the white light is making it bright enough for the human eye to see. However, the reality of the situation is quite different.

Without getting overly scientific, every object in the world contains a certain amount of molecular *energy*. As the electromagnetic energy, in this case the visible light energy, hits an object, the light energy is forced to interact with the molecular energy of the objects. For instance, the red sphere seen in Visual 5–10 is not a red object that is being lit by white light. On the contrary, the red sphere's molecular makeup is actually allowing all of the wavelengths of the visible spectrum, from approximately 400 nm to 650 nm, to be absorbed. In turn, the lower frequencies are being reflected or bounced back to the eyes of the observer.

Red Sphere Example

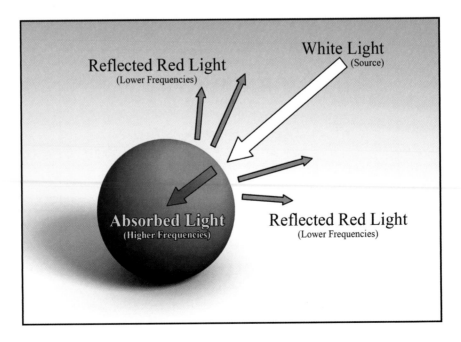

Therefore, it is the manner in which the light energy reacts and interacts that will determine the color and appearance of the object. In this particular case, the observer perceives the sphere to be smooth and red.

Building on Newton's discoveries, Albert Einstein developed the photon theory of light during the early part of the twentieth century. His theory was based on the fact that light could act not only in the Newtonian wavelike fashion but also as a particle. This elementary particle of EM Radiation or light, known as a photon, does not have mass and travels at a constant speed. The photon will continue to travel at this constant speed, the speed of light, until it interacts with an object in space. This interaction can affect the photon and, therefore, the object's appearance. It can be categorized into five distinct groups: *absorption, reflection, scattering, refraction* and *transmission*. These groupings will not only help to explain the nature of light but guide you down the road when creating lights and shaders for your digital scene.

Absorption

When the light energy of a photon entering into an object matches the molecular energy within the object, those particular wavelengths are absorbed within the object. Typically, the matching photons are destroyed releasing this energy into the object as heat. Visual 5–11 demonstrates a single photon being absorbed into an object.

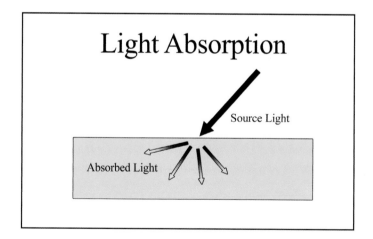

Absorption Diagram

Reflection

When the light energy of a photon entering into an object does not match with the molecular energy inside, the photon is bounced back out of the object almost immediately. Assuming that the surface of the object is smooth, the angle of

Reflection Diagram

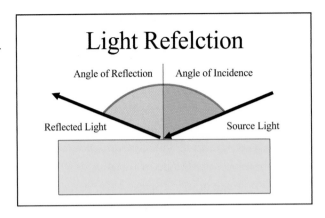

the reflected photon is identical to the angle of entry. This type of reflection, known as *specular*, produces an identical copy of the photos producing a perfect mirror image to the observer. Visual 5–12 demonstrates multiple photons being reflected from a mirrorlike object.

Scattering

Scattering of visible light or photons is very similar to reflection in that the energy is immediately bounced out of the object. However, the major difference between scattering and reflection is the type of surface the light is interacting with. Scattering, or diffuse reflection, occurs when photons hit an uneven or rough surface, causing the photons to bounce back in a haphazard fashion. The end result is an illumination effect rather than a mirror. For example, this is the reason why you can see yourself in the mirror, which is specular reflection, while brushing your teeth and not in the drywall, which is diffuse reflection or scattering, next to it. Visual 5–13 demonstrates multiple photons being scattered from an uneven surface.

visual |5–13|

Scattering Diagram

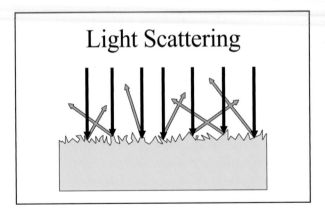

visual |5–14|

Subsurface Scattering

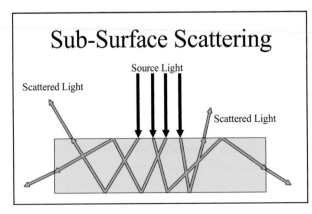

SubSurface Scattering

Subsurface scattering bounces back the photons in an uneven manner. However, unlike traditional scattering, the photons are allowed to enter the surface and bounce around inside multiple times before being released. The result is a glowing effect that emits from the object. Human skin/flesh is an object that allows for subsurface scattering. The thinner the object is, the more subsurface scattering is allowed. The perfect example of the effects of subsurface scattering is when you place an illuminated flashlight behind your hand. The light is allowed inside and bounces around producing an overall glow to your hand and fingers.

Refraction

Refraction of light energy happens when the photons closely match that of the object energy and is allowed to enter the object. However, unlike absorption, the energy is not destroyed but, rather, transformed slightly and then passed through the object. This transfer of energy not only slows down the speed of the photon but also changes its direction. This change of direction is known as the *angle of*

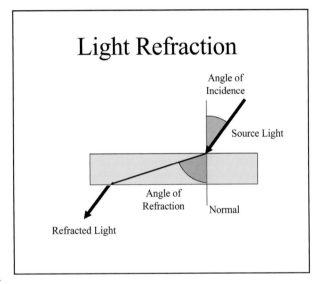

refraction and can be measured. For instance, glass and water have different indexes of refraction; each will bend light in different amounts. Visual 5–15 compares equal light energy entering objects with different indexes of refraction.

Transmission

Transmission of light energy happens when the light energy is extremely different from the object that it is interacting with. Therefore, the photons are virtually untouched and able to pass through the object unscathed. The result is a transparent-looking object to the viewer, the opposite of a mirror.

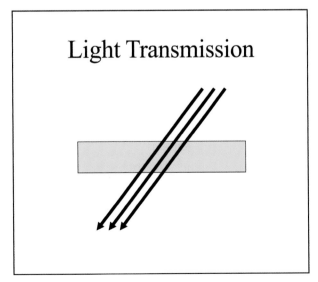

CHARACTERISTICS OF LIGHT

With some historical and scientific perspective under our belts, it is now time to turn our attention to the descriptive characteristics of light. One of the more difficult aspects of studying light and color are the endless terms that help define their characteristics. Terms such as *brightness, luminosity, hue,* and *color* tend to overlap in many ways. To add further confusion, some of the terms are *objective*, an unbiased, scientific measurement, whereas some of them are purely *subjective*, based on the individual viewer's perceptions. However, there are some terms that are more commonly used and therefore are more functional than others.

At the highest level, there are six characteristics of light that can be used to accurately describe almost any lighting setup or scenario. Almost everything that you will need to know about lighting will stem from these six core attributes:

1. Intensity
2. Contrast
3. Angle
4. Coverage
5. Animation
6. Color

Understanding the six characteristics of light will allow you to obtain the three skills that all great digital lighters possess: evaluation, communication, and translation.

Intensity

Intensity, often referred to as brightness, is one of the first characteristics that you will want to determine when developing a lighting setup for a scene. The intensity of the lights will play a big role in the atmosphere of the scene and the focus of the audience. For instance, most people will associate certain light intensities with particular, places, times, and moods. A shot of a couple eating a romantic dinner at a French restaurant will illicit a much lower light intensity than does a shot of a person getting their teeth cleaned at the dentist office, which is significantly higher. However, much like other lighting terms, intensity is not a strict quantifiable measurement. In fact, it is the combination of both objective and subjective components. Typically, intensity is determined by the total *illuminance*, or the amount of light energy that falls onto the objects in your scene, and the distance from those objects to the viewer or camera.

Illuminance, the objective part of the intensity equation, is measured in *lux* (lumens/m^2) to determine the total luminous power on a surface per unit area, and is measured with a *photometer*. Here are some common average illuminance levels for both natural outdoor and artificial indoor lighting conditions (Electro Optical Industries, Inc.).

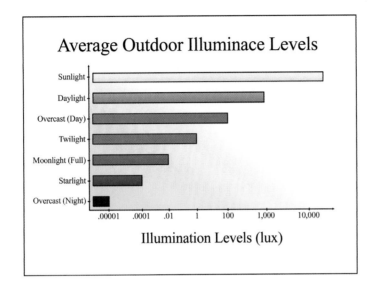

visual |5–17|

Average Outdoor
Illuminance Levels

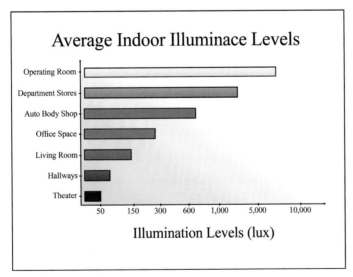

visual |5–18|

Average Indoor
Illuminance Levels

Although illuminance plays a major role in determing the overall intensity of a scene, there are other more subjective factors, such as the color and distance of other peripheral objects, that also contribute. For instance, the viewer's overall distance from the scence will greatly affect the percieved light intensity. Although the illuminance on a given object can stay the same, the distance from the camera will determine the percived intensity or brightness of the image. Visual 5–19 demonstrates the effects of distance on the percieved intensity.

Perceived Intensity

Attenuation

It is impossible to discuss illuminance, or the amount of light hitting a surface, without talking about the phenomena of attenuation. As light propagates through space, the total energy is inversely proportionally to the distance from the source. The further away the object is from the light, the weaker the light energy hitting the object will be. For instance, the sphere in Visual 5–20 is being lit by the same light with identical intensities. However, as the sphere moves farther away from the light, the more light energy *fall-off* occurs.

Attenuation

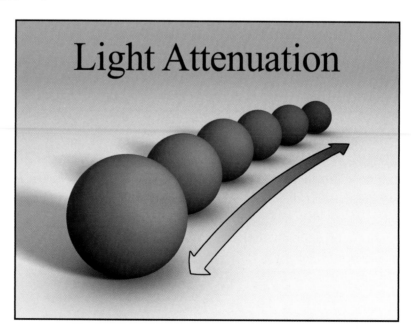

Light Attenuation

In the real-world, there is a specific formula to calculate how much fall-off will occur. Newton, who discovered the Inverse Square Law, stated that a light's illuminance is inversely proportional to the square of the distance from the light source.

The Inverse Square Law Formula

$$\frac{\text{Source Energy}}{\text{Distance}^2} = \text{Illuminace (lux)}$$

visual |5–21|

Inverse Square Law Formula (Illuminance = Source Energy ÷ Distance^2)

Therefore, in the real world, an object of the same size and material that is twice the distance from the light source will only receive one-quarter the illuminance. Visual 5–22 demonstrates the Inverse Square Law.

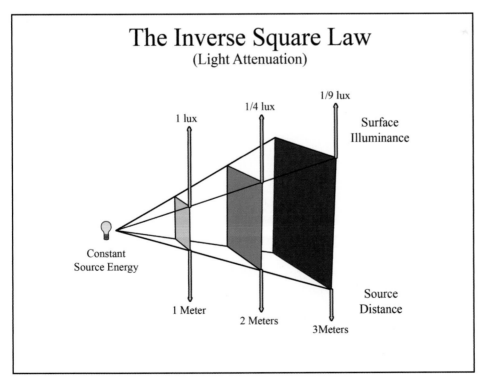

The Inverse Square Law
(Light Attenuation)

1/9 lux

1/4 lux

1 lux

Surface Illuminance

Constant Source Energy

1 Meter

2 Meters

3 Meters

Source Distance

visual |5–22|

Inverse Square Attenuation Diagram

Contrast

Light contrast, often referred to as the quality, is the next major lighting characteristic to consider when creating a lighting setup. Contrast, which typically is broken down into two major categories, hard or soft, is the way in which light envelops objects in the scene. Depending on which type of light quality is used, the viewer is given particular visual clues about the scene including weather and location, indoors or outdoors. The two major determining factors when working with light contrast are the distance from the light source to the objects and the size of the source. For instance, a floodlight from ten feet away will produce a much different contrast or quality than will the sun on a cloudy day.

Hard Light

Hard lighting occurs when a scene is illuminated by unobstructed single point light source. Some common examples of sources that can create hard lighting are flashlights, spotlights, camera flash bulbs, and the sun on a very clear day. Hard light is typically identified by its harsh edges and strong shadows caused by the directional nature of the light waves. In other words, the light rays are coming into the scene at one direction, creating very light portions of the object as well as very dark portions with little transition between the two.

Visual 5–23 shows a soccer ball illuminated with indoor hard lighting. You'll notice that there is a harsh division between the part of the ball that is in light versus the part that is in shadow. Furthermore, the shadow produced is not only hard-edged but shows very little visual detail.

visual |5–23|

Hard Light Example - Indoors

Visual 5–24 shows the same soccer ball only now light by the sun on very clear afternoon. Although the sun is larger and much further away, it produces the same single source direction light rays that cause the harsh edges and shadows with very little detail.

visual |5–24|

Hard Light Example - Outdoors

Soft Light

Soft lighting, the opposite of hard lighting, is created when using larger, diffused light sources. That is to say that there are more less-intense light waves hitting the subject from many different angles. The end result is a more inviting, flattering feel for the viewer. In fact, soft lighting is typically used in all commercial and fashion photography for that reason. Furthermore, soft light produces little to no shadow, allowing for greater vision of the entire subject. Although this produces a flatter-looking image, it can hide some of the small imperfections in an object that might otherwise be apparent.

Visual 5–25 shows a soccer ball illuminated with indoor soft lighting, similar to that of a spotlight with an *umbrella diffuser* attached. Notice that you can see much more of the ball's surface area as compared to Visual 5–24. You also should note that the transition from the lighter front side of the ball to the darker back side is much smoother.

Visual 5–26 shows the same soccer ball only now light by the sun on very cloudy after-noon. Although it is the same source as in Visual 5–25, the heavy clouds act much like the umbrella diffuser in the previous image, producing a soft, flat lighting scenario.

Angle

Much like light contrast or quality, the angle of your lights can serve both aesthetic and practical purposes within your shots. Depending on if there is natural light entering into your scene, the angle of your lights can help the viewer determine the particular time of day. For instance, an object lit with a spotlight that has a high angle will produce very short, well-defined shadows. If the light is intended to from a natural source, it will tell the viewer that the scene's timeframe is around midday, when the sun is at its highest point in the sky.

Mid-Day Lighting Angle

However, if the spotlight is brought down closer to the horizon line, or at a very low angle to the subject, the viewer will assume that is being shot either at the beginning or end of the day.

Beginning/End-of-Day
Lighting Angle

Furthermore, the direction of the lights can play a major role in determining the amount of perceived depth and texture detail an object is given. The closer the angle of the light is to the particular camera from which the scene is being shot, the flatter the image will appear. By contrast, the greater the light angle is away from the camera, the more depth and form will be created.

Front Lighting

Front lighting will create a very flat and, more often than not, an uninteresting image. Because the light is stemming from an angle that is very close to the camera's angle, the shadows are almost all hidden. Therefore, it can be very difficult to make out specific texture and depth detail. The best example of front lighting is from a flash camera, as the flash is always coming directly from the angle of the camera. This is especially noticeable when the flash is the only source of light in the scene. Visuals 5–29 and 5–30 demonstrate the effects of front lighting on our hero.

visual |5–29|

Front Lighting Diagram

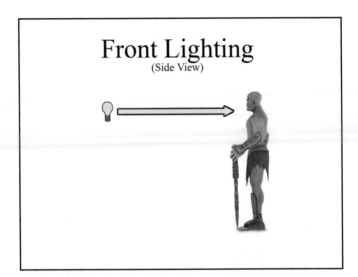

visual |5–30|

Front Lighting Example

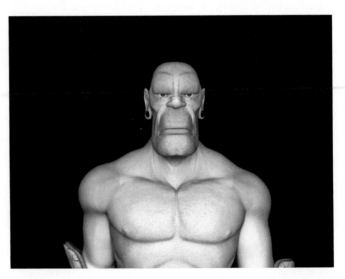

Side Lighting

Side lighting produces, in general, a much more dramatic image to the viewer. As the direction or angle of the light moves further away from that of the camera toward the 90 degree mark, the more the texture detail and shadows will appear. Visuals 5–31 and 5–32 demonstrate the effects of side lighting on our hero.

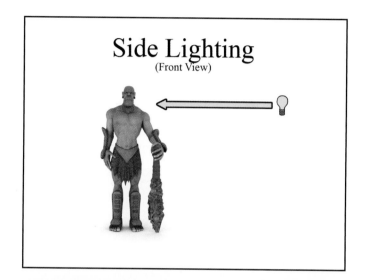

visual |5–31|

Side Lighting Diagram

visual |5–32|

Side Lighting Example

Back Lighting

As the light angle moves pas the 90 degree mark toward the back of the object, the less and less of the subject is seen. This produces an outline or silhouette effect on the subject, highlighting the positive and negative space within the shot. Often this shot is more about the particular pose or position of the subject rather than the specific details within. Visuals 5–33 and 5–34 demonstrate the effects of *back lighting* on our hero.

Back Lighting Diagram

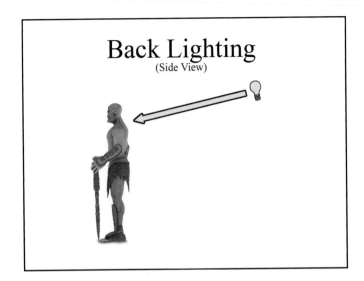

Back Lighting Example

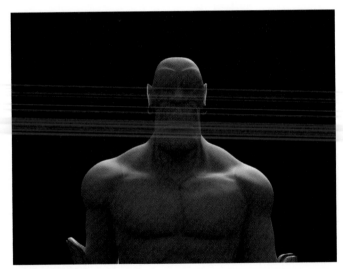

Low-Angle Lighting

Low-angle lighting is produced when the light angle is below that of the camera. The greater the angle of the light is between the subject and the camera, the more dynamic the image will appear. Typically, most low-angle lighting tends to give the subject an unnatural, menacing, or evil feel. You will see this type of lighting used often in the horror movie industry just for that reason. Most young children will grab a flashlight and put it underneath their chin to mimic this low-angle lighting when telling a spooky story. Visuals 5–35 and 5–36 demonstrate the effects of low-angle lighting on our hero.

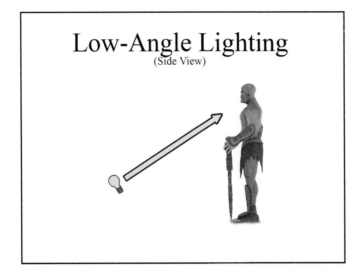

Low-Angle Lighting
Diagram

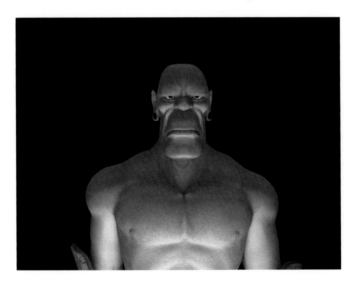

Low-Angle Lighting
Example

High-Angle Lighting

High-angle lighting is produced when the light angle is above that of the camera. Although both low- and high-angle lighting have an unnatural feel, high-angle lighting can imply an angelic or holy appearance. Visuals 5–37 and 5–38 demonstrate the effects of high-angle lighting on our hero.

High-Angle Lighting
Diagram

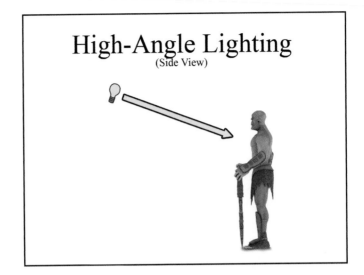

High-Angle Lighting
Example

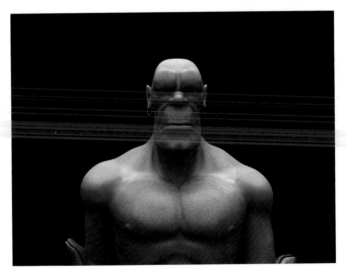

Coverage

The overall light coverage of scene is a deliberate decision by the director to determine which part(s) of the subject or scene is being illuminated and which are not. Coverage can serve both aesthetic and practical purposes. For instance, a director might choose to arrange a character in the front of a shot that is very well lit, while the background contains little to no light. This decision might be driven by pure aesthetic purposes, in that the hero just simply looks better in front of black. However, the decision might play a more practical role, in that the director might be hiding something from the character, the audience, or both. Furthermore, and maybe even more important for the digital filmmaker, the director may not have had enough time or resources to construct the particular backgrounds and sets that are required. Therefore, the black simply allows the audience to assume this particular background is present without having to build it.

Light Coverage Example

Animation

Light animation is simply the change of other five characteristic of light over time. Whether it is the light angle changing to mimic the movement of the sun over time or the light coverage to reveal a new object or character into the scene, animation is used most effectively when there is a clear purpose or intent to the movement. In fact, much like camera movements without clear direction and intent, ineffective light animation can cause viewer annoyance and discontent.

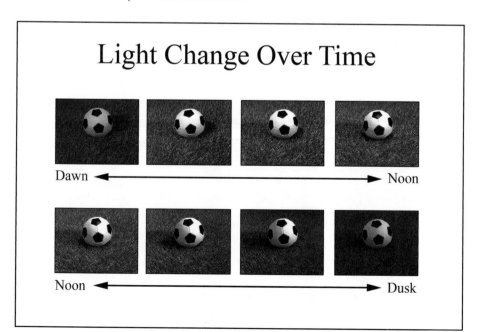

Light Animation – Time of Day Change

Color

The last, but certainly not least, of the six major light characteristics is the light color. Color is by far the most misunderstood and underutilized aspect of digital lighting. The color of the light interacts with so many different aspects of the production process including geometry, animation, materials, and rendering, so it is critical to understand when and how to use it correctly. Starting with the science, which we covered earlier in this chapter, you must build on that foundation by exploring the art and psychology behind color. This exploration, know commonly as color theory, will prove to be the road map for your lighting decisions.

COLOR TEMPERATURE

In the real world, every single source of light has its own unique *color temperature*. This color temperature is then perceived by the viewer as a particular color within the visible spectrum. Therefore, when creating lights within the digital world, it is critical to understand which colors are associated with which particular types of light sources.

Kelvin Scale

The color temperature of an individual light source is measured using the *Kelvin scale*, named after the nineteenth-century British physicist/mathematician *William Thomas Kelvin*. Kelvin discovered that you can distinguish an individual light source's color temperature by comparing it to the color of a heated *black-body radiator*. In Kelvin's particular case, the black-body radiator was a piece of black carbon. He quickly noticed that not only did the carbon glow when heated, but that it changed colors depending on the temperature. Visual 5–41 shows the range of colors that black-body radiator was able to produce in degrees Kelvin.

visual |5–41|

Color Temperature Scale

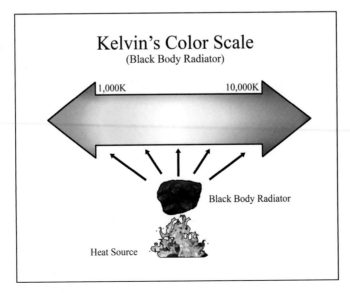

Kelvin's Color Scale
(Black Body Radiator)

1,000K   10,000K

Black Body Radiator

Heat Source

Building on the color temperature scale, you can determine the color temperature of an individual light source by matching its color with one on the scale. Visual 5–42 outlines some of the more common light sources that might be used in the filmmaking process with their corresponding temperatures and perceived colors.

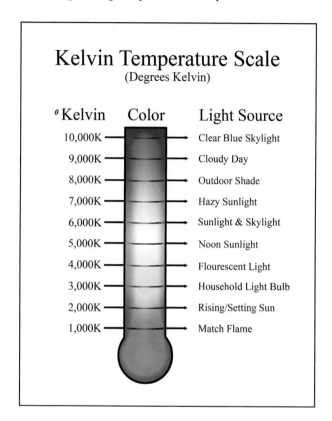

White Balance

As you will notice in Visual 5–42, lower temperatures produce a warmer red, orange, or yellow tone, whereas a higher temperature produces a cooler blue or purple tone. However, it is important to point out that as the temperatures transition from the lower, warmer tones into the higher, cooler tones they must fade through white. The white or white light, in the natural world represents the daylight sun on a clear afternoon. Therefore, this chart is considered to be white-balanced or adjusted to the daylight sun. Now, that might be ideal if you are actually creating a shot that is supposed to be taking place at noon on a clear day. However, if you are shooting at different times of day or indoors, you will need to adjust the white balance accordingly.

You may be familiar to the term *white balance* if you've ever dabbled in traditional photography. In fact, most cameras today will allow you to white balance the image either manually or automatically. In both cases, you are determining for the camera where that true white color will fall on the temperature scale. For instance, if you have a camera that is set to the outdoor settings, noon on a clear day, the colors in Visual 5–43 will work fine. However, if you bring that camera with the same setting indoors, the colors will appear very odd. The indoor tungsten light bulbs, which are probably creating most of the visible light, will appear very yellow and orange. Although this might be the look you are going for in certain situations, chances are that you will want to adjust the white balance from approximately 5500 degrees Kelvin (Daylight Sun) to about 3000 degrees Kelvin (Tungsten).

visual |5–43|

Adjusting the Color
Balance Scale

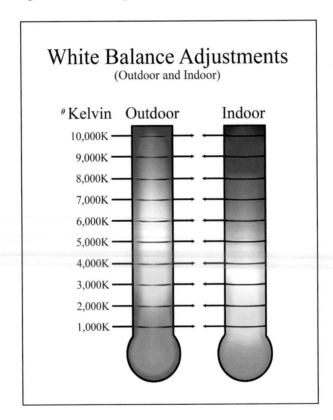

This will adjust the color of the *tungsten light* bulbs to appear white and therefore produce a more natural-looking scene to the viewer. The reality is that the human eye has the unique ability to naturally white balance itself depending on the situation. Therefore, it is important that you consider both the color temperature and white balance when determining the colors for your lights.

Photo that is White
Balanced for the
Daylight Sun

Photo that is White
Balanced for Indoor
Light Bulbs

COLOR THEORY

Although it was first mentioned two hundred years ago, it was Sir Isaac Newton's early-eighteenth-century book, *Opticks,* that began the modern practice of color theory. By definition, color theory is the blueprint to understanding the psychology behind and application of color and color combinations. These theories have evolved somewhat over the last few centuries, but the majority of the color theory principles have remained stable. However, the various mediums in which color theory is being used have exploded beyond anything that Newton could have imagined. Certainly it is still used heavily in the traditional fine arts, but with the advent of modern mediums such as television, motion pictures, animation, the Internet, and video games, color theory has never played a bigger role in the visual arts.

In the world of digital filmmaking, colors are delivered to the viewer via the texture maps and lighting. These color palettes and schemes will determine the overall mood, environment, energy, and focus of your film. Therefore, it is critical that you, as the digital cinematographer, understand how to mix and match colors according to the desired physical and emotional viewer reaction. Certain color choices undoubtedly will be determined by their real-world properties. An orange should more or less appear orange, for instance. However, there are many others that are left up to the artist. In fact, this is what will, in a many ways, will separate the good from the bad, the engaging from the mundane, and the unforgettable form the ordinary.

COLOR SYSTEMS

Color can be generated either by a physical object/surface or by a light source. For instance, the page on which this text resides is a physical object that has its own color parameters. It requires a third-party light source to illuminate the page so that the words and images can be seen. However, the computer monitor on which I am writing these words is its own light source and does not require any additional light for me to see it. Although the words and images look identical in both scenarios, the ways in which they are generated are quite different. In fact, these methods, or color systems, are the only two ways that color can be generated.

Available Color Systems

Additive (+)
Generates Own Light Source
Starts with Black
Mixes Colors toward White
Uses RGB Colors

Subtractive (-)
Requires Additional Light Source
Starts with White
Mixes Colors toward Black
Uses CMYK Colors

visual | 5–46 |

Color Systems Diagram

Additive Color System

The *additive color* system generates color with light and does not require any additional light sources. Televisions, LCD screens, and computer monitors are all examples of devices that generate color using the additive color system. Starting with the absence of light and color, this system creates color by adding various amounts of red, blue, and green light. Often referred to as the RGB color system, these colors can be used to create any color in the universe. If you add all three colors at their maximum strength, the resulting color is white. Therefore, the additive or *RGB color* system starts with black, or the absence of light, and works toward white, the result of adding all three colors (Ford).

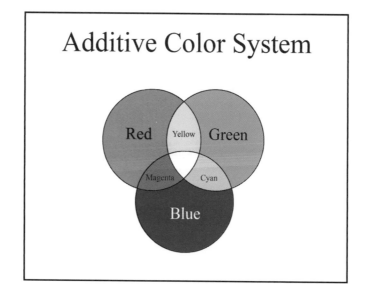

visual | 5–47 |

Additive Color System

Subtractive Color System

The *subtractive color* system is quite different than the additive in that it requires both a physical object and a light source. Print media, for example, magazines, newspapers, and photos, are all examples of mediums that use the subtractive color system. Starting with a white palate, this system creates color by adding various amounts of cyan, magenta, yellow, and black. Often referred to as the *CMYK color* system within the print industry, these colors can be used to create any color in the universe. If these colors are mixed together, in ink or paint form, at their maximum strength, the resulting color is black. Therefore, the subtractive or CMYK color system starts with white, or the absence of ink or paint, and works toward black, the result of mixing all four colors (Ford).

visual |5–48|

Subtractive Color System

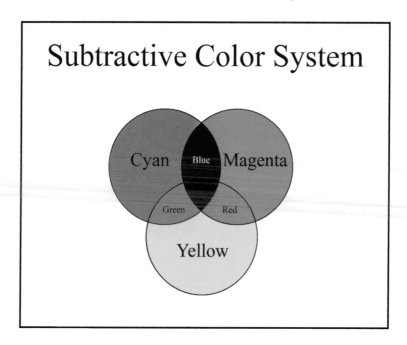

THE COLOR WHEEL

The *color wheel*, which was first theorized in Newton's *Opticks,* is the foundation for all color theory practices. Used first by artists, mainly painters, to create a visual resource for mixing paint colors, the color wheel is primary tool for creating effective color schemes and palates for almost every visual medium.

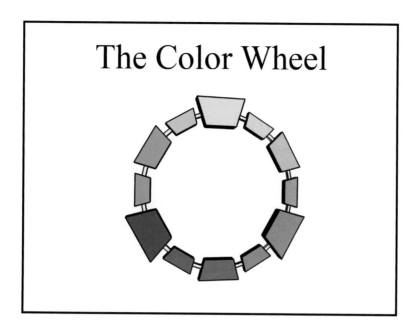

The Color Wheel

Primary Colors

Primary colors are, by definition, the raw colors that can not be created by mixing any other colors. The three primary colors are red, blue, and yellow. These colors can not be created by mixing any other colors. However, all other colors in the visible spectrum can be created by mixing these colors together. Visual 5–50 shows the primary colors within the color wheel.

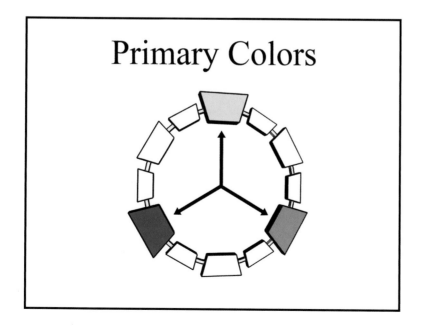

Primary Colors within the Color Wheel

Secondary Colors

Secondary colors result from mixing two primary colors.

visual |5–51|

Secondary Colors within
the Color Wheel

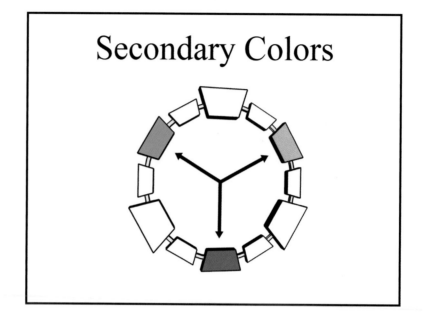

Tertiary Colors

Tertiary colors result from mixing a primary color with a secondary color.

visual |5–52|

Tertiary Colors within the
Color Wheel

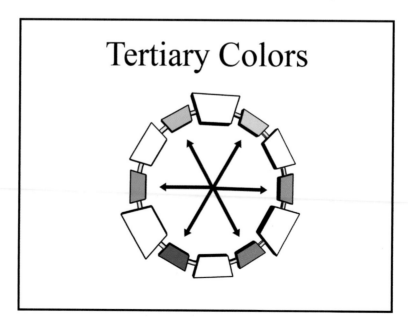

COLOR SCHEMES AND HARMONY

Do some colors work better with others? Whether you're picking out a tie to go with a shirt or the lights for your next shot, the colors you pick, individually and as a group or scheme, will illicit certain physical and emotional responses from a viewer. Although individual viewer reactions may vary slightly, the vast majority will agree that certain colors have better harmony and appear to match, while others clash. That being said, how then do you ensure that the colors used in the shot will work together?

Building on a basic understanding of the color wheel, you can start to form relationships between colors in accordance to their position within the wheel. Although there are endless possibilities for these relationships, there are four main groupings that can be used as the foundation when determining a color scheme, or *palette* for a project.

Complementary

Complementary colors are those opposite each other on the color wheel. These colors, when placed within the same shot, create high levels on contrast and energy. They are the most dynamic of the four main color schemes and therefore must be used with caution. Used correctly, they can bring an added level of focus and intensity to a shot. Used incorrectly, they can annoy and distract the viewer.

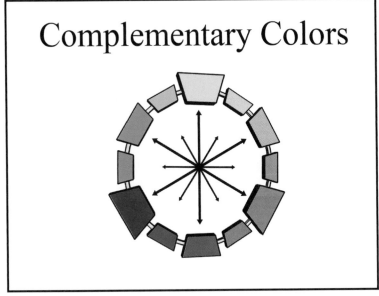

visual |5–53|

Complementary Colors

| NOTE |

Often a film's *color scheme* will define the overall look and feel of the entire project. Close your eyes and picture a shot from these two popular live actions films: the 1972 Francis Ford Coppola classic *The Godfather* and the 1985 Tim Burton cult classic *Pee-Wee's Big Adventure.* How do the color schemes compare? Now, imagine what the films would look like if you switched the color schemes. Even though nothing else about the films would change, do you think that these films would still be classics?

Analogous

Analogous colors are those adjacent to each other on the color wheel. Typically in groups of three, these colors create a pleasant and harmonious feel as a result of their close relationship within the color wheel. Analogous colors blend smoothly rather than producing contrast.

Analogous Colors

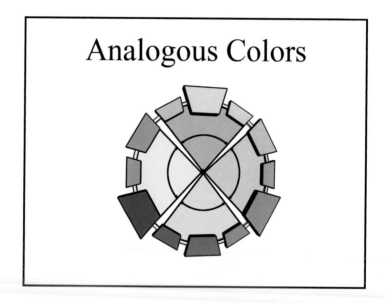

Triadic

Triadic colors are those that are equidistant or 120 degrees apart from each other on the color wheel. Typically in groups of three, these colors create both harmony and contrast. Used extensively in the fine arts world, triadic colors provide the perfect balance between complementary and analogous color schemes.

Triadic Colors

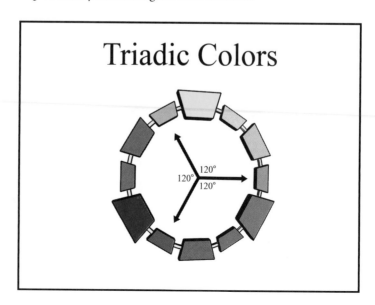

Split Complementary

Split complementary colors are typically in groups of three. Start with any color on the color wheel and pair them with the two colors that are adjacent to its compliment.

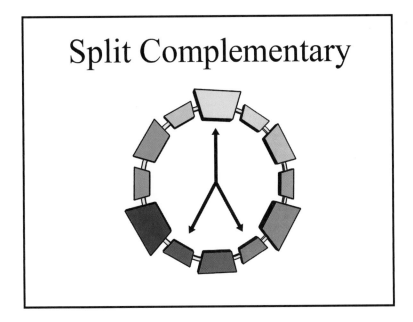

visual |5–56|

Split Complementary
Colors

COLOR TERMINOLOGY

Throughout this chapter, we have been referring to color as the list of possible colors found within the visible spectrum or on the color wheel. Although these color systems certainly represent the variety of colors that exist on a high level, they do not approach the vast array of variations that can be created within each of the specific colors. For instance, there are certainly many more types of red then the one represented within the color wheel. You will find that describing color is often confusing because most people do not have good grasp on color terminology. In fact, those not in the know will use these term inappropriately or interchangeably. However, the terms are very specific as far in terms of their creation and, in the end, how they are perceived by the viewer.

Hue

Hue is the most basic description of color. In fact, the term "color" is often used instead of the term "hue." Hue is what distinguishes red from blue and green from yellow.

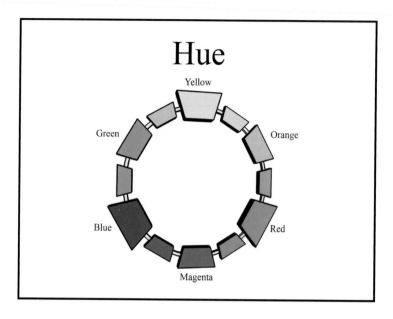

Saturation

Saturation is the measurement of the intensity of a given hue. Often referred to as the color's purity, the higher the saturation, the more lively and energetic it appears. The lower the saturation, the closer the color is to its gray equivalent.

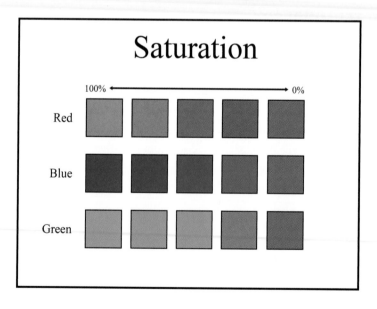

Value

Value describes a particular color's relationship between dark and light. In other words, value determines how close that color is to being white or black. If you desaturate (remove the saturation) from a particular hue, it becomes much easier to determine its overall value, as you can see its relationship with back and white.

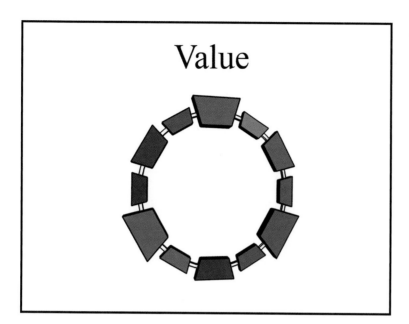

Value

HSV Color Model Used
within Adobe's Photoshop

Insider Info

The hue, saturation, and value (*HSV*) *color space* was developed in the late 1970s as a tool to define, create, and recreate a particular color easily. Most commonly used in conjunction with the RGB model, the HSV color model can be utilized in almost every computer applications that create visual media.

Tint

The *tint* is determined by the amount of white that is added to a particular hue.

Tint

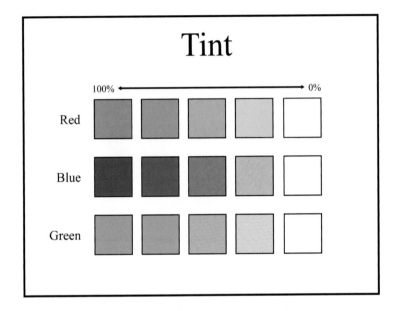

Shade

The *shade* is determined by the amount of black that is added to a particular hue.

Shade

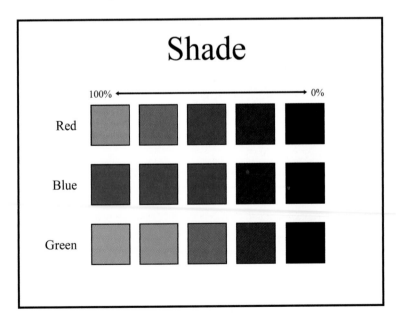

Tone

The *tone* is determined by the amount of gray that is added to a particular hue.

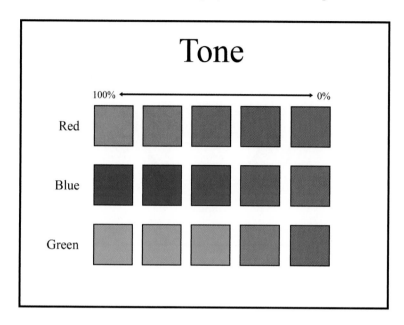

Tone

COLOR MEANINGS AND SYMBOLISM

Every color and color combination has a meaning and symbolism behind it. Some colors have a universal symbolism, like the ones found in nature. Green symbolizes growth and fertility. However, some colors vary quite drastically, depending on cultural and geographical differences. For instance, the color white often is associated with a wedding ceremony in the United States. However, in northern India, red is the color that is most associated with weddings, as it is the traditional color for a wedding dress. Therefore, it is vitally important to consider both the meaning and the audience when developing color schemes.

Warm Colors

The color wheel can be divided into half, separating the colors into the two major color groups: warm and cool colors. The *warm colors*, including reds, yellows, and oranges, represent the colors that you would find in nature associated with warmth and heat. These colors also tend to elicit feeling of intensity, energy, activity, and anger from the viewer. Visual 5–64 highlights the warm colors within the color wheel.

| NOTE |

You'll often hear the term *monochromatic* when discussing colors and color schemes. A monochromatic color scheme utilizes only one hue but includes all of the tints, shades, and tones.

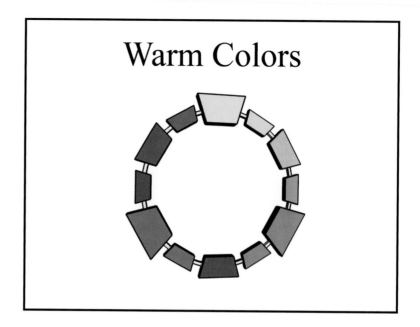

Cool Colors

Cool colors, including blues, greens, and purples, are named for the hues that are represented in nature with cold and ice. Most viewers will get a calming, relaxing sensation from a cool color scheme.

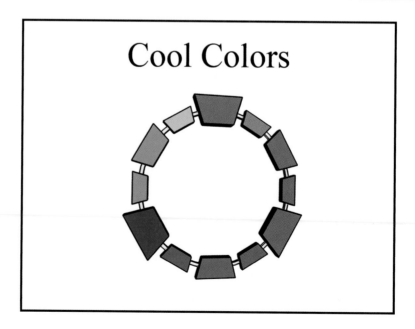

Individual Color Meanings

Beyond the high-level classifications or warm and cool, individual colors can symbolize many different things depending on the context in which they are used. For instance, the hue yellow, depending on its particular saturation, can mean everything from happiness and joy (for example, the yellow smiley face icon), to caution and concern (for example, a yield road sign). Visual 5–66 is a chart of the most common individual color meanings.

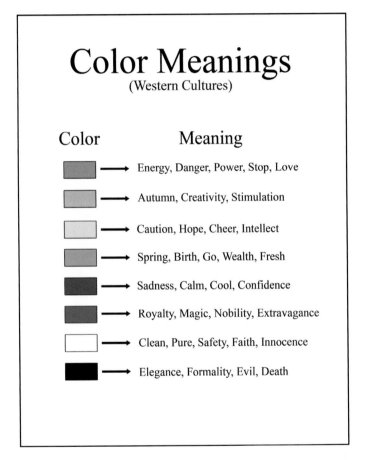

visual |5–66|
_____

Color Meanings

SUMMARY

The importance of the lighting process within digital filmmaking is often underestimated and overlooked until the very end of the project. However, the impact that light and color can have on a shot, scene, and film are far-reaching. Light and color add a dimension to your work that is difficult to achieve otherwise: illumination is transferred into atmosphere and color is transferred into depth. To fully unleash the power of both, one must first understand the science behind their creation and interaction with objects in space. This practical knowledge will be the foundation from which you can build the look and feel of your film, including light direction, placement, and color schemes.

▶ *in review*

1. What is electromagnetic radiation?

2. What is the visible spectrum and how does it relate to EM radiation?

3. Explain the correlation between wavelength and color within the visible spectrum.

4. What did Sir Isaac Newton discover about white light in the mid-seventeenth century?

5. What are the five main ways that light can interact with objects in space?

6. What are the six characteristics of light?

7. Explain the differences between hard and soft light.

8. Explain the concept of color temperature and how it relates to the Kelvin scale.

9. Explain the difference between the additive and subtractive color systems.

10. What is the purpose and function of the color wheel?

11. What is the HSV colorspace and how does it relate to digital filmmaking?

12. What are the major differences in symbolism between warm and cool colors?

exercises

1. Working with the characteristics of light, use a 3D character model that you have previously built to create a hard-light scenario by tweaking the level on contrast within the image.

    a. Without changing the model, textures, or camera angles, repeat the same exercise, but this time, create a soft-light scenario. What light parameters did you change? What are the overall differences from a viewer's standpoint?

2. Create a simple polygon model of an opened supermarket paper bag. Place it on a plane and arrange three lights around the bag. Determine a reasonable intensity for your three lights. The light should be the default white; change only the direction and angle of the lights to create the illusion of different weights and depth.

    a. Create a version in which the bag appears to be very heavy. What did you change?

    b. Create a version in which the bag appears to be very light. What did you change?

    c. Create a version in which the bag appears to be flat and thin. What did you change?

    d. Create a version in which the bag appears to be dimensional and thick. What did you change?

3. Using the same scene as in exercise #2, keep the light's angle and direction locked. Changing only the colors of the lights, create the illusion of different moods and atmospheres.

    a. Create a version in which the bag appears to be sinister. What did you change?

    b. Create a version in which the bag appears to be joyful. What did you change?

    c. Create a version in which the bag appears to be sickly. What did you change?

    d. Create a version in which the bag appears to be calm. What did you change?

CHAPTER 6

objectives

- Understand the difference between direct and indirect light
- Explore the concept of global illumination
- Explore the most common light types within film production
- Understand the link between shadows and spatial relationships
- Learn to create a traditional three-point lighting setup
- Understand key-to-fill ratios as it relates to three-point lighting

introduction

This chapter will build on the scientific understanding of light and color discussed in Chapter 5 and will explore the traditional production tools and techniques used in film lighting. Although it may be very tempting to jump right into the virtual world and start adding lights into your scene, it is critical that we take a step back and understand the traditional live-action concepts and processes that have been around since the early days of filmmaking.

The most common sources and types of lights used in production will be analyzed from both a physical and aesthetic standpoint. This will be immediately put into practice as we explore the launch pad for all lighting setups, the almighty three-point lighting. All of this will help tremendously when trying to navigate the complex waters of lighting within the virtual environment.

INTRODUCTION TO LIGHTING PRODUCTION

Quality lighting, like camerawork, is an often misunderstood part of the filmmaking equation for both amateurs and students. Although lighting has a bad reputation for being a mysterious process that it is much too complicated or time-consuming, the lighting process is just that: a process. In fact, most lighting setups are variations, albeit sometimes complicated, of the core techniques discussed later in this book. The reality is that most student filmmakers do not know where to start. They often make choices in a haphazard fashion, which lacks overall direction and motivation.

Lighting in a film can play as an important a role in determining the mood and atmosphere as the script and the characters. Lighting is a powerful tool that, when used correctly, can transform an individual frame into a work of art. Learning to light a scene involves learning how to see the real world first. For instance, when you learn to draw, you start with mimicking reality. It is only after you have grasped real-world perspective and proportions that you can move on to your own personal style. The same is true when it comes to lighting. Being able to visualize and recreate reality is the first step on the journey to developing your own lighting style. The following chapter will explore all the tools and techniques you will need while on that journey.

ILLUMINATION

Illumination, by definition, is the intensity of light falling at a given place on a lighted surface. However, the illumination that is generated from a particular source, such as the sun, light bulb, or candle, is only part of the equation. As we learned in Chapter 5, light interacts with all of the objects in world. Depending on the surface and color properties of those objects, they will reflect, refract, scatter, and bounce a certain amount of that light back into the scene. Therefore, only the combination of these two types will create realistic real-world illumination.

Direct Illumination

Direct illumination is light generated directly from a light source. The rays of light from that source travel in a straight line until they it an object in space. For instance, the diagram in Visual 6–1 demonstrates how the individual light rays from a single source cast direct light onto a spherical object.

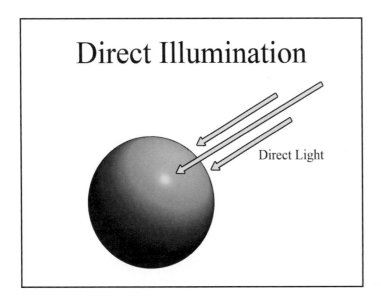

visual |6–1|

Direct Illumination
Diagram

Visual 6–2 shows a render of the same scenario in 3D using a soccer ball. Notice that because the ball is only illuminated with direct light, the bottom and left sides are in complete darkness.

visual |6–2|

Soccer Ball Lit with Direct
Illumination

Although there may be specific situations in which you would want this type of look, for the most part, using only direct illumination will make the scene look artificial. In fact, in the early days of computer graphics and animation, direct illumination was the only option in lighting because of the relatively straightforward calculations needed to create it.

Indirect Illumination

Indirect illumination is light that has bounced off another object in the scene. For instance, the diagram in Visual 6–3 builds on Visual 6–2 by adding indirect illumination.

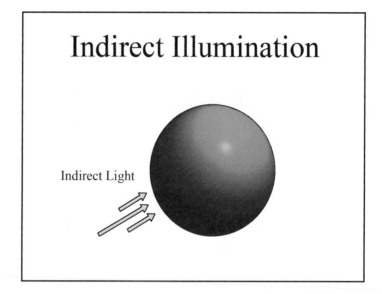

Notice that the light rays that hit the floor in front of the sphere do not simply die on contact but bounce back up to illuminate the underside. Although some of the intensity of indirect light typically is lost in the bounce, it should still be noticeable to the viewer depending on the type of surface that it is reflecting off. Visual 6–4 shows a 3D render of the soccer ball utilizing only indirect illumination. Notice that there is now light illuminating the bottom and left side of the ball. Furthermore, indirect illumination also transfers color information depending on the reflecting surface.

This transfer of light and color, often referred to as *radiosity*, will continue well beyond the first bounce. In fact, indirect light never dies but continues to bounce indefinitely. However, because the intensity drops off with every bounce, the human eye can only perceive a few of the bounces. Visual 6–5 demonstrates how the indirect light from the *ground plane* is transferred in the bounce back onto the bottom of the sphere.

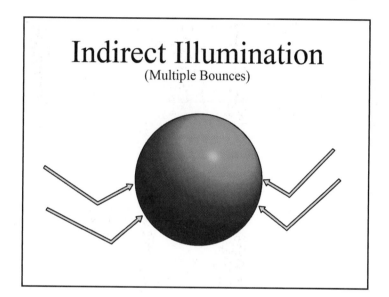

visual |6–5|

Indirect Illumination with Multiple Bounces

Global Illumination

Global illumination, also known as GI, is a term that has become widely used in the 3D animation community over the last few years. It is the incorporation of both direct and indirect illumination within a scene. Although it is often associated with outdoor or day-light lighting scenarios, global illumination is the term used to describe photo-realistic or real-world lighting.

It has only been in recent years that GI has become an option for 3D artists. As you can imagine, it requires much more computer horsepower to calculate the complex algorithms needed to determine light ray information with both direct and indirect or bounced light. Visual 6–6 is a diagram demonstrating a scenario taking both direct and indirect illumination into account. GI will be discussed at greater length in Chapter 7.

visual |6–6|

Global Illumination
Diagram

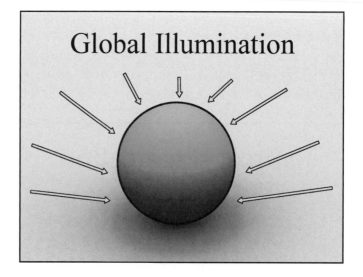

visual |6–7|

Soccer Ball Lit with
Global Illumination

SOURCES OF LIGHT

It is very rare that a single light source generates the total illumination for a given scene. In fact, I challenge you to find a situation throughout your day in which there are not multiple sources of light contributing to the overall illumination. Whether it is multiple versions of the same lights, different types of lights, or a mix of natural and artificial, these combinations will produce different colors and contrasts eliciting different moods from the viewer.

Image with Multiple Light Sources

For instance, close your eyes and imagine yourself sitting in one of those fancy high-end coffee shops. I'm writing this chapter in one right now. What does the lighting look like? Now, imagine if you replaced all the lights with only one huge ultrabright light on the ceiling. Although the illumination would be sufficient for the employees and customers to see what they are doing, would it be comfortable? Would you like to sit down and spend an hour slowly sipping your latte under this one bright light? On the flip side, there are plenty of situations in which bright harsh lighting is very appropriate: in an emergency room, for example. In this case, comfort is not as important as total visibility and illumination. The type and quantity of lights in your scene dramatically affect the emotional and physical responses from the viewer. Therefore, it is critical that you understand the various lighting options that exist and how they interact with each other.

Natural Light

Natural light, also know as *available light*, is generated by the sun, stars, and reflected off the moon. Although natural light produces the key energy necessary for human, animal, and plant life to exist, it also creates a byproduct of complex and beautiful lighting scenarios. In fact, natural light is a living breathing organism that is constantly changing and adapting depending on the time of day, location, and weather conditions. The endless variety of colors, contrasts, tones, and depths is what makes natural light so dynamic and interesting to the viewer.

Natural Light Diagram

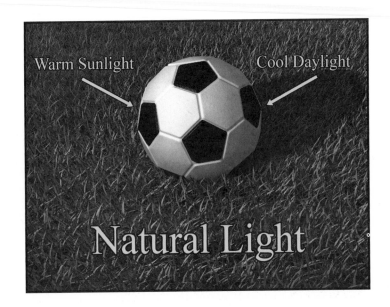

The positives of using natural light within a production are huge. Not only is the quality and diversity outstanding, natural light is cost-effective, that is, it's free! However, because filmmakers, or anyone for that matter, have little control over natural light, including time and weather, it can be very difficult to plan and produce shots revolving solely around natural light.

Image with Natural Light

Combustion Light

Combustion light occurs when there is a chemical reaction in which heat and light are the by-product. Combustion light can create dynamic lighting scenarios. Some common examples of combustion lighting include fire, candles, gas lanterns, and torches.

Typically, combustion light is on a much smaller scale than natural light, and it produces a more localized illumination effect.

Combustion Light Example

Artificial Light

Once electricity and the *incandescent light bulb* were invented in the nineteenth century, artificial, or man-made, light sources have become a cornerstone to civilization as we know it. Although it is difficult to achieve some of the same effects that natural light can produce, especially on such a mass scale, *artificial light* is both versatile and dependable. Barring the occasional blown bulb or fuse, artificial light can be a filmmaker's best friend, because of its unwavering consistency. Unlike natural light, which is constantly changing and adjusting, a completely artificial lighting setup can be used and reused independent of time and weather, giving the cinematographer and director greater flexibility when shooting.

There are three main categories of artificial light used today: incandescent, *halogen*, and *fluorescent*. Each of these produces light in different ways, and, therefore, has very different visual end results. It is important to understand what those differences are when developing the various lighting scenarios for your film.

Artificial Light Example

Incandescent Lights

The incandescent light is the most commonly used of all artificial light sources. From the ordinary household light bulb to more elaborate lamps, light is generated through a process called incandescence. Four main components are required for this process to take place: an envelope (usually a glass bulb), a gas (usually argon or nitrogen), a thin tungsten filament, and an electric current. The filament, which is enclosed within an airtight gas-filled glass bulb, is heated with electricity to the point at which light is generated. Visual 6–13 shows a basic diagram of the typical incandescent light bulb.

visual |6–13|

Incandescent Light Bulb
Diagram

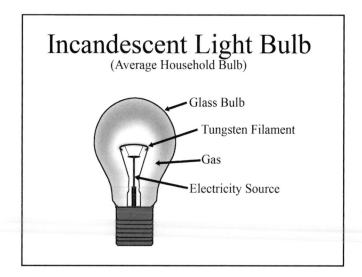

Incandescent Light Bulb
(Average Household Bulb)

Glass Bulb

Tungsten Filament

Gas

Electricity Source

The light emitted from the typical incandescent light bulb runs at temperature of about 2800 degrees Kelvin. Visual 6–14 refers to the Kelvin scale we discussed in the last chapter. Notice that it runs at about half the temperature of the mid-day sun and therefore falls into the warmer tones of the scale. Typically, incandescent light will cast a yellow/orange tint to a set. In general, this elicits a more comforting and relaxed feeling from the viewer and, therefore, is the light source used in most homes.

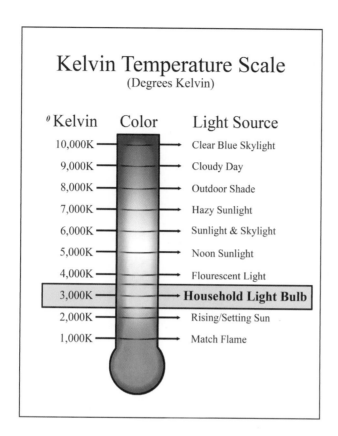

Kelvin Scale –
Incandescent

Visual 6–15 shows the soccer ball scene lit only with incandescent sources. Notice the white in the ball takes on a more yellow/orange tone, simulating overhead track lighting, as does the table.

Soccer Ball with
Incandescent Lighting –
One Source

Soccer Ball with
Incandescent Lighting –
Two Sources

Halogen Lamp

The halogen lamp, a close relative to the incandescent light, was developed to outlast the rather inefficient normal light bulb, which has a lifespan of only about 800–1,000 hours in standard use. This is because the tungsten filament evaporates over time and eventually burns out. However, the halogen light uses a much smaller envelope filled with a halogen gas, which allows the tungsten to regenerate itself within the heating process.

Halogen Light Diagram

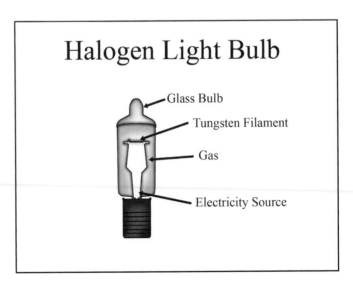

Therefore, the lifespan of the filament and the lamp is about twice that of the incandescent light, lasting on average about 2,000 hours. Because of these efficiency modifications, the halogen lamp is able to run at a higher temperature, approximately 250 degrees

Kelvin higher (3020 degrees Kelvin) than the incandescent bulb, and thus casts a slightly cooler tone onto a scene. However, it still falls into the warm tone category of lighting and therefore is used frequently in homes. Visual 6–18 demonstrates the effects of halogen lamp lighting on the soccer ball scene.

visual |6–18|

Soccer Ball with Halogen Lighting

Fluorescent Light

The fluorescent light is a complete departure from both the incandescent and halogen lamps from a light generation standpoint. Instead of using a heated filament, the fluorescent light sends an electrical charge through an ionized gas-filled tube to excite mercury and phosphor atoms, which release visible light. Visual 6–19 is a simplified diagram explaining this process.

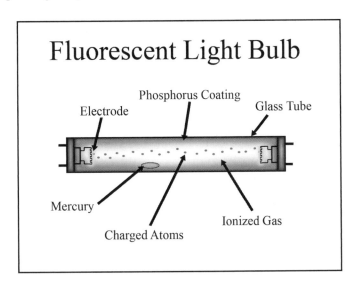

visual |6–19|

Fluorescent Light Diagram

Incandescent bulbs waste about 95 percent of its total energy on heat, leaving only 5 percent for the light output. However, fluorescent light does not require heat and, therefore, is about 400 percent more efficient. Not only will a fluorescent light put out more total light with the same energy, but also it will last up to ten times longer than the average incandescent light bulb.

Therefore, the fluorescent light bulb has been and will continue to be the most popular light source used in business/office settings throughout the world. You may be asking if it is brighter, cheaper, and lasts longer, why don't we use it in our homes? Although it is certainly a more efficient and cost-effective light source, it comes down to aesthetics. The normal fluorescent tube runs at about 3500 degrees Kelvin, which is significantly higher than an incandescent bulb. As you can see in Visual 6–20, the higher temperature brings its color almost completely out of the warm tones. Most will say that the average fluorescent tube will cast a sickly pale green color onto a scene. Also, because of its oscillating electrical currents, fluorescents can create a slight flickering affect, which can be very unpleasant to the viewer. For those reasons, most people will sacrifice efficiency for the warmer tones of the incandescent bulb in their homes.

visual |6–20|

Soccer Ball with
Fluorescent Lighting

visual |6–21|

Light Source Comparison –
Incandescent, Halogen, and
Fluorescent

PRODUCTION LIGHTS

Now that we have a solid foundation of both the theoretical and scientific aspects of light and color, let's turn our attention to their practical application as relates to film production. Although there are an endless variety of lighting equipment available to today's cinematographer, most can fit into one of four categories; *directional, omni-directional, spotlights,* and *area lights.* You will find that most 3D software packages use the exact same methodology and, with an understanding of their real-world applications, the transition to the virtual world should be seamless.

Directional Light

Directional light, also known as infinite light, is created from an extremely high powered and distant source. In the real world, the most common example of a directional light is the sun. The light emitted from the sun, or any directional light for that matter, arrive at the earth's surface as parallel rays. The farther away any light source is from the receiving surface, the more parallel the light rays will become.

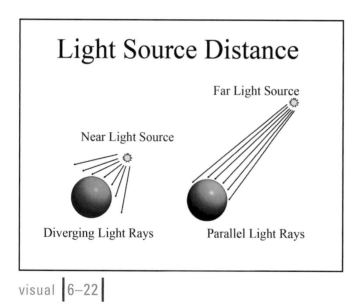

visual |6–22|

Light Source Distance Diagram

Therefore, it typically takes a powerful source, such as the sun, to create the unique combination of intensity and parallel rays. In fact, directional lights are considered not to have an exact position in space. They are so far from the surface that is being illuminated that it is not important to know what the exact location is. However, they do contain direction, color, and intensity information.

Directional light illuminates all surfaces from the same direction because of its parallel rays, creating an extremely uniform look and feel to the scene. Visual 6–23 shows the effects of a singular, isolated, directional light illuminating multiple soccer balls. Notice that the light's direction, color, and intensity are uniform to all of the surfaces independent of their location.

Directional Light Example

Sunlight/Daylight

Although the image in Visual 6–23 is a great example of directional light, in reality it is not an accurate representation of the most common directional light: the sun. *Sunlight* is white light that contains all the colors of the visible spectrum. As the sunlight enters the Earth's atmosphere, the shorter wavelengths, or the cool tones, are more easily scattered by the atmospheric particles and, therefore, the reason the sky is blue. This scattered light from the sky, or *skylight*, is emitted from all directions as if from a giant blue dome. This additional ambient light softens the effects of the direct sunlight. The combination of both sunlight and skylight is what is referred to as *daylight*. Visual 6–24 shows the soccer ball scene lit with midday daylight.

The closer the sun approaches the horizon line, at dawn and dusk, the longer the sunlight has to travel through the atmosphere to reach the earth. This extra distance allows for most of the shorter, cooler, wavelengths to be scattered away completely, isolating the warmer yellow and red tones, creating a typical sunrise/sunset. Visual 6–25 shows the soccer ball scene lit during a sunset.

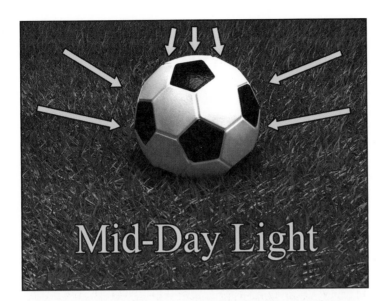

Daylight Example –
Mid-Day

Daylight Example –
Sunset

Omni-Directional Light

Omni-directional, or *omni lights* radiate from a single point in space, evenly distributing light in all directions. The most common real-world example of an omni light is an incandescent light bulb. Although a light bulb doesn't fully radiate in all directions, it contains color, intensity, and position information. However, because the light rays are distributed from every angle, a light bulb, and omni lights in general, do not have direction.

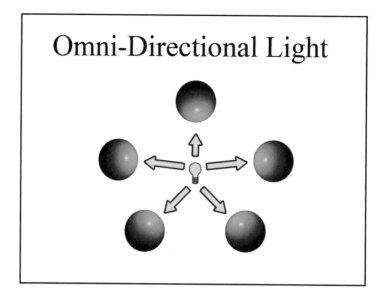

Omni-directional lights, because of their physical and aesthetic properties, tend to give off a warm and inviting quality to a scene and, thus, are the most popular choice for lighting homes. Visual 6–27 shows the soccer ball scene lit with an omni-directional light. Please note that omni lights are often diffused by something, for example, a lamp shade. This further enhances the soft and warm quality.

Spotlights

Spotlights are, by far, the most common type of light used in the production of both traditional and digital films. Similar to an omni-directional light in that the illumination emanates from a specific point in space, the spotlight has a housing that focuses the light rays into a conelike shape. Spotlights have direction, position, color, and intensity, which provide a high level of control to the cinematographer when designing a lighting setup. Depending on how wide the cone angle is opened, the spotlight can be used as the major source of illumination in a shot as well as to spot-fill some specific dark areas.

Spotlights cast light in a very distinct fashion. There is an inner cone, also known as the hotspot, in which 100 percent of light's intensity is transmitted. There is also the outer cone, or the falloff, in which the light intensity evenly diminishes outwardly. The size of both the hotspot and the falloff are determined by the shape of the spotlight's housing cone. Visual 6–28 demonstrates a typical spotlight illumination cone.

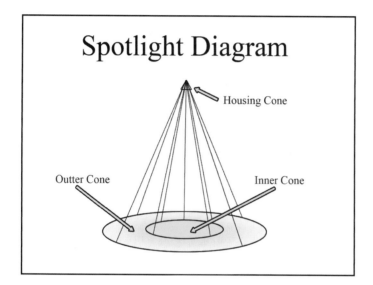

visual |6–28|

Spotlight Illumination Cone

Using the soccer ball scenario, we will use two different variations of a spotlight to light the scene. Notice in Visual 6–29 that the spotlight on the left has a narrow cone angle as well as a very small dropoff. The end result is a hard-edged, focused beam of light. You will often see this type of light used in theatrical productions to highlight a particular actor or object on stage.

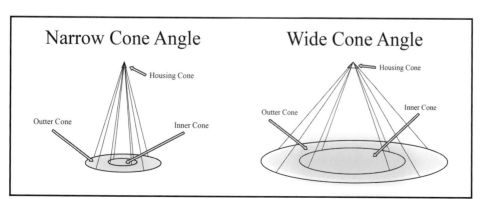

visual |6–29|

Cone Angle Comparisons

In contrast, the spotlight on the right uses a much wider cone angle and a large dropoff. You will notice that it not only illuminates a greater portion of the scene but also that there is a much softer transition from the inner to outer cone. You will see this used quite a bit in film production, as it gives you great coverage as well as focus.

Area Lights

Area lights, unlike spots or points, emit light rays evenly across a flat surface rather than from a single point. Therefore, the area light is similar to a directional light in that the light rays are parallel. This produces a consistent illumination across all objects in the scene, as well as creating a softer edge and shadow. However, unlike a directional light, an area light has a definite position in space. Therefore, objects closer to an area light will be more illuminated than those that are not. Visual 6–31 shows a diagram of a typical area light.

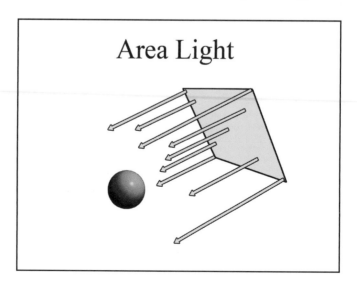

Area Light

Although area lights can be any 2D shape, more often then not they are rectangular. Some common real-world examples of area lights are large flat-screen televisions, electric billboards, and overhead industrial lighting. In production, area lights often are used on a set to mimic a real-world phenomenon such as a large reflection from a window. Visual 6–32 shows the soccer ball scene lit with an area light. The left side mimics an overhead light, whereas the right image mimics a window reflection.

visual |6–32|

Soccer Ball Illuminated by an Area Light

LIGHTING ACCESSORIES

Although it is possible to achieve amazing results with the lights as they exist, there are an array of lighting accessories that can help shape the light even further adding even greater flexibility and control to the cinematographer. These accessories, used in both indoor and outdoor scenarios, can reflect, diffuse, remove, and refocus the light rays on to very specific parts of a shot. More often than not, they are used to counterbalance a particular light source, or lack thereof, that is out of the director's control; bright sunlight and harsh fluorescent lighting for example.

Reflectors and Bouncers

Reflectors and *bouncers* are used frequently when shooting outdoors or on-location. Their sole purpose, not surprisingly, is to redirect light onto a specific location within the shot. Although they are most commonly used to reflect natural or available light, they can be used with complicated artificial lighting setups as well. Card reflectors, as seen in Visual 6–33, are typically thin pieces of light colored fabric or cardstock and are either rectangular or circular in shape. The light color of the reflector, as we learned in Chapter 5, absorbs very little of the light energy, bouncing it back on to the scene.

visual |6–33|

Card Reflector

Visual 6–34 shows the soccer ball lit mainly by harsh mid-afternoon sunlight. The shot requires that the sun be behind the ball leaving most of its front in shade or darkness. However, if you use a card reflector, shown in the wide-angle view of Visual 6–35, the resulting image is much more aesthetically pleasing. Visual 6–36 shows the before and after image of the soccer ball being lit with and without the use of a card reflector.

visual |6–34|

Soccer Ball Scene – Harsh
Available Light

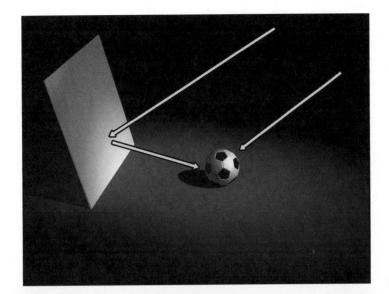

Wide-Angle View of Scene
Using a Card Reflector

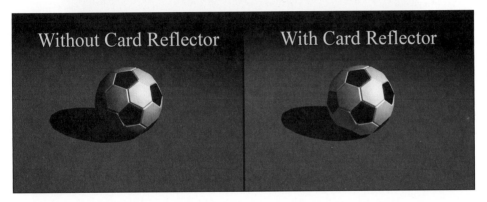

Without Card Reflector   With Card Reflector

Before and After Example
of Card Reflector Use

Umbrellas and Softboxes

Umbrellas and *softboxes* are similar to reflectors in that they are used to refocus light back into a scene. However, they work specifically with artificial sources as opposed to natural or available light. Umbrellas look identical to the standard rainproof versions in that they form a round cuplike shape. However, instead of the typical handle, it has an artificial light, usually a spotlight, attached that points directly toward the deepest part of the umbrella. Therefore, the light is actually pointed 180 degrees away from where the light is needed. The light colored fabric of the umbrella not only reflects the light back onto the scene, but also the cuplike shape diffuses the light significantly, producing a much softer light.

Umbrella Reflector

Softboxes, by contrast, are self-contained units that shine a light, or series of lights, through a semitransparent piece of fabric. Although the lights point directly in the direction of intended area, the light rays are scattered significantly as they pass through the light colored fabric. The end results are very similar to that of the umbrella, creating soft light and edges reducing unwanted hotspots on the scene objects. The larger the umbrella or softbox, the more scattered the light will become and the softer the light will appear. Visual 6–38 demonstrates a typical softbox in use.

Softbox Example

Scrims

Scrims are large pieces of translucent fabric that are placed in front of artificial lights as a diffuser. They work in a similar fashion to a softbox but are usually much larger and helpful in outdoor shooting situations.

visual |6–39|

Scrim Example

Gobos

Gobos ("go-betweens"), are black card reflectors that intended to remove or reduce rather than add light from a scene. They are extremely helpful for minimizing the effects of natural light or reducing the size and strength of another reflector or diffuser within your lighting setup.

visual |6–40|

Gobo Example

Barn doors

Barn doors are supplemental attachments placed on the opening end of an artificial light. Typically used with spotlights, barn doors consist of four adjustable flaps on the top, bottom, left, and right of the light. They can be used separately or together to limit and focus the light rays being emitted. Barn doors are great for illuminating very small areas within a scene or for minimizing hotspots on particular troublesome objects and surfaces.

Barn Doors Example

SHADOWS

Not just by-products of light, shadows are an extremely valuable tool for the director and cinematographer. For instance, in Frank Miller's 2005 feature film *Sin City*, the shadows were as important as the objects and lights themselves. Because of its black and white, graphic novel aesthetic, the shape, size, and placement of the shadows provided compositional strength and beauty as well as vital visual cues for the audience.

Shadows are an often overlooked and underutilized portion of the lighting process for amateur filmmakers. This is mainly because shadows, at least in traditional live-action filmmaking, are not something you need to create specifically. In other words, they are a natural phenomenon that occurs when light is blocked by an object in space. However, it is important to note that although shadows will appear naturally, they can be tweaked and manipulated to enhance the overall shot, scene, or film. This is especially true in digital filmmaking, where shadows are optional and highly malleable. We will discuss 3D shadows in greater detail in Chapter 7.

Shadow Components

Shadows, by definition, are the relatively darker areas created by the lack of direct light from a specific light source caused by an object in space. Visual 6–42 depicts a sphere being lit by a single spotlight.

visual |6–42|

Shadow Example

As the light rays travel from right to left across the scene, they come into contact with the sphere and are absorbed and/or bounced back. As you can see in the Visual 6–43, the light rays (labeled A) are not able to penetrate the sphere, so the area of the ball opposite of the light, as well as the corresponding area on the surface plane, is in shadow. The light rays that do not come in contact with the sphere (labeled B), are unobstructed until they reach the surface plane. The resulting shape on the surface plane (labeled C), known as the cast shadow, is determined by the shape of the object casting the shadow as well as the type and position of the light source.

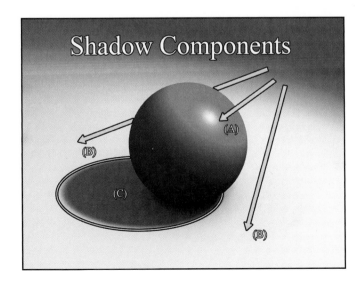

visual |6–43|

Shadow Components

Shadow Casting Object

Concentrating just on the sphere, or *shadow casting object*, for the moment, you will notice that there is an illumination shift from lighter (right) to darker (left).

Illumination Shift

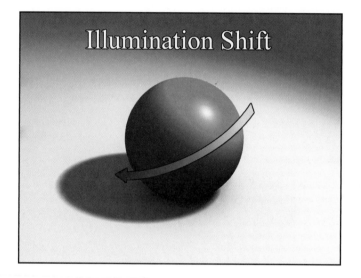

This transition of light across the object can be separated into three distinct areas depending upon the angle of the light source. Visual 6–45 demonstrates the three categories of illumination on a shadow casting object. Moving right to left in the direction of the light rays, the first section (labeled D) is considered the object's area of direct illumination. This part of the object is, as the name suggests, the part that is receiving unobstructed light rays from the particular light source. Therefore, this part of the object will appear the brightest to the viewer. The second section (labeled E) is known as the *terminator*. It forms a dark ringlike shape around the object as it is, in most cases, the area of the surface that is receiving the least amount of light. This is because the surface area that comprises the terminator is exactly, or very close to, parallel with the light rays.

Direct Illumination,
Terminator, and Shadow

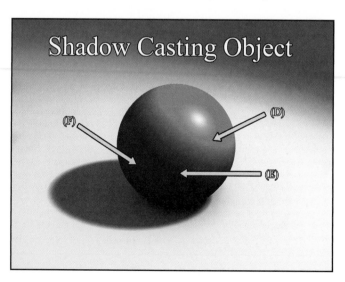

The last illumination component to the shadow casting object is the shadow area. This section (labeled F) is the part of the surface that is not being directly affected by the light source. However, it is more illuminated than the terminator as a result of the bounce light from other objects in the scene. In this particular case, it is the white light from the surface plane that is slightly illuminating the shadow area of the shadow casting object.

Cast Shadow

Let's focus on the shadow area that appears on the surface plane. This area is known as the cast shadow because its shape is entirely determined by the shadow casting object. Similar to the shadow casting object, there are three main components that combine to form the *cast shadow*: the *contact shadow*, cast shadow, and *shadow edge*. Although the size, shape, and intensity of the three components will vary depending on the given lighting setup, all three are always present. The only exception to that rule is with the contact shadow, which is only present when the shadow casting object is in contact with another surface.

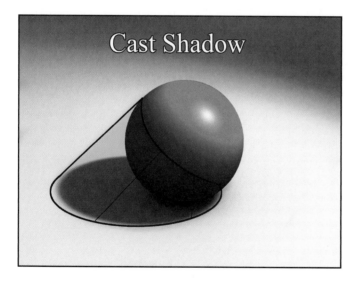

visual | 6–46 |

Cast Shadow

Visual 6–47 shows the same sphere and spotlight scenario but from both front and top views to see all three of the components. The contact shadow (labeled G) is the small dark ring around the bottom of the sphere. The contact shadow, similar to the terminator on the shadow casting object, it the darkest portion of the cast shadow. The area directly around where the shadow casting object and the ground surface intersect is considered the contact shadow. This small dark area is what cues the viewer that the object is sitting directly on the surface plane. The second component, and the one that usually takes up the most surface area, is the main cast shadow. This area (labeled H) is the direct responsibility of the shadow casting object and what most people consider the objects shadow. Finally, the shadow edge (labeled I) is the outline transition between the cast shadow and the fully illuminated surface plane. This transition typically is an even gradient the size of which is determined by the light source.

Contact Shadow,
Cast Shadow, and
Shadow Edge

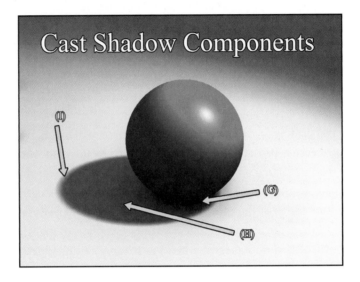

Cast shadows often are categorized by their edge detail. The larger the edge of the shadow, the softer the shadow will appear. By contrast, the smaller the edge of the shadow, the less transition and, therefore, the harder the shadow will appear. This is determined by type, size, and distance of the shadow-casting light source in the scene. In general, the smaller and closer the source of light, the harder the shadow will appear. Visual 6–48 shows a spotlight that is very close to its subject, which produces a hard-edged shadow.

Hard-Edged Shadow

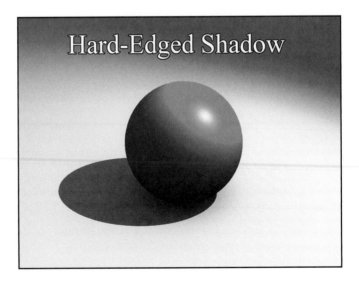

Visual 6–49 shows the same scene but this time lit with an area light that is about three times farther away. Notice the size of the shadow edge is significantly larger, producing a longer transition from the cast shadow to the illuminated surface.

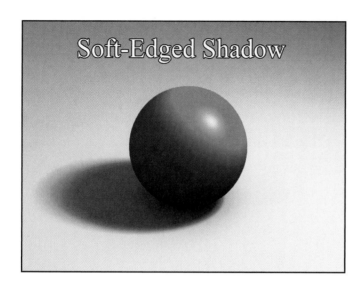

Soft-Edged Shadow

Spatial Cues

Beyond adding visual complexity and interest, shadows can provide valuable spatial information about the shot to the viewer. For instance, Visual 6–50 is a series of three images depicting a soccer ball bouncing up and down. Although the light source does not change direction, angle, or intensity, notice the differences in the shadow.

visual |6–50|

Shadow-Defined Spatial Relationships – Ball Bouncing

In the first frame, the ball is on the way down approximately two feet above the ground surface. How do I know this? There are two important visual cues that allow me to make that assumption. The first is the overall size and scale of the objects in the scene. Because I recognize the object as a soccer ball, I can only assume that this is a normal regulation size ball. Along with the size of the ball, I can tell how far off the ground it is because of the shape, size, and edge detail of the shadow. Notice that the shadow is fairly dark but does not contain a contact shadow.

Ball Bounce – Above the Floor

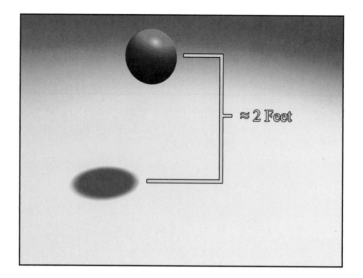

The second frame shows the ball as it hits the ground. This time, the ball is obviously in contact with the ground plane because it has changed shape significantly; utilizing one of the twelve principles of animation, squash, and stretch. Notice the changes that take place with regard to the cast shadow. A contact shadow is now obvious around the bottom of the ball, which becomes the main visual cue that places that ball onto the floor. Also, the edge detail becomes significantly more defined, producing a much harder shadow, another clue that the ball is closer to the ground surface.

Ball Bounce – Hitting the Floor

The third frame shows the ball on the back up at approximately four feet off the ground. The ball is now in the opposite shape, stretching toward the sky. However, it is the shadow that tells us the most information about the ball's location. The shadow is now without the dark contact shadow area, much larger in shape overall, lighter in color, and much softer in edge detail. Visual 6–53 shows two versions of all three images; one with the shadows as normal and one with the shadows completely removed. Although you get the basic drift of what is happening in the top three images, the shadows add a sense of visual comfort and familiarity that just simply does not exist without them.

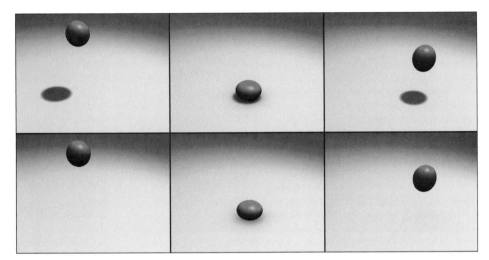

visual |6–53|

Ball Bounce – With and Without Shadows

Shadow Color

One of the biggest lighting misconceptions involves shadow color. Most student/amateur filmmakers would probably tell you that all shadows are either completely black or a shade of gray. Although it is true that shadows appear darker, relatively speaking, than their surrounding areas, they almost always have a level of color. How do you determine what the color of a particular shadow will look like? The first step is to determine all of the various light sources in a particular shot. Visual 6–54 depicts two images of soccer ball being lit by late afternoon natural sunlight. However, Image A has a shadow that contains no color information, whereas Image B takes more realistic approach.

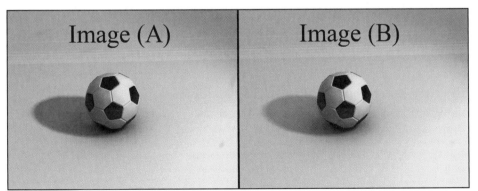

visual |6–54|

Shadow Color Example – Late Afternoon Sunlight

Notice that in both images, the warm tones of the direct sunlight are hitting the right side of the ball, which creates a cast shadow on the surface plane on which it is resting. However, the cast shadow has taken on a decidedly different hue. Although both cast shadows help with spatial definition, only Image B seems to feel natural. This is because the cast shadow is taking on a cool bluish tint, which is the opposite of the warm sunlight. This is highlighted in Visual 6–55.

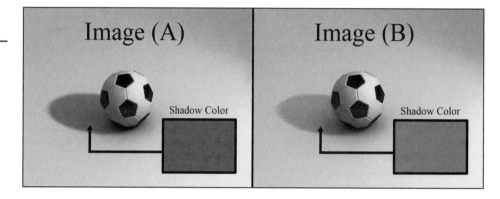

Where are the blue tones coming from? The shadow color is determined by two factors in the scene; surface color and the remaining available light. In this particular case, the

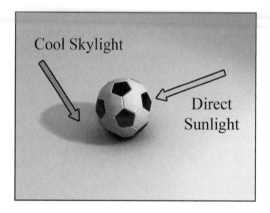

surface color is white, so it will pick up the hue of almost any light source available. As far as the remaining light sources are concerned, we have to look beyond just the direct light of the sunlight. Although the shadow is unaffected by the direct warm hues, it is affected by the scattered, diffuse blue skylight. Visual 6–56 demonstrates the effects of skylight on the shadow color.

The same holds true for artificial lighting situations as well. Visual 6–57 depicts a soccer ball that is lit by two spotlights. The spotlights, for demonstration purposes, have been given different hues: green and yellow. Notice how the green spotlight's light rays on the right side of the image are able to reach the cast shadow on the left, creating a green tint. Furthermore, the left-hand spotlight is able to tint the cast shadow of the right-hand soccer ball a pale yellow.

Shadow Color Example –
Two Spotlights

Cookies and Assumed Objects

In the real world, shadows or patterns of light add rich detail and visual interest to the space around us. *Throw shadows* or throw patterns can stem from almost any off-screen shadow casting object. For instance, Visual 6–58 depicts a character that is being lit primarily from a window that we can assume has Venetian blinds attached. Although it is not important that the viewer ever see the actual window, the unique pattern of light that the window blinds produce adds a unique aesthetic twist to the shot.

However, when it comes to filmmaking, traditional or digital, budget and time are always a consideration. Therefore, unless you are directing a huge blockbuster

visual |6–58|

Window Throw Pattern –
Venetian Blinds

Hollywood film, chances are you have to look for ways to cut corners. One of the most useful time- and budget-saving production techniques is the use of assumed objects with light cookies. *Cookies*, a nickname for the traditional term *cucoloris*, are flat objects that have holes cut out to mimic their real-world counterparts. Visual 6–59 is an example of the cookie used to create the shadows in Visual 6–60.

Notice how simple this object needs to be, because it will never be seen by the viewer. All that is important with cookies are the size and proportions of the holes that allow light to pass. Although the end results are identical, creating a cookie rather than an actual window with blinds is much more time- and cost-effective. Visual 6–60 shows all of the elements involved with the scene. Notice that the cookie is positioned in front of the light source that is shining through the assumed window.

Some other common examples of cookies used in the filmmaking process are shapes resembling people and trees as well as random shapes used to break up the light and create visual interest.

THREE-POINT LIGHTING

Much like working with the camera, there is an endless array of options that a cinematographer must wade through when determining the lighting scheme for a particular shot, including source, type, color, and position. Although these choices allow the cinematographer to realize almost any look and feel that they can imagine, it can leave the amateur filmmaker overwhelmed and unsure as to where to begin. However, much like the rule of thirds or the 180 degree rule, there are some basic guidelines and formulas to help even the most timid of lighters. *Three-point lighting* is the most commonly used lighting scheme in filmmaking production.

Developed back in the heyday of Hollywood productions, three-point lighting became the foundation on which all lighting schemes were built. Each light, or light function, serves a very unique and important role within the shot. When these three lights are combined correctly, the end results are considered to be universally more aesthetically pleasing to the viewer. The power of three-point lighting lies within its enhanced modeling of the objects in the scene. Although the term "modeling" is used to describe the creation of geometry within the 3D universe, it is used in terms of lighting to describe the degree of dimensionality that the light adds to the shot. In other words, objects are well modeled when they appear more three-dimensional to the viewer. For instance, compare Visuals 6–61 and 6–62. The two images contain the same exact scene objects; only the lighting has changed. However, the object in Visual 6–61 appears to be very shallow and flat. On the contrary, the object in Visual 6–62 appears to have depth and dimensionality.

Which figure delivers the most information about the scene? Which one is more visually appealing? Although there may be specific reasons that call for a very flat image, more often than not, greater modeling with light will produce more engaging imagery.

visual |6–61|

Flat Lighting

The three lights, or light functions, that are involved in creating a three-point lighting scheme are the *key light,* the *fill light,* and the *rim light.* These light are placed at various positions in relation to the camera around the scene. They contain important differences in their intensity and color that help to create the light variation across an object's surface. Visual 6–63 highlights the surface variation differences between three-point lighting on the left and flat lighting on the right. It is exactly this variation of light and color or modeling that helps to bring out or emphasize certain portions or qualities of the object while setting back or hiding others.

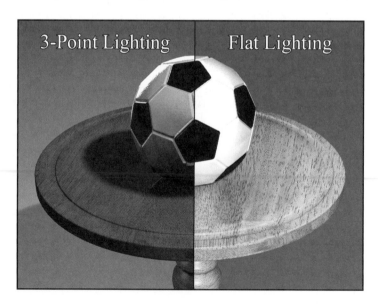

As we explore the inner workings of three-point lighting, we are going to use spotlights as the default light. Although there are many options for lights available to the cinematographer, sticking to one light type will help to demonstrate the power of the lighting setup rather than the differences in the light source. Furthermore, almost everything can be achieved with spotlights, especially in digital filmmaking. Thus, learning how to light first with spotlights only will force you to fully understand the power and process rather than confusing the situation with other light types.

Key Light

The key light, also known as the main light, is the source that will supply the overall direction as well as the majority of the intensity and shadows for your shot. This is the light that you would use if you could only use one light in your scene. However, using only one light can be extremely limiting and there are only very few circumstances in which you would want to go that route.

Because the key light will provide the majority of the illumination in your shot, you will want to make sure that you pick the appropriate cone angle and distance so that the light is able to affect the entire scene. Although the angle and distance will depend on the specific size of the scene, Visual 6–64 diagrams, from a top view, the approximate cone size and distance needed. It is important that the key light is able supply light to the entire scene without an unsightly cutoff. However, feel free to adjust the hotspot and edge detail to provide even more surface variation.

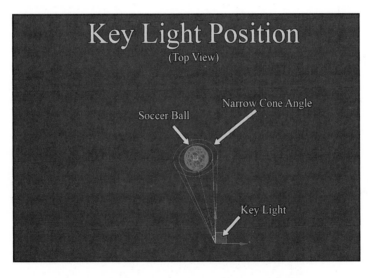

visual |6–64|

Key Light Cone Size and Distance – Top View

Once you have adjusted the key light to accommodate all of the scene objects, it is now time to adjust its position relative to the camera. Notice that in Visual 6–64 the light is pointing straight on and is not taking the camera into consideration. Assuming that the camera is in the same position as the light, the resulting image would appear flat and uninteresting, as in Visual 6–65.

Key Light Positioned
Straight-On

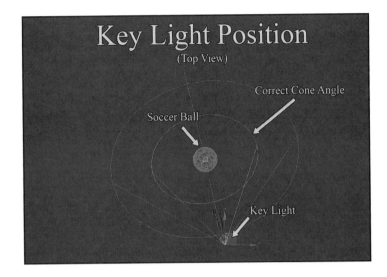

Keeping in mind that the entire purpose behind three-point lighting is surface varia-tion and modeling, we must further adjust the light position according to the position of the camera. Visual 6–66 shows the same top view but this time incorporating the camera, which remains straight on. However, the key light is now moved off center to create surface light variation. Which side the key light falls on does not matter; this is a personal aesthetic decision made by the cinematographer. However, the further you move the angle from the center, the greater the surface variation will appear. In my opinion, the best results are achieved somewhere in the 15-degree to 45-degree range.

Key Light Angle –
Top View

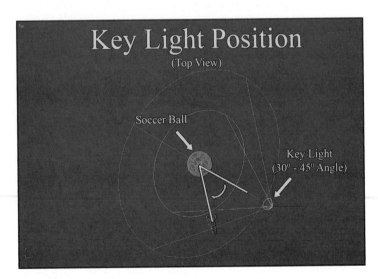

To add even further modeling to the object, let's adjust the profile angle of the spot-light; moving the light above the ground plane. Notice that in Visual 6–67 the same principles apply as they did from on the top view. The further you move the camera above or below the ground plane, the more surface variation occurs. Again, the best results are achieved with an angle between 15 degrees and 45 degrees.

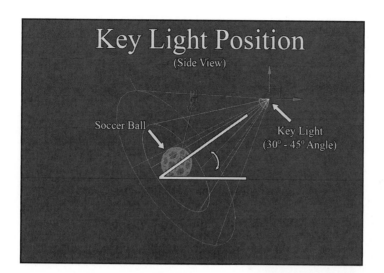

Key Light Angle – Side View

To further demonstrate the correct position and placement of the key light, Visual 6–68 shows the evolution of the process we just described. In the first frame, the spotlight has not been adjusted to fit the scene. Notice that not all of the objects are being illuminated. The second frame shows the correct adjustment of the cone angle and distance. However, because the light is straight on, it produces a rather flat image. In the third frame, the light angle has been adjusted from the top view perspective. This adds a great amount of surface variation as the scene objects start to appear more dimensional. The last frame demonstrates the results of adjusting the light's profile angle. Notice that the object appears well modeled, with even further depth and dimensionality.

Key Light Evolution

Fill Light

The fill light is the source that is used to balance out the surface variation created with the key light. Although surface variation is important to the modeling of an object, we do not necessarily want parts of the object to go into complete darkness. The fill light, less intense and a different hue, will mimic the effects of bounce and ambient light that would often occur with natural light. In fact, when shooting outdoors with natural light, the cinematographer often will use a reflector to enhance the fill light in a scene.

As with the key light, the fill light will have to be adjusted to accommodate for all of the objects in the scene. However, from a positioning standpoint, the fill light should be close to a mirrored image of the key. Visual 6–69 shows both a top and side view of a typical fill light setup.

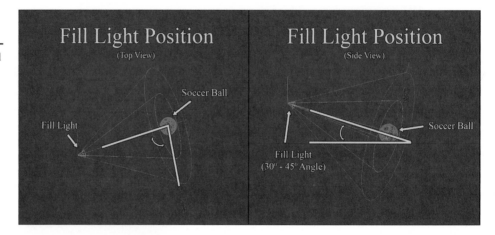

Notice that other than being pulled slightly further away from the object, the fill looks remarkably similar to the key light. However, you will want to adjust the angle, within the 15-degree to 45-degree range, so that the appropriate amount of light is filling the darker sides of the scene objects. Using the same scene as in the previous visual, Visual 6–70 demonstrates the evolution of the fill light.

Rim Light

The rim light, or back light, is the source that is used to highlight the surface edges of the scene objects. Although the rim light only provides approximately 5 percent to 10 percent of the total light that is visible in the shot, it can be the difference between good and great lighting. Designed solely for aesthetic reasons, the rim light tends to make the objects pop out toward the viewer, creating even further depth and dimensionality.

From a positioning standpoint, the rim light can prove to be difficult to control, especially for the amateur filmmaker. Its position in space has everything to do with the camera and almost independent of the key and fill. For the most part, the rim light will be almost 180 degrees away from the camera, on the back side of the scene objects. However, it cannot be a perfect mirror copy because you would never see the light, as it would be completely blocked by the objects.

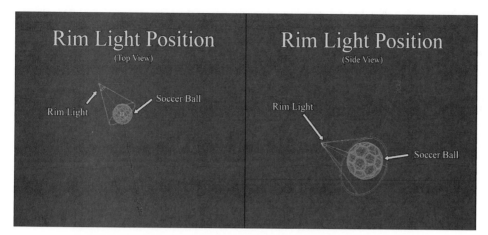

visual |6–71|

Rim Light Angle

Therefore, you must move the rim light position so that the light seems to be just illuminating the rim or edge of the object. Typically, you can get good results about 15 degrees of center from the top and about 45 degrees of center from the side. However, and I cannot stress this enough, it will depend completely on the size and shape of the objects in the scene. Visual 6–72 shows the results of the rim light.

visual |6–72|

Rim Light Example

Double Rims

There are certain artistic scenarios in which you might want even further edge/background separation. To achieve this, you may use *double rim* lights. The effect is rather unnatural-looking. However, it is unique and will grab the attention of the audience.

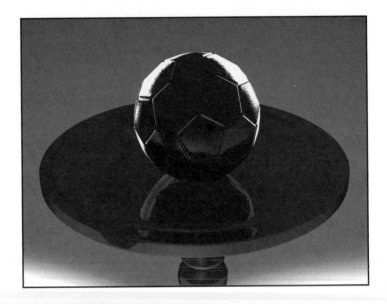

Putting It All Together

Up until this point, we have discussed the key, fill, and rim lights as separate and distinct units. Although each has very specific roles and responsibilities within the three-point lighting scheme, they are only really useful when put together. However, separating them out is extremely useful and is the process in which you should use when developing your own. In other words, do not start by throwing the three lights into the scene and adjust from there. Much like the evolution images in Visuals 6–68, 6–70, and 6–72, start with complete darkness and adjust one light at a time independent of each other. This will allow you to see the true effects that each is having on the scene. Otherwise, it will be very difficult to make adjustments, as the light will naturally overlap.

With the position of the lights set, it is now time to start thinking about the intensity ratios between the three lights. It makes the most sense to start first with the key light. Adjust the intensity so that there is sufficient illumination. Avoid overillumination, which creates large hotspots and flattening of the image, as well as underillumination, which will not provide the amount of visual information necessary for the viewer.

Once the key light intensity has been determined, you can use some basic guidelines to adjust the intensity of the fill and rim. In general, the average fill light should be approximately 10 percent to 20 percent of the total illumination of the key light. Although this is just a guideline, these ratios seem to provide the best results. You will want the fill light to be noticeable by the viewer, but it should never compete with the key light. Visual 6–74 shows an image with both a key and fill light added.

Key and Fill Lights

This relationship between the key light and fill light is often referred to as the *key-to-fill ratio*. For instance, the higher the key-to-fill ratio is, the greater the difference between the light's intensities. Visual 6–75 demonstrates a high key-to-fill ratio.

High Key-to-Fill Ratio

By contrast, a low key-to-fill ratio is the result of similar intensities for both the key and the fill. A low key-to-fill ratio creates a flatter-looking image and, in most cases, defeats the purpose of three-point lighting.

Low Key-to-Fill Ratio

The rim light, however, is typically more intense than the key light. Because its purpose is to produce a controlled hotspot of sorts, it can range anywhere from 150 percent to 300 percent of the key's intensity. However, this will depend on the surface properties of the objects. For instance, shiny metallic objects, will not need as much to produce a hotspot, whereas diffuse objects, such as clothing, will need more. Visual 6–77 shows all three of the lights in the scene.

Key, Fill, and Rim

The Color Shift

Color is a critical tool that can be used to enhance the surface variation and modeling within a shot. In general, creating a shift of color over the objects, known as *the color shift*, will create visual interest and increased depth. Although the rim color can be important, it does not affect as much of the object surface area as the key and the fill. Therefore, you will want to use the key and the fill as the main source of the color shift.

The basic concept is to shift from a warm hue to a cool hue. This is the same affect that happens naturally during a sunset. One half of the sky is emitting warm colors, while the other half is emitting the cooler hues. However, it is important to note that the shift should be more of a hint of color rather than strong and overpowering. Visual 6–78 shows the complete effect of three-point lighting, taking position, intensity, and color into consideration.

Complete Three-Point Lighting

Beyond Three-Point Lighting

Although three-point lighting is an amazing tool for the amateur filmmaker, the reality is that most lighting schemes go well beyond the simple three-light setup. The lighting functions, especially the key and fill, are almost always used in some way, shape, or form. For instance, the key light might be the sun or a combination of artificial light sources in a particular shot. However, there is still a definite direction is which the majority of the light is being transmitted, that is, a key light. In fact, the fill light might not be an actual light at all. In many outdoor scenes, the fill light is created with a reflector that bounces some of the natural light back onto the subject. The point is to not be so literal with the use of three-point lighting but to adapt and revise the scheme to fit your shot's particular needs.

SUMMARY

The digital cinematographer must first explore how light and color work in the real world before a single virtual light ray is cast. Developing a critical eye that recognizes the often subtle differences that exist within light and shadow is only half of the equation. In fact, the most successful cinematographers have a deep understanding of the traditional lighting tools and options that will allow them to not only mimic reality but go well beyond, developing a unique personal style. These skills will not only make you a better lighter but also make for a much smoother transition into the virtual world.

in review

1. What is the difference between direct and indirect illumination?

2. Explain the concept of Global Illumination and how it relates to available light.

3. What are the four main components of the incandescent light bulb?

4. Compare the color temperatures of incandescent, halogen, and fluorescent light.

5. Why are directional lights considered to be an infinite light source?

6. What types of production lights have direction, color, and intensity?

7. What is an area light and how does it emit light?

8. Explain the difference between a reflector and a gobo.

9. Explain the importance of shadows within a lighting scheme.

10. What are the three components to a shadow?

11. What does the term modeling refer to with regard to lighting?

12. What are the three components to three-point lighting?

13. What are the visual differentiators between high and low key-to-fill ratios?

▶ *exercises*

1. Using the Internet, search for an image of an indoor public space such as a department store or a bus station.

   a. Create a list of all the light sources that you believe are illuminating the scene.

   b. What types of production lights would you use to recreate this scenario on a Hollywood sound stage?

2. Illuminate a preexisting character model with a single spotlight. Create a cookie that resembles a tree branch with leaves.

   a. Repeat the same scenario, but instead create a cookie that resembles another human character.

3. Using a simple ground plane and sphere, set up a three-point lighting scheme.

   a. Focusing only on position and intensity, create a key, fill, and rim light using the process outlined in this chapter. Hint: Do not place them all into the scene at once.

   b. Create a warm to cool color shift using the key and fill lights.

   c. To add further complexity, create another primitive object into the scene. How does this affect the current lighting scheme? What adjustments will you have to make to the light positions?

   d. Create a double rim around the sphere.

CHAPTER 7

objectives

- Explore the transition from real-world lighting to virtual lighting
- Understand the common parameters within 3D light sources
- Defy real-world limitations with the use of negative light
- Understand the various ways virtual shadows are calculated and created
- Discover the various way to light your virtual characters and sets
- Learn to fake global illumination within your shot

introduction

This chapter serves as the bridge between the color theory and real-world lighting techniques discussed in the previous chapters and their application within the digital environment discussed in the final chapter. You'll find that the deeper your understanding of these core fundamental theories and practices, the easier this transition from traditional to digital will be.

There are aspects of digital lighting that are much easier, adjusting positions for example, or only possible to create in the virtual environment, for example, negative light. However, there are lighting scenarios, for example, global illumination, that occur naturally in the real world. It is often very difficult and time-consuming to recreate real-world lighting digitally. Therefore, it is critical that the virtual lighter understand the possibilities and limitations of working within the 3D environment, exploiting its ease of use while working around the more challenging situations.

VIRTUAL LIGHTING

INTRODUCTION TO VIRTUAL LIGHTING

Mastering any aspect of the digital filmmaking process first requires a deep understanding of real-world, or traditional, filmmaking. Software manufacturers have taken painstaking measures to make the digital lighting process as close to the traditional lighting process as possible. In fact, the top packages have meticulously included all of the various controls, parameters, and options that are available in the physical environment.

visual |7–1|

Lighting Example –
Kitchen Set

TRANSITION TO THE 3D ENVIRONMENT

When beginning work on a new project, most animators do not immediately jump into the lighting process. This is quite understandable. The first thing you see when you open up any 3D software application are the empty viewports.

visual |7–2|

Empty Viewports

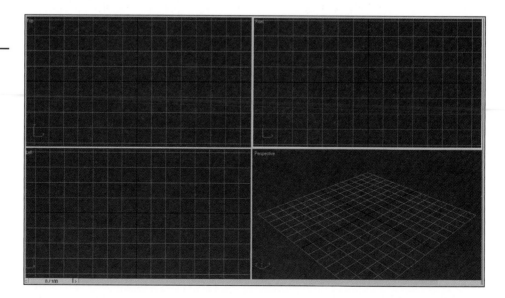

Therefore, it is logical that you would build 3D assets before you can start to light them. However, it does not make sense to wait to the end of the production process, either. Lights are not only used to create the final look and feel of your film but actually to see what you are creating during the other phases of production along the way.

Without some form of light in your scene, you will not be able to see the geometry that you are trying to work on. Although most software applications build in a form of default lighting so that your geometry will never be in complete darkness, this often needs to be supplemented or removed completely. Therefore, you must approach lighting as a three-phase process: *default lighting*, *production lighting*, and *final lighting*.

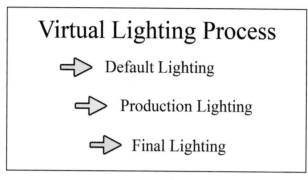

visual |7–3|

Lighting Phases Diagram

Production lights are used during the modeling, texturing, and animation phases to see exactly what it is you are creating. Think of these lights as the industrial lights that might be used in a craftsman's workshop. These have a utilitarian purpose and, thus, they are often not the most flattering lights, or lighting schemes, in the world. However, they are intended to make every face or polygon visible to the artist, high-lighting all of the imperfections, so that they can be adjusted early on.

visual |7–4|

Production Lighting

The final lighting setups are what most people think of when they think of lighting. These are the lights that will be used during the final rendering of your film. They are as much an artistic tool as they are illuminating the scene. For instance, there may be shots in which particular scene objects will need to be in shadow or complete darkness for storytelling/aesthetic purposes. Although this lighting looks great for the final shot, it would be extremely difficult to use when modeling or texturing.

VIRTUAL LIGHTS

3D lights are similar to virtual cameras with respect to their ease of use, unlimited supply, and functionality that rivals their real-world counterparts. To fully explore the power of digital lighting, you must be able to decipher the lighting terminology used in the advanced parameter rollouts. This terminology is, whenever possible, identical to those used with traditional lighting equipment. Therefore, understanding traditional concepts is critical to your success in the virtual environment. This is a step that is frequently overlooked in the production process. The artist, confused by the many choices available, often ignores the most powerful options all together or haphazardly picks and chooses which to adjust and manipulate.

Often, the biggest mistake a lighter can make is at the very beginning of the decision tree. Which type of light should I use for which purpose at which stage in production? The answer lies within the understanding of the various light types that are available for use. The following light types are those that are found in almost every 3D software package on the market. Although there are some slight differences in some of the terminology from package to package, the functionality is nearly identical.

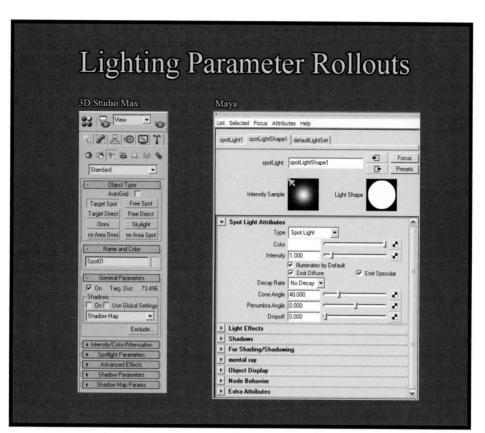

Lighting Parameter
Rollout

DEFAULT LIGHTING

A visualization tool more than anything, *default lighting* is used when there are no
lights in a scene. Without default lighting, the user would not be able to see anything
they start building in a shaded viewport. Much like in the real world, everything would
appear black without a source of light. Therefore, the software manufacturers have created a default light source to get the artist going. In most circumstances, the default
light is a shadowless version of a direct light.

Default Lighting within
the Active Viewport

Because the default lighting is permanently attached to the renderable camera, there is no 3D representation or icon that can be seen or manipulated in the viewports. Therefore, the default lighting is constant and is not able to be changed. Therein lies its biggest weakness. Although it is certainly helpful to have generic illumination in the very early stages of the production process, its power is quite limited. In fact, because the light is always shining directly at the object or objects at which the camera is looking, it tends to flatten out everything. This not only looks unrealistic but can be detrimental even early on in the modeling phase.

The use of default lighting should be kept to a minimum. In fact, it is best to think of it as a last resort. It is recommended that you use one or more of the other standard light sources, such as an omni or spotlight, for at least the production stage of your film.

visual | 7–8 |

Render Utilizing Default Lighting

STANDARD LIGHT SETS

In any 3D animation software package, *standard lights* are the computer-generated simulations of real-world lighting sources, both artificial and natural. They are non-physical-based solutions that do not take physical size and intensities into consideration. Although this makes them technically less accurate from a light/photon creation/calculation standpoint, they offer a wide variety of distribution options that, when used correctly, can imitate almost any lighting scenario in the real world.

Common Parameters

Regardless of which 3D software package you choose, there are four common parameters that are available for use with all standard lights as well as in some of the advanced lighting features.

These parameters, which include intensity, color, decay/attenuation, and shadows, are the main controllers that will define the basic look and feel for the particular light. They are designed to recreate real-world options in the traditional filmmaking setting. You will notice that standard lights are easier to manipulate and change on the fly than physical lights, and they provide near-instant feedback to the digital cinematographer.

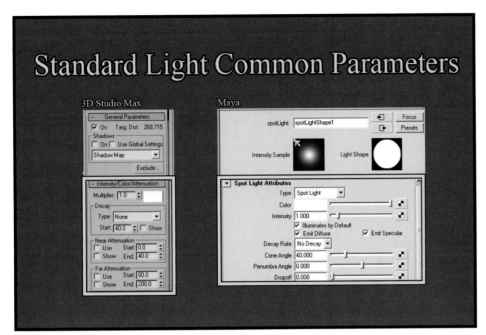

Intensity

The light's *intensity* is usually one of the first attributes that will appear in the parameter roll-out. Although intensity does not specifically relate to an exact scientific calculation of light illuminance (foot-candles), it will control the overall brightness of the light. Using generic units, the default intensity for most lights is set at 1. An intensity level set at 0 will produce no light, and a level of 2 will appear twice as bright as the default setting.

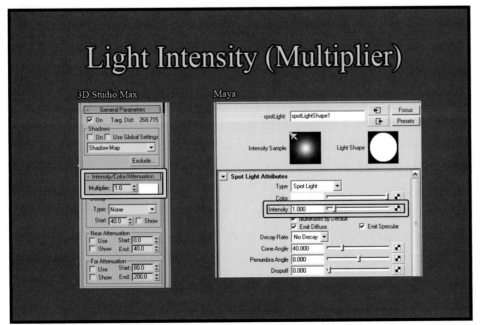

Visual 7–11 demonstrates a series of four images in which the light intensity, starting at the multiplier setting of .5, is doubled each time. Notice how the surface properties of the objects in the scene are affected, ranging from not enough light to an overabundance.

Color

Color is another option that will appear at the top of the parameter dialogue box. Similar to intensity, it does not relate to a specific scientific calculation of light color, in that color temperature is not taken into consideration. However, the digital cinematographer is able to choose the color independent of the source and temperature. Although this adds a great deal of flexibility in the creative process, it is critical that the lighter refer back to the color temperatures as well as color theory when deciding on what to use and when. Visual 7–12 shows a typical color dialogue box in which an interactive color chooser is available as well as the option to enter in specific RGB or HSV number values.

visual |7–11|

Light Intensity – Four Images

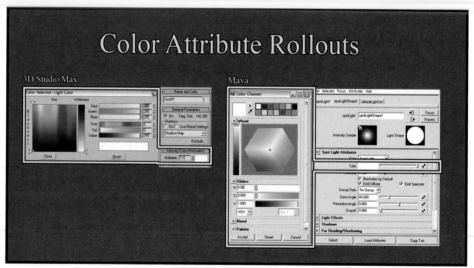

visual |7–12|

Color Attribute

Visual 7–13 demonstrates a series of three images in which the light color is adjusted according to times of day. Please note that the only light attribute that is changed in each image is the color.

Light Color – Three Images

Decay and Attenuation

In the real world, the brightness or intensity of light lessens over the distance from the point of source. Often referred to as the amount of *decay* or *attenuation* that the light has, the intensity will decrease proportionally to the square of the distance to the source. This equation, known as the inverse square law, is the closest to a realistic light simulation and is available in all of the major 3D software applications. Visual 7–14 demonstrates the effects of this type of attenuation, often referred to as quadratic decay, within the virtual environment.

visual |7–14|

Light Decay Example

Most software packages have the light decay turned off by default. This means that the lights intensity is not affected by the distance to the source. This option is not only less computationally intensive, which produces shorter rendering times, but allows for more flexibility for the light placements in the 3D scene. Most artists find, at least when first learning how to light, that the quadratic decay appears too dark and is harder to work with.

visual |7–15|

No Decay versus
Quadratic Decay

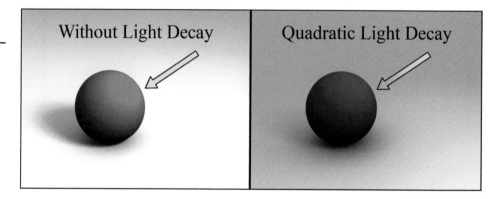

There are several other options for computational or equation-driven decay rates that are available to the artist. Although they are not realistic, they can provide decay that fits to the particular scale necessary in your scene. These decay rate options include:

- Linear Decay — Intensity decreases in a linear, straightforward manner, which is a slower process than in reality.

- Quadratic — Intensity decreases proportionally to the square of the distance to the source, the inverse square law, which is the most realistic approach available.

- Cubic — Intensity decreases proportionally to the cube of the distance to the source, which is a faster process than in reality.

3D lights allow you to control the light attenuation from a non-equation-driven standpoint, giving the digital cinematographer the ultimate control over the decay. Although this is far from a realistic simulation, it can be very useful for pinpointing the light illumination within a scene. Attenuation of 3D light sources can be broken down into two categories of control; near attenuation and far attenuation.

Near attenuation controls the light decay from zero intensity, or complete darkness, at the source through full intensity. Far attenuation controls the decay from full intensity through complete darkness. Both near and far attenuation attributes have a start point and an end point that can be adjusted by entering in specific units of distance from the source. Visual 7–16 illustrates a typical virtual spotlight utilizing both near and far attenuations.

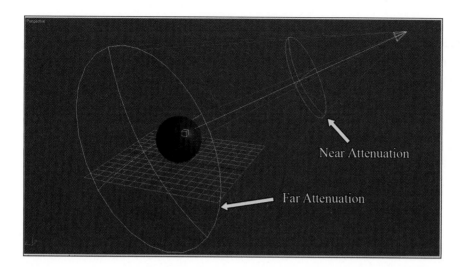

3D Spotlight Using Near and Far Attenuation

Shadows

Shadows are formed by the absence of light due to an obstruction of the light rays. By default, standard virtual light sources have the shadow creation option turned off. This is because shadows can cause significant render time increases. However, you will find that you will use shadow casting lights in almost every shot you create, especially those that have an element of realism.

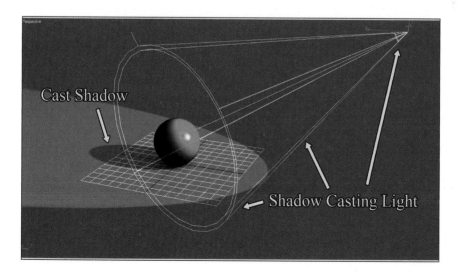

Shadow Casting Light

SPOTLIGHTS

The *virtual spotlight* is nearly identical to its real-world equivalent in that it emits light from a single point, constrained by a virtual light housing, that creates a cone-shaped light pattern. Unlike the traditional spotlight, the 3D spotlight can be easily replicated and positioned anywhere within the virtual environment. They include a wide variety of adjustable options and parameters that allow the digital cinematographer all of the flexibility and creativity of the traditional variety used on the stage and screen, and there are additional features and benefits. Therefore, the 3D spotlight is the most commonly used standard light in the digital cinematographer's tool chest. In fact, most software packages will use a spotlight icon to represent the entire standard light set.

visual |7–18|

Spotlight Icons

Located within the standard light sets in most 3D software packages, a spotlight can be created easily by dropping one into a camera viewport. Visual 7–19 demonstrates the look of an unaltered standard 3D spotlight.

visual |7–19|

Standard 3D Spotlight - Unaltered

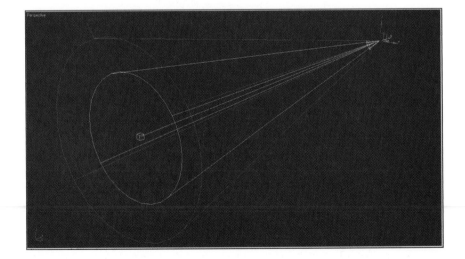

Spotlight Components

There are two major components and two subcomponents to the standard 3D spotlight. The two major components, shown in Visual 7–20, are the *main spotlight* (A) and the *target* (B).

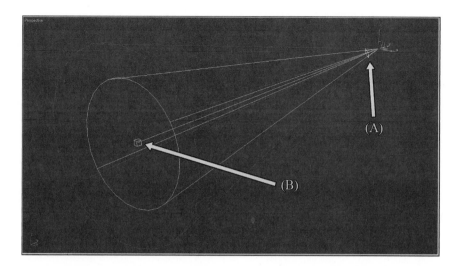

Standard 3D Spotlight –
Major Components

The main spotlight represents the light source as well as the virtual housing. The main spotlight is what contains all of the vital information regarding the light. You will want to pick this in the viewport to access the many options and parameters available. Although this controls all of the common properties available to most light sources, it also contains the ones unique to the spotlight. Chief among these is the cone angle. The wider the cone angle, the more light is shed onto the scene.

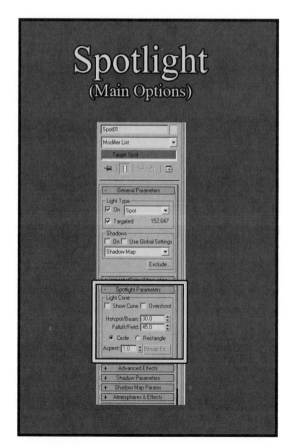

Main Light – Options

The spotlight target (simply, the target), is what controls the direction of the main light source. You should pick both the main light and target within the viewport to make large-scale movements and adjustments to the light. However, you will want to use the target to make finer adjustments.

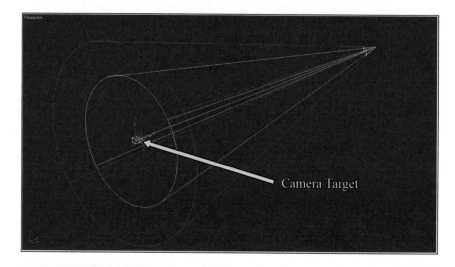

The spotlight's subcomponents, highlighted in Visual 7–23, consist of the *inner cone* or *hotspot* (C) and the *outer cone* or *falloff* (D). These are controlled through the main spotlight, but they are located on the same plane as the target. Therefore, position is determined by the target and visual properties are determined by the main spotlight.

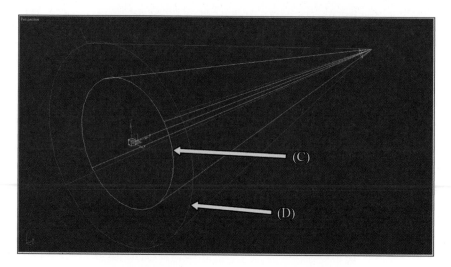

The hotspot determines the area that will receive the full intensity of the spotlight, whereas the falloff radiates outward and determines the distance that the light intensity will fall off or fade out to darkness. Visuals 7–24 and 7–25 demonstrate results of two spotlights with opposite major and subcomponent properties. The spotlight in Visual 7–24 has a very narrow cone angle. Notice that this results in a very thin circle of light with a relatively sharp edge. By contrast, the spotlight in Visual 7–25 has a very wide cone angle with equal distribution of hotspot and falloff. This resulting image is a very wide light circle with a very smooth transition from full intensity to darkness.

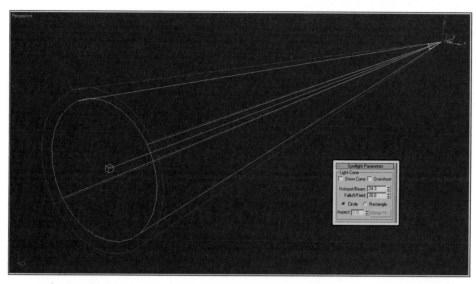

visual |7–24|

Standard 3D Spotlight – Narrow Cone Angle with Dialogue Box

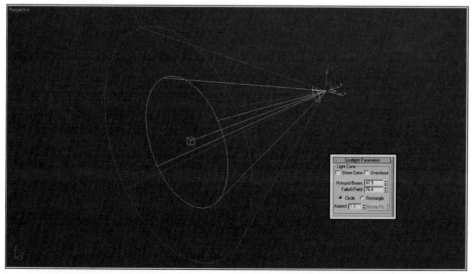

visual |7–25|

Standard 3D Spotlight – Wide Cone Angle with Dialogue Box

| NOTE |

A Technical Director at Pixar once told me that you can achieve almost any desired lighting look and feel in 3D using only spotlights. Although there have been some amazing strides in lighting options available to digital cine-matographers in the eight years since he spoke those words, the basic sentiment remains true. It is critical, especially when first learning how to light, that you under-stand the various options available and their visual ramifications. Throwing too many different types of lights into your scene can create confusion and chaos, distracting from the true task at hand. Take a tip from the folks at Pixar and limit your light source palette at first. Learn to light with spot-lights only and slowly build out from there. This is where I started, and am thankful for that tip almost every time I start to cre-ate a light rig.

DIRECTIONAL LIGHTS

The *virtual directional light* mimics a natural light source unlike the artificial spotlight. As we learned in Chapter 6, directional lights create an infinite light source with parallel light rays. Directional lights do not have position per se; they only have intensity and direction. Although you can position a directional light anywhere in the viewport, its distance to specific objects in the scene is irrelevant. Therefore, the digital cinematographer should be concerned with the angle and intensity only.

visual | 7–26 |

Direct Light at Different
Distances

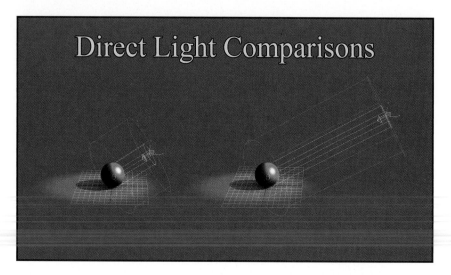

Visual 7–27 shows the typical 3D representation of a direct light. Notice that is has similar components, major and sub-, as the spotlight; the main light (A), target (B), hotspot (C), and falloff (D).

visual | 7–27 |

Standard Direct Light
Components

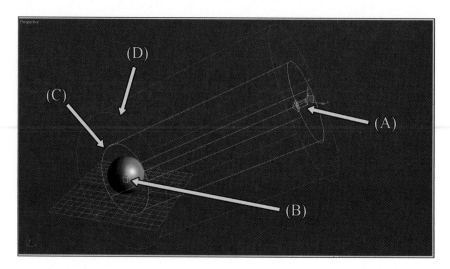

However, unlike the signature cone shape that the spotlight produces, the direct light can take either a cylindrical or cubic shape in which the light rays emanate evenly from the inside the top cap segment. As with the spotlight, increasing the hotspot/falloff size will, in turn, enlarge the area of the cylinder/cube and increase the amount of light emitted into the scene.

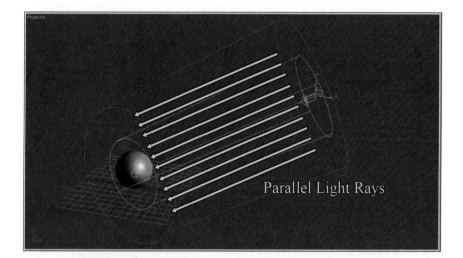

visual |7–28|

Standard Direct Light – Parallel Light Rays

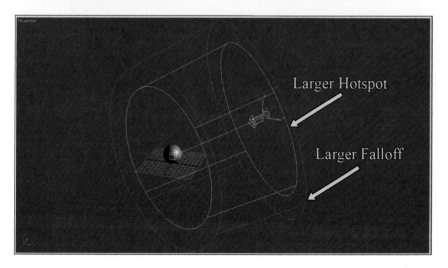

visual |7–29|

Increased Hotspot/Falloff

OMNIDIRECTIONAL LIGHTS

Omni lights, also know as *point lights*, emit evenly from a single point with a full 360 degree spectrum. They are similar to spotlights, without the virtual housing that limits the illumination to a cone shape. Therefore, the virtual omni light has no direction but only position and intensity. The 3D representations reflect this lack of direction typically using a bulbous uniform shape. Visual 7–30 depicts some common icons used to identify a virtual omni light.

Standard Omni Light 3D
Representations

Because the light has no direction, it does not require a target. Therefore, there is only single component to an omni light: the main light. Visual 7–31 depicts an omni light placed inside a closed box. Notice that the light hits the walls on all sides evenly.

Omin Light within a
Closed Room

VOLUME LIGHTS

A *volume light* is something that does not appear in the physical world either naturally or artificially. Therefore, it is a computer-generated light source. As the name suggests, a volume light is a light source that fills a specific three-dimensional space. Available in most of the primitive modeling shapes such as spheres, cubes, cylinders, and cones, the volume light emits light from the surface of a shape either inwardly or outwardly.

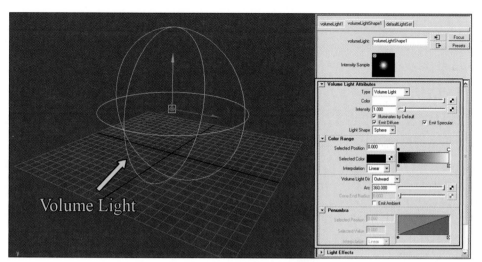

Volume Light

Because the shape of the volume defines the light emission, the volume light can be easily manipulated by adjusting the surface as you would with the standard modeling tools. This makes it very easy to create specific light shapes. Visual 7–33 depicts a long cylindrically shaped volume light similar to a fluorescent tube.

visual | 7–33 |

Volume Light –
Fluorescent Light Tube

SKYLIGHTS

Skylights are akin to direct lights in that they both try to replicate a natural light source. Whereas the direct light simulates the direct light emitting from the sun, the skylight mimics the diffused light that emanates from the entire sky during daylight hours. To achieve this look and feel, the skylight creates a virtual half-dome within the scene that emits a large number of low intensity light rays. Visual 7–34 demonstrates, diagrammatically, how the skylight effect is achieved in the virtual environment.

However, the actual arrays of low intensity lights are kept invisible to the user for organizational purposes. In fact, they are represented within the virtual environment as a simple half-dome icon. It is important to note that the skylight only contains intensity data; its position and direction are always fixed.

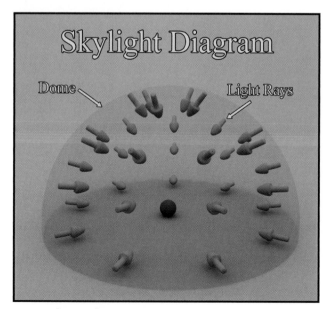

visual | 7–34 |

Skylight Diagram

Skylight Icon

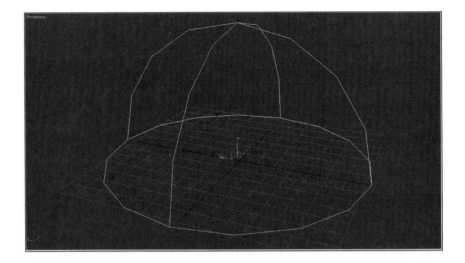

These light rays, because they are emitted from all directions, produce the very soft and diffused light and shadow that are the hallmark of midday skylight in the real world. Visual 7–36 demonstrates the results of using a skylight.

visual |7–36|

Skylight Example

DIGITAL SHADOWS

Digital shadows are one of the biggest determining factors for developing a photo-realistic lighting setup. In fact, the shadows, or areas of relative lack of light, are as important as the light itself. Although most casual observers cannot describe particular shadow qualities at great length, they certainly notice when they are off or unnatural-looking. Therefore, it is critical that the digital cinematographer understand how realistic shadows are created and how to transfer that knowledge into the virtual environment.

SHADOW QUALITY AND GENERATION CALCULATIONS

In the virtual world, shadows are controlled by the individual lights sources, both their existence and appearance. A major portion of the overall look and feel of the shadow is determined by the way in which one decides calculate its generation within the 3D software. Depending on which of the two options are chosen, the shadows will not only appear quite different in terms of edge quality, soft or hard, but also will have a dramatic impact on the overall rendering times.

Shadow Maps

The default shadow calculation method for most 3D software packages is with the use of *shadow maps*, also know as *depth maps*. To create the shadow, a map is generated, before rendering, from the light's point of view, which approximates the various distances from the light source to the scene objects. This map is then utilized during the actual rendering process to determine where the shadows should appear in the shot.

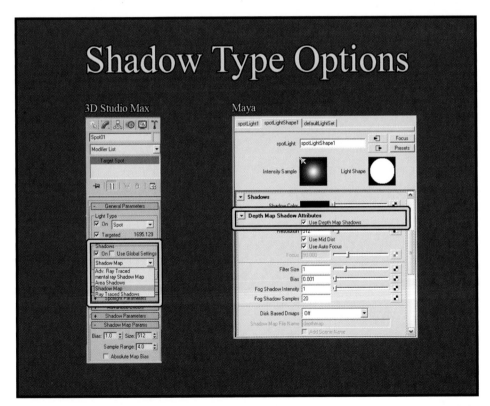

visual |7–37|

Shadow Type Options

Because the shadow maps are an approximation, a slightly less accurate shadow generally is produced. Therefore, the visual results can be somewhat flawed. However, the maps produce a softer-edged shadow and can be used multiple times, creating a good balance between shadow quality and rendering speed. Visual 7–38 demonstrates the use of shadow map shadow generation within a scene.

visual |7–38|

Shadow Map Render – 512

Map Size

The default pixel size of a depth map is typically 512. This tends to give enough visual information to adequately calculate most shadows. However, this size can be increased to produce more visual information, and, in turn, more accurate shadows within your shot. Please note that the larger the *map size*, the longer the render and calculation times.

Shadow Map Transparency Handling

Because the shadow map creation technique is a depth-based approximation, it cannot calculate for material transparency. In other words, it can only look at the raw geometry in the scene and not any transparency/opacity maps that may exist. Visual 7–40, for example, is a simple window created out of a primitive box. Although it looks like there is transparent glass in between the sills, the shadow map cannot distinguish between the opaque wood and the transparent glass.

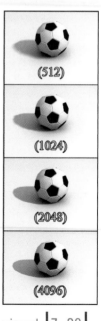

visual |7–39|

Shadow Map Size Progression – 512, 1024, 2048, and 4096

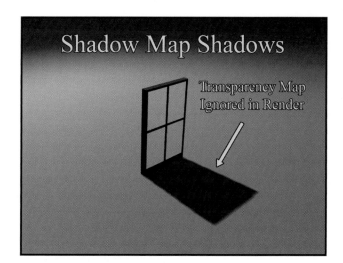

Shadow Map
Transparency Problems

Raytraced Shadows

The individual light rays from each source are tracked, determining which objects should receive light and which should be in shadow, creating *raytraced shadows.* This pinpoint accuracy tends to create a much harder-edged shadow. The processing is done at the time of render and cannot, like shadow maps, be recycled. This should be factored into the total production timeline. Visual 7–41 demonstrates the use of raytraced shadow generation within a scene.

visual |7–41|

Raytraced Shadows

Raytraced Transparency Handling

Because raytraced shadows use individual light rays to calculate cast shadows, transparency/opacity map data should be taken into consideration. This could be a major determining factor when deciding on which type of shadow calculation technique should be used. Visual 7–42 revisits the simple window created from a primitive box that was illustrated in Visual 7–40. Notice that raytraced shadows produce the correct shadows.

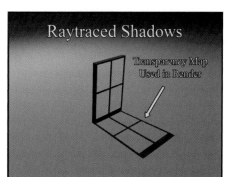

visual |7–42|

Raytraced Shadows
Transparency Handling

Bias

The *shadow bias*, or ray bias for raytraced shadows, is the relative distance between the shadow and the shadow-casting object. The closer the bias unit is to 0, the closer the shadow will appear to the shadow-casting object. Visual 7–43 depicts shadows with varying degrees of shadow bias.

Filter or Sample Range

The *filter* or *sample range* of a shadow will determine the overall edge detail. Typically ranging from 0 to 4, the higher the number, the softer the shadow will appear. Visual 7–44 depicts shadows with varying degrees of sample range.

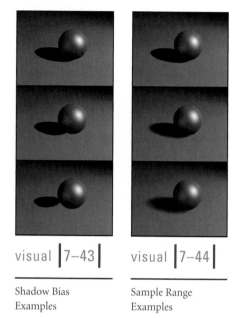

visual |7–43|

Shadow Bias
Examples

visual |7–44|

Sample Range
Examples

ADVANCED OPTIONS

Digging a little deeper into the attribute editors for digital lights, you will find some advanced features that, when utilized properly, can take your lighting rig to the next level. Although some of these are not an option in real-world lighting schemes, they can be used to add realism into your CG shots. This section will explore three of the more useful advanced 3D light options available.

Light Exclusion and Inclusion

One of the more useful tools that the digital cinematographer has available when working with 3D lights is the ability to pick and choose which lights affect which objects within a scene. Defying real-world physics, a virtual light easily can be customized on a per-object basis to either cast, or not cast, illumination, shadows, or both. To achieve something even remotely close in traditional filmmaking, the cinematographer would have to build elaborate light cookies or scrims to purposely avoid particular objects. However, in the 3D environment, it is as easy as the click of a button. Visual 7–45 shows a typical exclusion/inclusion option box.

Notice that you can either pick objects by the ones you would like to include, which the light will affect, or exclude, which the light will not affect. This makes it very easy, depending on the number of objects in your scene, to quickly adjust the lights to the specific needs of the shot.

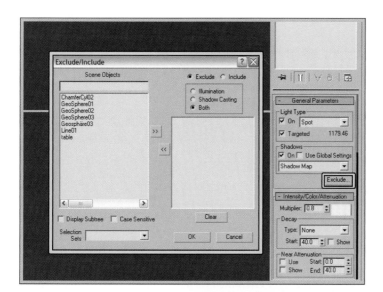

Light Exclude/Include
Dialogue Box

One of the more common uses for light exclusion is to avoid strange light patterns on a particular object. For instance, in Visual 7–46, you will notice that the soccer ball is lit well but that the cone of the spotlight used for the fill light can be clearly seen on the table it is sitting on.

To quickly remedy this problem, choose the fill light within one of the viewports to access its attribute editor. Navigate to the exclude/include option box, and turn the illumination off for the table (see Visual 7–47).

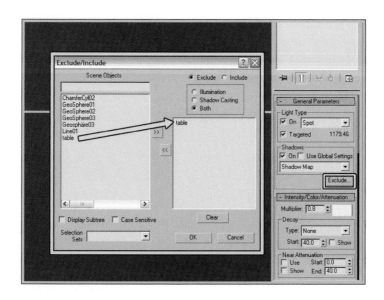

Soccer Ball before Light
Exclusion

Soccer Ball – Exclude Table

Soccer Ball – Exclusion
Render

The floor will still receive illumination from the main light but without the unnecessary additional light from the fill. However, the light's affect on the soccer ball remains unchangeit as we did not highlight it in the exclude dialogue box. Visual 7–48 shows the resulting rendered image.

Negative Lights

Another physics-defying light attribute available to the digital lighter is the ability to cast *negative light*. Most amateur 3D artists would not even realize that they could manipulate a light's intensity in the negative direction, or that it would make a difference even if you could. The fact is, as easy as you can create a virtual light that emits light into a scene, you can create one that sucks light out. To achieve this, enter a negative number into the intensity multiplier for any light in your scene.

Negative lights are one of the great under-utilized resources for the digital lighter. They can be used effectively on both a macro-level, to darken specific portions of an environment or set, for instance, as well as on a micro-level, to minimize a highlight or hotspot on an a particularly shiny object. However, one of the best uses of a negative light is to create the often difficult to achieve contact shadow. Let's revisit the soccer ball shot we used to describe light exclusion in Visual 7–48. Although the shadows certainly make it look like the ball is sitting on the table, it can be made to look even better with a more well-defined contact shadow. To achieve this, a spotlight is positioned directly above the ball, allowing the cone to define the size. Notice that there is very little falloff used to create the relatively sharp edge of the contact shadow.

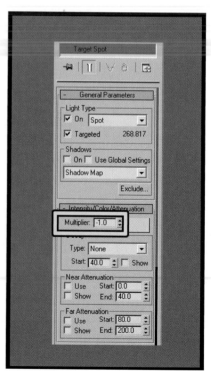

Negative Light – Negative Light Intensity

A Spotlight with Negative Intensity Used to Create a Contact Shadow

The spotlight's negative intensity draws the light away from underneath the ball, creating a well-defined contact shadow. Notice the difference that the shadow makes in the final render as is compared to the previous version illustrated in Visual 7–48.

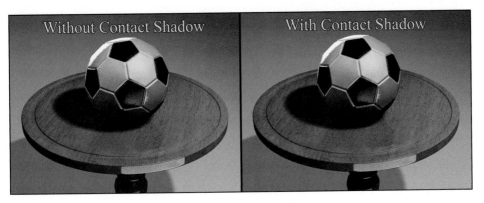

Negative Light Comparison

LIGHTING'S RELATIONSHIP WITH GEOMETRY

The quality of light in any shot has as much to with the light being bounced off the objects in the scene as it does with the raw light being emitted from the source. Therefore, the surface properties of the objects to be illuminated must be considered when developing a lighting scheme. In particular, the degree of smoothness over an object in many ways will affect how the object and lighting is perceived by the viewer. For instance, Visuals 7–52 and 7–53 show two spheres of similar size being lit by identical spotlights. The sphere in Visual 7–52 appears very smooth as a result of high-level of geometry. This is because each light ray that bounces of the sphere is slightly different then the one next to it.

visual |7–52|

Smooth Sphere

visual |7–53|

Faceted Sphere

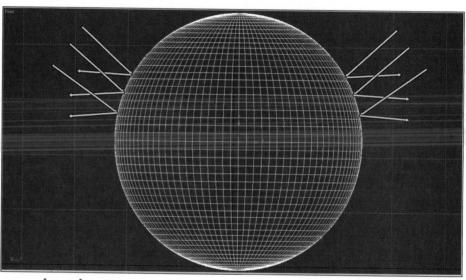

visual |7-54|

Smooth Sphere's Geometry

In contrast, the sphere seen in Visual 7–53 appears extremely hard-edged and clunky. In fact, the individual polygons that form the sphere are large enough to be easily seen by the viewer, creating what is known as faceting. There simply is too little geometry being used to form the surface area of the object. In Visual 7–55, entire groups of light rays are being bounced back to the viewer at identical angles from the polygons, creating the hard-edged look.

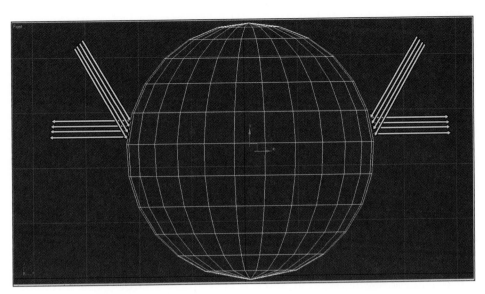

Faceted Sphere's
Geometry

Rounded Edges

Outside the main surface area, a digital lighter also must consider an object's edge quality when developing a lighting rig. Although it is very easy to create perfect, razor-sharp edges when modeling in 3D, very few surfaces in reality are, in fact, that way. Most surface edges have a certain degree of *rounded edge*.

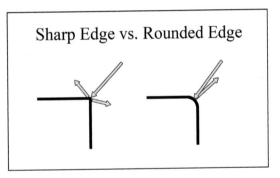

visual | 7–56 |

Sharp Edge versus
Rounded Edge Diagram

Although some surfaces edges appear to be sharp, like a new countertop. For example, if you look at them at an extremely close distance, they do have a rounded edge. It is this rounded edge that allows for a condensed part of light rays to bounce back toward the viewer, creating an object highlight.

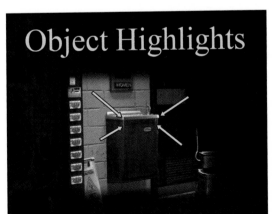

visual | 7–57 |

Object Highlights
Example

This highlight not only provides an extra level of detail, including depth and surface quality, but also is universally considered more appealing to the viewer. For example, Visual 7–58 shows a standard, hard-edged, primitive 3D cube under normal three-point lighting conditions. Although the lighting scheme is set up correctly, this results in a rather flat and boring image.

By contrast, if the edges of the cube are rounded out, a dramatically different result is achieved with the same lights.

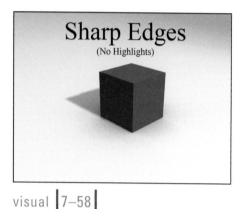

visual |7–58|

3D Cube – Sharp Edges

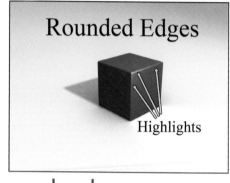

visual |7–59|

3D Cube – Rounded Edges

DIGITAL OBJECT AND PRODUCT LIGHTING

3D artists often will spend exorbitant amounts of time creating their models and textures. However, when it comes time to show off the fruits of their labors on a portfolio or demo reel, often the lighting scheme used does more harm than good. Bad lighting can make even the best models and textures look flat and uninteresting. For instance, Visual 7–60 shows a model of a wireless drill that you could see on the shelves at almost any home improvement store. The image, lit with only one dim light at an awkward angle, is far from dynamic and eye-catching.

However, we can revise the lighting scheme and approach this model much as if it were appearing in a high-quality magazine or billboard advertisement.

visual |7–60|

Wireless Drill – One Light Source

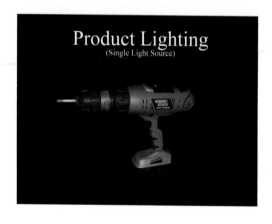

In general, there are some rules of thumb used when shooting product photography that can help any 3D artist when creating quality renders of their models:

- Create an interesting camera angle when showing off the product.
- Start with the standard three-point lighting setup and build from there, depending on the needs of the shot.
- Make sure the key-to-fill ratio is appropriate for the type of surface and material of the object.
- Create a well-defined rim light, which is critical to enhancing the three-dimensionality of the object.
- The background should be of a singular hue and without edges.
- The cast shadows should be soft or nonexistent.

Visual 7–61 shows the updated lighting scheme for the drill taking the principles of product photography and lighting into consideration. Notice that there are now five distinct lights being used. In addition to the three standard three-point lights, there is an additional rim light as well as a background light. Visual 7–62 shows the much more attractive end results.

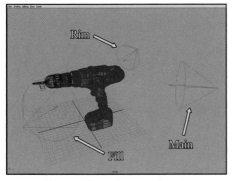

visual |7–61|

Drill – Product Lighting 3D Viewport

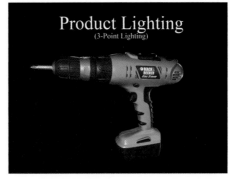

visual |7–62|

Drill – Product Lighting Final Render

CHARACTER LIGHTING

Following these lighting principles will serve you well on any digital filmmaking endeavor. However, there are some special considerations that will need to be made when lighting specific types of subjects or environments. Character lighting, for instance, should be treated differently than a product shot. Although both lighting

schemes may start off as a standard three-point lighting setup, they have unique qualities that will guide you toward or steer you away from certain light qualities, angles,
and shadow types.

Character Lighting
Example

Most digital cinematographers create films that revolve around one or more characters. Therefore, it is critical to understand how light affects the human form, especially
the face. This section will focus on the some of the more common character lighting
scenarios and how to achieve the best results.

The Headshot

For the most part, digital filmmaking revolves around character action and interaction. Therefore, the cinematographer inevitably will need to plan for a great deal of
camera close-ups or headshots, which are used extensively during dialogue sequences
to provide the viewer with added visual detail about the character's face, eyes, and
expressions. These are all critical
components to telling stories.

Storyboard of Character
Headshot

A headshot cannot be treated as
just another object to light on
the set. Although light direction
and corresponding cast shadow
placement mean a great deal
when dealing with inanimate
objects, they can actually change
an audience's perception of a
character.

Visual 7–65 shows a headshot of male character that is currently lit by default lighting only. The lack of lighting and shadows does not do much for the aesthetics of the shot. Therefore, any snap judgments that are made by the audience about the character's personality are purely based on his physical appearances and not on any external factors.

Character Headshot with Default Lighting

To start building a lighting scheme for this character, insert a standard three-point rig into the shot. Notice in Visual 7–66 that spotlights are used for the main, fill, and rim lights.

visual |7–66|

Headshot – Three-Point Lighting Wireframe

The three-point lighting adds a tremendous amount of detail and visual interest. Visual 7–67 shows a side-by-side comparison of the new render with the previous, default lighting–only version. However, the standard three-point lighting, although a definite quality upgrade, does not add any further information about the character.

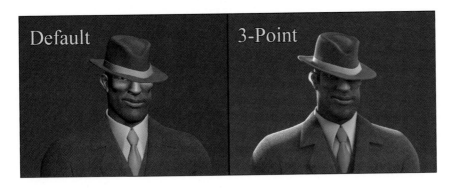

visual |7–67|

Headshot – Three-Point Lighting versus Default

In order to create a lighting scheme that will contribute to the character's perception, adjustments to the main and fill lights will need to be made in order to create a different illumination/shadow pattern across the character's face. By doing this, the light will start to highlight particular facial features while hiding others. This character, in particular, has a couple of unique features that will have to be considered when lighting. The very pronounced cheekbones and a low-angled hat have the potential to create very unflattering or unwanted cast shadows across the face, as seen in Visuals 7–68 through 7–71.

visual |7–68|

Headshot – Unflattering Lighting Example # 1

visual |7–69|

Headshot – Unflattering Lighting Example # 2

visual |7–70|

Headshot – Unflattering Lighting Example # 3

visual |7–71|

Headshot – Unflattering Lighting Example # 4

However, shadows across the face are not always a bad thing. With some slight adjustments to the angles and key-to-fill ratio, the shadows provide a level of intrigue and mystique the character that did not exist with the standard setup.

visual |7–72|

Headshot – Frontal Lighting Scheme

visual |7–73|

Headshot – Side Lighting Scheme

visual |7–74|

Headshot – Back Lighting Scheme

visual |7–75|

Headshot – Profile Lighting Scheme

LIGHTING INTERIORS

The environment in which a character or an object resides is as important to the overall quality of a shot as the lighting. Because most characters and objects exist somewhere in space, there is a high likelihood that you will have to develop a lighting scheme for a virtual set. However, the approach is much different then the typical three-point studio setup.

visual |7–76|

Interior Set Sketch

Light Inventory

Most beginning digital filmmakers have a difficult time figuring out where to start when lighting an interior virtual set. Unlike the three-point setup, an interior's light sources are critical to the overall look and feel of the shot. Not only are they often nonuniform in shape, size, and color, they often appear in the actual shot. Therefore, the first step in determining the lighting scheme for a virtual interior set is to do a complete *lighting inventory* of the scene. That is to say, you should create a list of all the various light sources that will be contributing to the illumination of the shot, no matter how large or small their intensity.

visual |7–77|

Light Inventory List

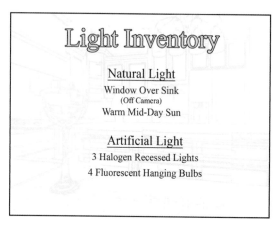

In this particular case, there were three main sources of light in the scene; three overhead halogen recessed lights, four hanging incandescent bulbs, and the middday sunlight coming in from the window (off-camera) over the sink. Visual 7–78 shows the final render.

visual |7–78|

Final Interior Render

The Simple Box

To begin to learn how to create realistic interior lighting schemes, it is important to understand how to light the simple box. All digital cinematographers must be able to light a simple room with four walls and a window convincingly.

The light inventory for this shot is quite simple. The main source of illumination into the scene will be the sunlight and daylight that will shine through the window. Next, there will be a great deal of ambient or bounced light around the room because of the size of the windows and the light color of the walls.

To recreate this lighting scenario, we will use four light sources; two target directional lights to mimic the sunlight and skylight, a target directional to mimic the bounce light from the floor, and an ambient-only omni light to mimic the overall ambient light in the room. By checking the ambient-only option in the attribute editor, the light ignores the specular and diffuse portions of the surfaces. Visual 7–81 shows a wireframe view of the scene with these four lights.

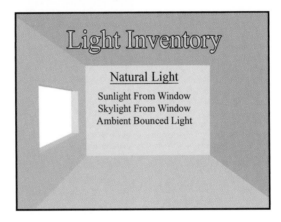

visual |7–79|

The Simple Box with Default Lighting

visual |7–80|

The Simple Box – Light Inventory

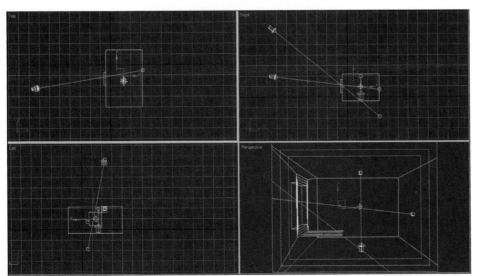

visual |7–81|

The Simple Box – Lighting Scheme Wireframe

Visual 7–82 illustrates the progression of the room's scheme as each of the lights are added, starting with the ambient-only omni, the target directional from above, and, finally, the two directional lights.

The Simple Box –
Lighting Progression

Insider Info

When lighting interior sets, it is important to pay attention to the little details with regard to the corners and edges of the walls and floors. Beginner lighters often will throw a wide main light into their scene to ensure sufficient illumination. However, that ends up producing very evenly lit surfaces. In the real world, there is almost always some variance in the illumination patterns across the walls of an interior space. In fact, the corners of the rooms should always appear slightly darker than the rest of the surface area of the wall. To achieve this, you can use a ambient-only omni, which has its far attenuation set to the height and width of the room. This will ensure that the corners are slightly darker. Also, small omni or spotlight with negative intensities can be placed into the corners to achieve similar results.

visual |7–83|

Dark Corners

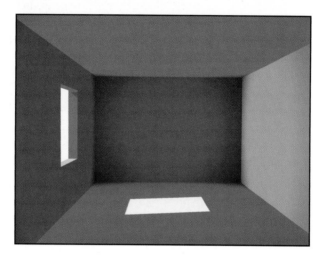

Faking Radiosity

To take the small box example a step further, let's add a scene object into the set to see how it affects the lighting scheme. In this case, we will add a large red sphere in the center of the room.

Light rays do not simply stop at the first surface they encounter. In fact, light rays will bounce infinitely, transferring a diminishing amount of light and color each time. This concept, known as radiosity, is difficult and time-consuming to achieve in 3D. However, there are some simple ways to fake this phenomenon with the tools that we are already using.

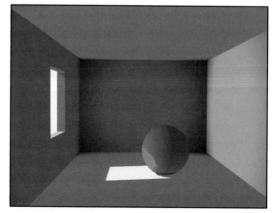

visual |7–84|

The Simple Box with Red Sphere

The Simple Box –
Radiosity Diagram

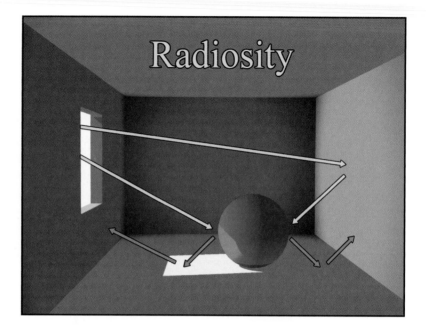

To simulate the red sphere transferring red light back onto the floor, we will add another ambient-only omni light into the scene at the center of the sphere. Adjust the near attenuation to start at the surface of the sphere and radiate outward. We do not want this light to add anymore light onto the sphere. Next, adjust the far attenuation to affect about twice the diameter of the sphere. Visual 7–86 shows the new light configuration in the viewport.

Faking Radiosity with a
Ambient-only Omni Light

The end result, seen in Visual 7–87, is a side-by-side image of the sphere scenario with and without the omni light mimicking the effects of radiosity. Notice that the image on the right is a far more convincing representation of how the lighting would appear in reality.

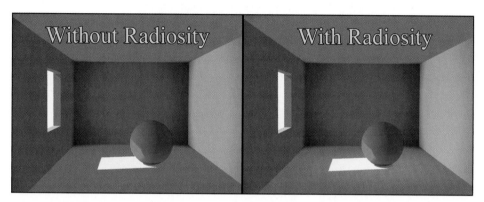

visual |7–87|

Final Radiosity Render Comparison

Time of Day

One of the major considerations when lighting interiors is the incorporation of exterior natural light. Natural light sources, such as windows or skylights, exist in most interior environments. For filmmaking purposes, having natural light enter into an interior set or environment provides increased light and color contrast as well as a visual clues to the viewer. As humans, we are able to decipher a great deal of information from the appearance of this natural light, including weather conditions and time of day.

Visual 7–88 shows a virtual set modeled after a typical kitchen in a newer suburban home. Although it is an interior scene, it has two large sources of natural light: the window over the sink as well as the glass door on the left-hand side. In fact, the natural light is the only light source for this shot. Therefore, it is easy for the viewer to determine, from the light's color, intensity, and direction, that this shot is taking place at around noon on a clear day.

Using the information about light angles and color temperatures that we discussed in the last

visual |7–88|

Interior Kitchen Set

chapter, Visuals 7–89 through 7–92 demonstrate how changing the light parameters can providing very different moods and atmospheres as well as visual time clues to the viewer. In this particular case, the lights have been adjusted to mimic midday sun, sunset, moonlight, and also a combination of artificial interior and moonlight.

visual | 7–89 |

Interior Kitchen Set – Midday

visual | 7–90 |

Interior Kitchen Set – Sunset

visual | 7–91 |

Interior Kitchen Set – Moonlight

visual | 7–92 |

Interior Kitchen Set – Artificial and Moonlight

Visual 7–93 strings all the renders together to get closer look at the differences that the time of day makes on the set.

Interior Kitchen Set –
Midday, Sunset,
Moonlight, and Artificial
and Moonlight

LIGHTING EXTERIORS

Outdoor illumination is provided either by a combination of sunlight and skylight during the day or the reflected light off the moon at night. Either way, the colors, angles, and cast shadows produced by natural outdoor light is unique and extremely difficult to achieve with man-made equipment. For that reason, the average viewer can easily differentiate exterior and interior lighting. Therefore, it is critical, when working with virtual outdoor sets and environments, that you take the time to create a lighting scheme that is able to approximate these qualities.

Faking Global Illumination

Although it is fairly easy to recreate the sharp parallel rays created by the sun in 3D using a target direct light, it can be challenging and time-consuming to recreate the soft diffuse light and shadows of skylight. However, there are some cheap and easy ways to fake global illumination that can be incorporated into almost any exterior set.

Let's start with a simple plane with a primitive sphere in the center, as seen in Visual 7–95. To mimic the dome lighting effect of global illumination, we will create an array of ten low-intensity target direct lights, with shadows turned on, that surround the sphere in the top viewport.

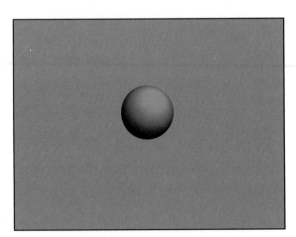

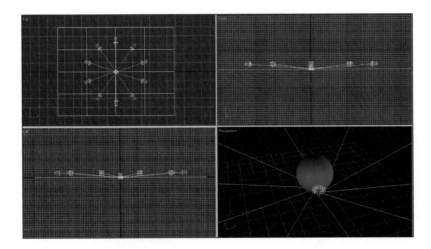

Global Illumination
Fake – Step 2

Select all the lights without their targets and create a new group and rename it "light array 1." Copy, move, and scale the light array twice to create a dome shape above the ground plane.

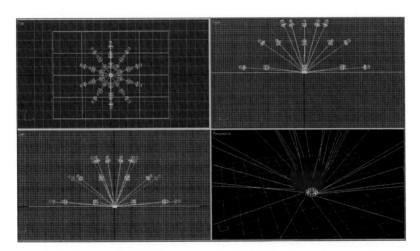

Global Illumination
Fake – Step 3

The end result, seen in Visual 7–98, is a fantastic approximation of the effects of skylight. To add even further realism to your shot, add another target direct light to the scene that will mimic the light from the sun. This will add a single distinct shadow, telling the user the time of day.

visual |7–98|

Global Illumination Fake – Skylight Render

visual |7–99|

Global Illumination Fake – Sunlight and
Skylight Render

Time of Day

Above everything else, the time of day will be the greatest factor in determining the look and feel of your outdoor shots. The angle at which the sun is able to illuminate the earth will affect both the light and shadow appearance. Visual 7–100 shows a typical outdoor patio environment with lighting intended to mimic the midday sun.

visual |7–100|

Exterior Patio Set –
Midday

Visuals 7–101 through 7–103 demonstrate the effects that lighting can have on a virtual set. Note that only the lights have been adjusted in these just to mimic the effects of sunset, moonlight, and the combination of moonlight and artificial light.

visual |7–101|

Exterior Patio Set – Sunset

visual |7–102|

Exterior Patio Set –
Moonlight

visual |7–103|

Exterior Patio Set –
Moonlight and
Artificial Light

Visual 7–104 strings all the renders together to get closer look at the differences that the time of day makes on the set.

visual |7–104|

Exterior Patio Set –
Midday, Sunset,
Moonlight, and Artificial
and Moonlight

SUMMARY

Digital lighting involves much more than placing lights into your camera viewports. You should have a deep understanding of color theory and traditional lighting techniques before attempting to create a lighting scheme in the virtual environment. This foundational knowledge is the key that will unlock the power of digital light, as it directly relates to almost all of the options and parameters available to the digital cinematographer.

artist SPOTLIGHT   *shane acker*

Director/Animator, Focus Features – feature film based on the Student Academy Award–winning short film *9*

Shane Acker was born in Wheaton, Illinois, and grew up along the East Coast. He received dual Master's degrees for Architecture (2000) and Animation (2004) from UCLA. Shane has taught 3D design and animation as well as freelanced in the motion picture, television, and video game industry since 1998. *9*, Shane's thesis film from UCLA's Animation Workshop, is his third award-winning short. He is currently a 3D artist, director, and independent filmmaker freelancing in Los Angeles. You also may see his work on his Web site at http://www.shaneacker.com.

visual |7–105|

Shane Acker

Credits:
2005–Present
Feature Film for Focus Features – Director
2004–2005
Guild Wars (Video Game) – 3D Artist
2004
9 – All Aspects of Production including Animating, Story, Directing, Modeling, Rigging, and Lighting.
2003
Lord of the Rings: The Return of the King – Character Animator

Artist Spotlight with Shane Acker
Looking Back at the Making of His Award-Winning Film *9*

Q. While lighting plays a critical role in every film, it seems to be especially important within *9*, not only from an illumination and color standpoint, but there are actual lights, lamps, and bulbs used as props in the film. What was your overall philosophy when developing the lighting for the film?

visual |7–106|

9 – Shane Acker

A. I use light in many ways in the short, not only to illuminate, but to create mood and symbolically to help support the theme of the movie.

Light is a symbol of knowledge; it is a pivotal tool in the development and survival of the Rag dolls. Much the same way fire was a pivotal tool in humankind's development. By creating light from a watch battery, wires, and a light bulb, 5 passes this knowledge on to 9. The illuminating of the light bulb is a metaphor for an idea, and this metaphoric "light" will now allow 9 to see into the darkness and formulate a plan to defeat the Beast.

From a design standpoint, the light staff that 9 carries allows me to create a space around my main character, a pocket of warm key light that helps separate my character from the environment. It helps focus the audience's eye on what's important, and to provide a motivated light source for the darker shots in the film.

The two glowing talisman halves are objects that bind the Rag dolls and the Beast in a constant game of cat and mouse. The Beast uses its half to hunt for the Rag dolls and the dolls, in turn, use their half as a beacon, a warning device that glows when the other half is near. I use this relationship to build tension and suspense in the film. Whenever this device glows with its eerie green light, the audience knows that the Beast is approaching. It's a simple but very effective way of using light to get an emotional response for the audience. I borrowed this idea from James Cameron, who used blips on a motion sensor prop to create in the audience's mind a space station full of aliens.

Nothing organic is still alive in the world of *9*. Plants, animals, and even humans have all died or disappeared. All that's left is a ruined civilization. I relied heavily on sound, atmosphere and light to make this dead world seem "alive." For example, I would animate slow-moving noise patterns and textures in my lights and set keys on the light's intensity to give the effect of light passing through mist and to make objects in the light "breathe" a little.

Lighting is also a great way to create a feeling of complexity in simple sets. When 9 is running from the Beast, he is passing through patterns of light created by the sun shining through the windows. But there is no sun and no windows. It's an illusion created by an image being projected through the light source. This cheat makes the world off-camera seem much bigger and more complex than it really is. Having the characters move through light patterns also creates a very dynamic shot, without being very computationally expensive.

Q. Since there was no dialogue in your animation, the story had to be delivered in other ways. While the acting played a huge role of course, how much of that story delivery do you think was the work of the lighting?

visual |7–107|

9 – Shane Acker

A. I used light as a way of concealing and revealing information to the audience. I also used light to focus the audience's eye to details or objects that are important to the story. In the beginning of the film, when 9 is setting traps for the Beast, the only light source is his light staff. I only allowed the lighting to reveal a small portion of the set, and small bits of action. So I could give the audience small clues while at the same time concealing things that I want them to discover later.

I was also on a tight budget, so letting the environments fall off into shadow meant there was that much less to build, light, and to render.

Q. I stress to my students the importance of understanding how to use "real-world" or traditional lights before jumping into the 3D environment. Do you agree? If so, how much do you pull, lighting-wise, from traditional, live-action filmmaking or photography?

A. I couldn't agree more. While I don't have a tremendous amount of experience working with real lights, I have a solid foundation on how different light sources work. Knowledge of color temperature, three-point lighting technique, the latitude of film, key to fill ratios, color theory, and how light works in the real world is key to achieving compelling results in a 3D production.

When lighting a scene I generally use the three-point lighting technique with some variation. It just works so well. I use key lights to define the light source and to provide the main color temperature for the scene. Fill lights round out the forms, pull details from the shadows, and can be used to fake light bouncing. Usually these lights have a little bit of color in them. I'll do this to compliment the key light, to push more depth or to imitate the color of light bouncing off of other objects. I use backlights to separate the characters from the backgrounds, or sometimes I'll fake a rim light by using a shader to wrap light around the edges of objects.

I'll also place little lights near the characters eyes to brighten them. This draws the audience to the characters face, where the emotional center is. I use depth of field and rack focus techniques to imitate real cameras and to create more dimensional shots. I'll even let objects blow out or light bloom from time to time to suggest the latitude of a film stock or to fake a camera filter. All these tools can be used to make the world seem more believable.

Q. Visual 7–108 shows a behind the scenes screen shot of the image in Visual 7-107. Describe the lighting process, in as much detail as possible that was used for this shot. What types of lights did you use and why?

A. In this shot, 9 is woken from a horrible memory by the glowing talisman. The glowing talisman warns of the approaching beast, which leads us into the third act of the film. I knew I wanted low key lighting for the shot to create a foreboding mood. I created a warm spot light to screen left of the character to represent the light coming from his light staff. I supplemented this with an omnidirectional light that had linear falloff to make objects closer to the light staff appear brighter. I placed these nearly perpendicular to the character almost like a rim light to keep the front of the character in shadow. Then I created several low-level direction lights with cool colors and I aimed them into the set from different angles. This helped to fill in shadows and fake bounce light. Some of these had soft shadows to help contacts and to round out the forms.

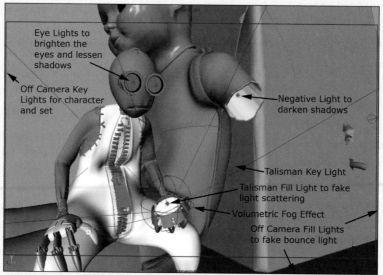

Eye Lights to brighten the eyes and lessen shadows

Off Camera Key Lights for character and set

Negative Light to darken shadows

Talisman Key Light

Talisman Fill Light to fake light scattering

Volumetric Fog Effect

Off Camera Fill Lights to fake bounce light

visual |7–108|

9 – Shane Acker

When the shot begins the talisman is dormant. 9's face and the front of his body are almost completely in shadow. I added two omni (point) lights in his eyes to brighten them so even in shadow the audience can see the emotional state of the rag doll. When the talisman glows, it creates an intense green light that floods over the character. This sudden contrast in lighting heightens the intensity of the shot, creating visual excitement and accentuates the story point that the beast has returned. The talisman glow is achieved by animating the intensity of a pre existing spot light aiming out of the talisman. I used a volumetric fog effect in this light to create an atmosphere, and I set keys on both the incandescent channel and the glow attribute of the shader assigned to the talisman glass to give the illusion it was a glowing light source. Then I placed a low-intensity point light (with falloff) a little above the surface of the talisman to fake light bouncing. Finally, a negative light was added inside the broken arm of the doll to keep it dark and some low-level lights were added to the fill in the background.

Q. 3D lights have all the flexibility of traditional lights as well as some options and features that are simply not available in the real world, such as negative intensities. What were some of the advanced features that were used throughout the production of *9*?

A. Well, I don't know how advanced these features are anymore, but there are several techniques I used to help control the lighting in the short. The tool I used the most by far was light linking. It's a way of controlling what objects are affected by which lights in the scene, so you can have absolute control over the lighting object by object. With this method, objects can have the same key light, to provide uniformity to light direction and shadow fall, but then you can add fill lights and little kickers that effect each object independently. You can also control the lighting on the surface of an object by using diffuse maps. I would apply a gray scale diffuse

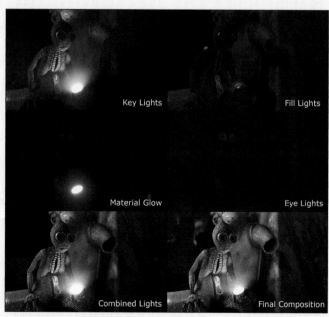

visual |7–109|

9 – Shane Acker

map to objects to control what parts of the surface were affected by light and which part would always remain in shadow. It's a way of faking a kind of global illumination, and it helped to keep the area inside the character's mouths dark for a clearer read of their expressions. Having the ability to turn off a light's shadow casting abilities and adjusting the falloff are great tools for controlling lighting as well, and something you can't do in the real world.

You mention negative lights, which are a great way to suck light out of areas in the scene, but can be a bit cumbersome to control. Foot contacts can be particularly hard to achieve, especially with lights casting depth map shadows. To solve this problem, I created a little rig composed of two lights. One of the lights had a positive intensity and would cast shadows. The other light had a negative intensity proportional to the first, but wasn't casting shadows. I would place these lights on top of each other such that the intensity of the light would be negated, but a shadow would still be cast if placed over an object. Then I would have this rig follow along with the character's feet to create crisp shadows on the ground in shots where the characters contact with seemed too ambiguous.

visual |7–110|

9 – Shane Acker

Q. The undeniable success of the film has led to collaboration with Tim Burton to create a feature film version of *9*. What has that process been like so far, and what can we expect from the film?

A. It's an incredible experience. I feel honored to have this opportunity to work with such amazing artists. Somehow I've arrived at this place I only dreamt of and I feel incredibly fortunate. But at the same time it is the most challenging thing I've ever done. One of the hardest things for me is fighting the impulse to want to do it all myself. When things aren't quite working or if one of the production artists are struggling with something, my impulse is to just sit down and start working through it myself. But if I did that the film would never get done, because I am the bottleneck, the filter that everything has to be squeezed through. I've moved from being the maker to becoming a mentor, a guide, and a critic.

The feature is not really an expansion of the short, but a different story based on the world of *9*. We'll be seeing more of the rag dolls and follow them on a journey of self-discovery as they seek the truth for who they are, and why these mechanical beasts are hunting them. Soon they discover the tragedy that has befallen humanity, and become locked in a desperate struggle for the future of the world … or something like that. It's really quite ambitious.

Q. What suggestions would you make to student's who are about to create their first animated short with regard to lighting, production processes, and self-promotion?

A. Keep it simple and keep it short! Set your goals on something that is achievable. Something that allows you to learn the process and the tools, but that won't bog you down too technically. I would suggest a film that involves one character, one set, and under thirty seconds. You are going to learn so much from going through the process. Then, if you still enjoy making films, take what you've learned and apply it to something more ambitious.

Looking forward, I would say that you should always be your own worst critic. Push yourself; don't settle for "good enough," or mediocrity. If you can see mistakes in your own work others will, too, so strive for perfection.

Professionally you should present yourself with confidence, don't be arrogant, but also don't sell yourself short. Always respect your peers, classmates, and the people you work with. The animation industry is actually quite small, and these are the people you are going to be working with for the rest of your career. In a team environment, good will goes a long way; It might even get you your next job.

Nowadays there are lots of ways of getting exposure. I spent a lot of time and a fair amount of money submitting my films to festivals, and making a concerted effort to create an online presence for myself. Like everything, it takes a lot of energy to get the ball rolling, but once the film started to getting seen it took off on its own. Soon other film festivals started requesting to see the film (and would waive their submission fees) and I was invited to attend. I made an effort to go to as many festivals as I could and I would go to industry events to meet other professionals. All this legwork led to me meeting an agency who then started sending me out to meet producers and film studios, which has now led to the making of *9.*

in review

1. What is the difference between production and final lighting?

2. How should default lighting be used within the digital filmmaking process?

3. What are the three most common light decay rate options?

4. Explain the difference between the inner and outer cone of a standard spotlight.

5. What is a skylight and what does type of light quality does it produce?

6. Explain the major differences between shadow map and raytraced shadows.

7. How does the bias attribute affect a shadow's appearance?

8. What is a negative light and how can it be used most affectively?

9. What are rounded edges and how can they affect your lighting scheme?

10. Explain the process of setting up a product shot.

11. What is radiosity and how can it enhance your interior lighting schemes?

12. How does the time of day affect natural lighting scenarios within the virtual environment?

exercises

1. Using a preexisting inanimate 3D model, set up a typical product shot using a nonedged background element such as a drop cloth.

   a. Create a standard three-point lighting scheme.

   b. Add two more lights to the scene to create a back light and a double rim on the object.

2. Using only primitive modeling objects, create a simple box with a hole for a window to simulate an interior environment.

   a. What types of lights would you use? Where would you place them and why?

3. Create a simple plane with a sphere on top. Create a simulated global illumination lighting scheme using 30 target direct lights; three layers of ten.

   a. Add another target light to simulate the effects of sunlight. Adjust the intensity, color, and angle of the light and shadows to mimic a sunset shot. What parameters did you adjust and why?

   b. Adjust the same scene to mimic a moonlight scenario. What parameters did you adjust and why?

CHAPTER 8

objectives

- Understand the difference between diffuse and specular reflections
- Explore the seven types of shader algorithms
- Learn to navigate the material editor or multilister
- Discover the best uses for bitmap and procedural texture maps
- Learn to add realism with dirt maps
- Understand the most commonly used rendering algorithms and engines

introduction

Quality lighting is determined by two things: the light emitted directly from the source and as the surface properties of the objects in the scene. Therefore, even the most outstanding lighting rigs can only solve half of the illumination equation. To obtain true lighting beauty within your shots, the digital cinematographer must have a deep understanding of real-world surface reflection, color and texture, and, more importantly, how to recreate their effects using materials and maps within the virtual environment.

INTRODUCTION TO MATERIALS AND TEXTURE MAPS

In many ways, 3D modeling is similar to sculpting objects out of clay. Typically, you start off with a primitive hunk of geometry, or clay, and use some basic modeling tools to start to carve out an object. While the resulting surface shape will vary depending on your skills, the surface properties of the object remain unchanged.

visual |8–1|

Raw Geometry – Head versus Soccer Ball

However, given the exact same lighting scheme, relatively soft human skin will act and interact with light differently than a hard-surfaced bowling ball. In fact, each object has a unique surface identity.

visual |8–2|

Final Head Render

Within the 3D universe, all the information regarding an individual object's surface properties exists within the *material* or *shader* that it is assigned. Everything including color, texture, shininess, reflectivity, and *opacity* are determined within the material properties.

| CHAPTER 8 | **287**

Production Flow

The production flow for creating the perfect material for a 3D object is a three-step process. Starting with the basic *shader algorithm* preset available in all 3D software packages, the digital artist will tailor the surface properties by adjusting the various common parameters found in the material editor as well as creating custom *texture maps*. Visual 8–3 shows the production flowchart for creating typical material or shader.

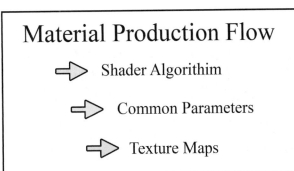

visual |8–3|

Production Flow for
Creating Surface Materials

Shader Algorithm

The first major decision that needs to be made when starting the material creation process is the shader algorithm type. The shader algorithms, a series of seven mathematically driven shading presets, are a set of instructions for the software on how a surface should react to light. The shading algorithms deal mostly with the shape and strength of their highlight or hotspot. For instance, a shiny metallic object will have a small well-defined highlight, as opposed to a rubber object, which will have larger, less intense, hotspot.

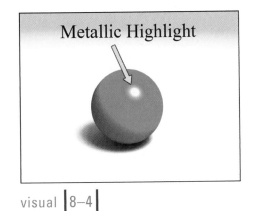

visual |8–4|

Metallic Object Highlight

visual |8–5|

Rubber Object Highlight

Common Parameters

There are some basic options that are available for tweaking in almost every shader that you create. In addition to the highlights, these common parameters allow you to adjust some of the object's most basic of surface qualities including color, glossiness, and opacity. Visual 8–6 shows identical objects with identical shading algorithms assigned to them. However, the common parameters have been adjusted to give the objects very different appearances.

Common Parameters
Comparison

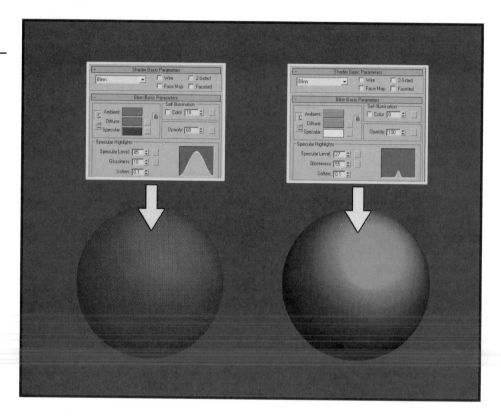

Texture Maps

Texture maps are applied to the surface of a 3D object to add a greater level of detail to your renders. In fact, texture maps are able to affect an object's appearance on both a 2D and 3D level by using a *UV coordinate system,* which allows specific points on the

Texture Map Comparison

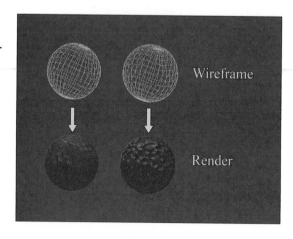

geometry to be assigned with specific points on an image. This image, or texture map, can customize the color, *specularity,* and opacity as well as the texture, or smoothness, of the surface. Most often, texture maps are used to add surface detail without additional core geometry to keep modeling and rendering times at a minimum. Visual 8–7 shows a side-by-side image of the same core geometry with different texture maps applied. Notice the extreme disparity in their shapes even though the mesh is unchanged.

SURFACE REFLECTION

Although it may be tempting to jump right in and pick a shader algorithm to start working with, it is important that we take a step back and revisit the topic of light reflection that was first discussed in Chapter 5. Light rays emit from a source and interact with the scene objects, which, in turn, illuminate the object and allow them to be seen by the viewer. Therefore, the fashion in which they interact with a particular surface will determine, in large part, how the viewer perceives that surface.

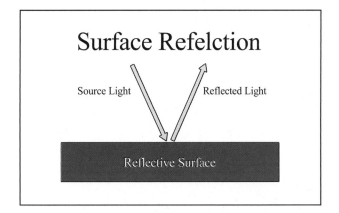

Depending upon how smooth or rough a surface is, the light rays will either bounce back uniformly or be scattered haphazardly.

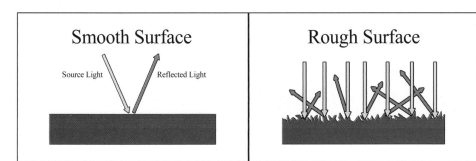

Specular Reflection

Specular reflection is the reflection of light waves in a uniform, mirrorlike fashion off a surface. The light waves will leave at the same angle at which it arrives at the surface of the object. To achieve this, the surface must be extremely smooth, as seen in Visual 8–10.

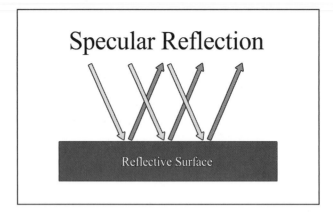

The visual results of specular reflection are that of a shiny, reflective, and often metallic-looking surface. In fact, the closer the surface approaches absolute smoothness, the more uniform or mirrorlike the object will appear. Visual 8–11 shows a character looking into a surface that has a great deal of specular reflection.

visual |8–11|

Character Looking into a
Surface That Has Specular
Reflection

Diffuse Reflection

Diffuse reflection is the result of surface that reflects light rays in a nonuniform, haphazard fashion. The light waves will leave at dramatically different angles because of the various ins and outs of the surface. Visual 8–12 shows a typical diffuse reflection caused by an object with a rough or uneven surface.

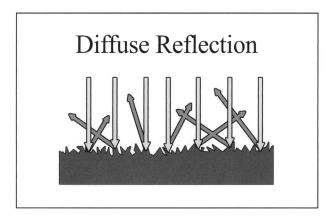

Diffuse Reflection
Diagram

Diffuse reflection causes objects to appear dull and nonreflective. In fact, the rougher a surface, the more matte the object will appear. Visual 8–13 shows a character looking into a surface that has a great deal of diffuse reflection.

Character Looking into a
Surface That Has Diffuse
Reflection

Mixed Surfaces

Most objects in the real world do not fall into just one category of surface reflection. The majority, in fact, have a combination of both specular and diffuse reflection. The exact ratio between the two types of surface reflection is what will make that particular surface unique. Visual 8–14 diagrams a typical combination of both diffuse and specular reflection, which results in *total reflected light*.

Mixed-Surface Reflection
Diagram

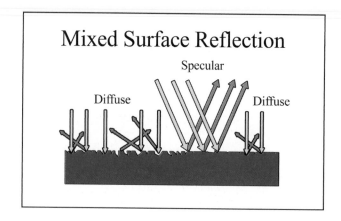

Diffuse

Using the primitive sphere seen in Visual 8–15, let's break out the components of a mixed-surface reflection model. Notice that the head model has only diffuse reflection and therefore looks dull and matte.

Diffuse Material on
the Head

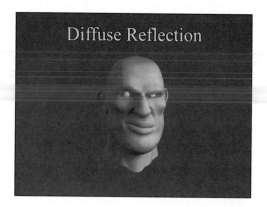

Specular

Visual 8–16 uses the same sphere model seen in the previous image. However, this time the head emits only specular reflection and, therefore, has a shiny or glossy appearance.

Specular Material on
the Head

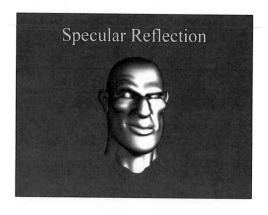

Total Reflected Light

The model seen in Visual 8–17 is a mixed-surface one and, therefore, has a combination of both diffuse and specular reflection, which results in the total reflected light of the surface. The resulting render is a far more realistic and interesting portrayal of the head.

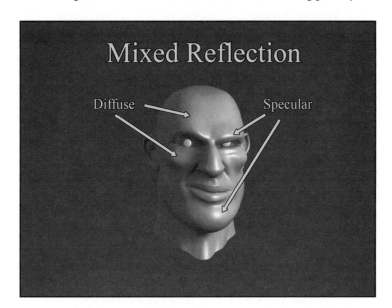

Mixed-Surface Material on the Head

SHADER ALGORITHM OPTIONS

There are seven common shading algorithm presets that exist in most high-end 3D animation software packages, which provide digital filmmakers with an excellent foundation for building custom materials and shaders. The algorithms have varying formulas for calculating surface light reflection and thus lend themselves better to mimicking particular types of real-world materials.

From a production standpoint, the 3D artist must first assess the surface reflection properties of the object they are trying to recreate. This will allow them to match it up with the closest available shading algorithm. However, it is critical that you understand the similarities and differences of the shading algorithms.

Blinn

The default shading algorithm for software programs such as Autodesk's 3D Studio Max, the *Blinn* shader provides a fantastic foundation for mixed surfaces such as shiny plastics or metals. Uniform circular hotspots are the hallmark of the Blinn shading algorithm, as seen in Visual 8–18.

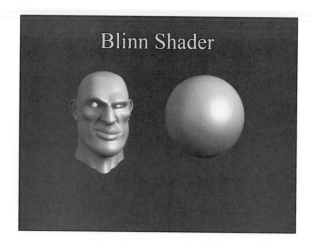

Phong

The most commonly used shading algorithm, *Phong* shaders calculate light reflection using three forms of illumination: specular, diffuse, and ambient light. Although the formula is not physically based, it provides great flexibility to the user and results in a high-quality render. It is closely related to the Blinn shader but tends to produce highlights that are harder-edged but less uniform in shape. Visual 8–19 uses identical geometry and light sources to those used in Visual 8–18, but it switches to the Phong preset.

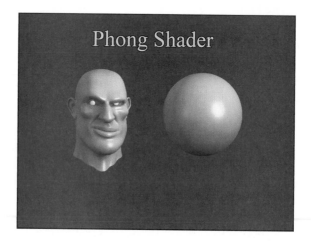

Lambert

The default shading algorithm for Autodesk's Maya software, the *Lambert* shading preset uses only diffuse light in its reflection calculation and does not create specular highlights. Therefore, it is great for matte or nonglossy surfaces such as chalk and notebook paper. Visual 8–20 uses the sphere model to display the properties of the Lambert reflection model.

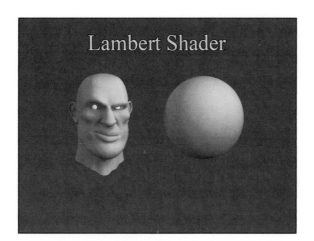

Lambert Shading
Algorithm

Anisotropic

Similar to a Phong shading algorithm, the *Anisotropic* reflection model uses ambient, diffuse, and specular light to calculate the render. However, the shape of the highlight or hotspot is dramatically different. Deviating from the traditional circular representation, the Anisotropic specular highlight is elliptical. The purpose behind the unique shape is to mimic the highlights from a grooved surface such as a CD or DVD. The shader will allow you to adjust the size and direction of the grooves that, in turn, will affect the highlight on the object. Visual 8–21 demonstrates the results of anisotropic reflection.

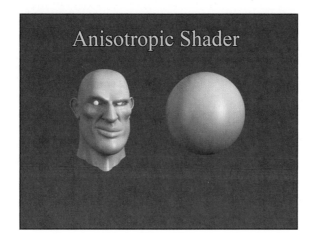

visual |8–21|

Anisotropic Shading
Algorithm

Multi-Layer

A variation on the Anisotropic algorithin, the *multi-layer shader* provides the exact same functionality with one major exception—two specular highlights. Although the highlights are still an elliptical shape, they can be manipulated independently of each other. This allows the digital artist to have an enormous amount of control over the object's hotspots, which can be extremely useful when creating materials for more complex geometry.

Multi-Layer Shading
Algorithm

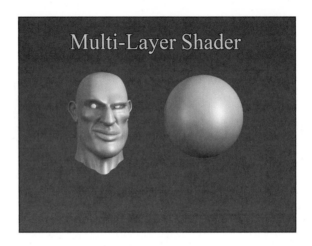

Orean-Naynar-Blinn

With roots in the Blinn shading algorithm, the *Orean-Naynar-Blinn* reflection model has all of the same visual characteristics but with a softer edge. This is a great choice for fabric-based surfaces such as clothing, drapery, or carpeting. Visual 8–23 demonstrates the softer highlights produced by the Orean-Naynar-Blinn material.

Orean-Naynar-Blinn
Shading Algorithm

Toon/Ink 'n' Paint Shaders

A complete departure from all of the other shading algorithms that attempt to mimic the real-world interaction between light and surfaces, a *toon shader* tries to emulate the look of 2D hand-drawn animation. This relatively recent additional to most 3D software packages has steadily gained popularity with students and studios alike. It provides a unique blend of the spatial accuracy that 3D provides with that traditional ink 'n' paint look.

To achieve this look, the toon shader divides every object into at least three basic components; the object outline, fill color, and highlight color.

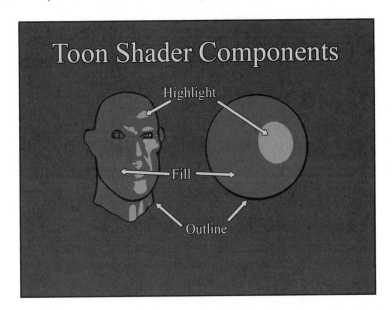

Although you can increase the number of iterations of both the fill and highlight components, at least one of each is required. Visuals 8–25 and 8–26 show the results of increasing the number of iterations to two and three, respectively.

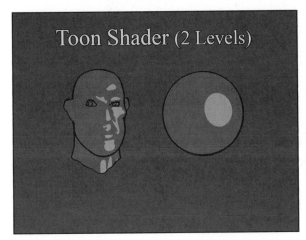

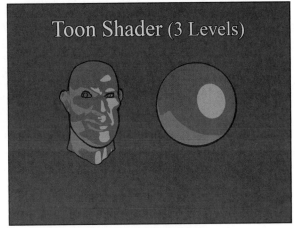

visual |8–25|

Toon Shader – Two Iterations

visual |8–26|

Toon Shader – Three Iterations

Insider Info

You may have noticed that most of the shading algorithms have a unique naming convention. Phong, Orean, Nayar, and Blinn are certainly included in most animator's everyday vocabulary. That is because they are named after the individuals that created the actual algorithm behind the shader. Individuals such as Dr. James F. Blinn, graphics fellow at Microsoft Research, and Dr. Bui Tuong Phong, noted computer graphics researcher, are still active parts of the CG community. In fact, do not be surprised to see some of these guys walking the convention floor at the next ACM/SIGGRAPH convention.

COMMON PARAMETERS

Once you have decided on the particular shading algorithm for the material that you are building, it now time to adjust some of the many common parameters available. These parameters are easily accessed through a project's material portal often referred to as the *material editor* or *multilister,* depending on which software platform you are using. Visual 8–27 shows 3D Studio Max's material editor, whereas Visual 8–28 show's Maya's Multilister interface. Notice that they are slightly different in appearance but allow the digital artist an easy to use graphical interface from which to manipulate their materials.

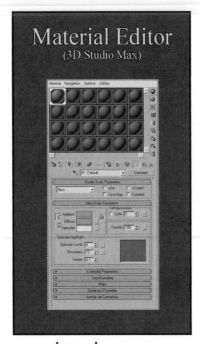

visual |8–27|

Material Editor – 3D Studio Max

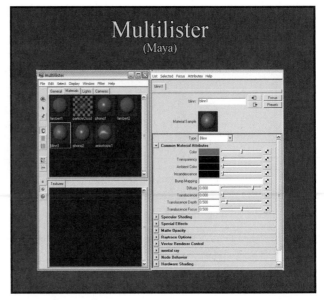

visual |8–28|

Multilister – Maya

Color

The foundation of all the common parameters, the color of an object is typically one of the first two visual qualities used by humans to describe an object. Along with the shape of the geometry, the color of the material will play a major role in how the viewer relates to that particular object. For this reason, you will see this at the very top of the options listed within the common parameters of your material portal.

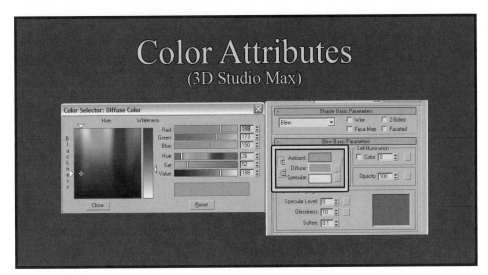

visual |8–29|

Color Attribute –
Material Editor

The color parameters are similar to those used in the more popular photo/graphic editing software on the market such as Adobe's Photoshop or Illustrator. For a more creative graphical experience, the color can be manipulated through the use of an interactive color spectrum or slider, as seen in Visual 8–30.

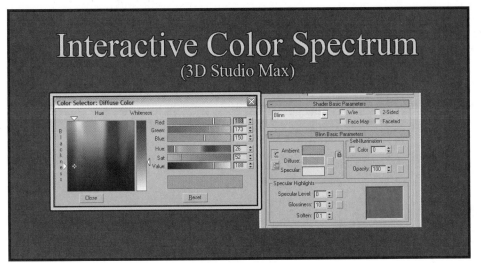

visual |8–30|

Interactive Color
Spectrum

For a more precise approach to color picking in the material editor, most software packages allow the digital artist to enter the specific hue, saturation, value (HSV), or red, green, blue (RGB) numeric values. This is helpful when recreating a specific color used in an image that was created in a different software package.

Precise Color Value Editing

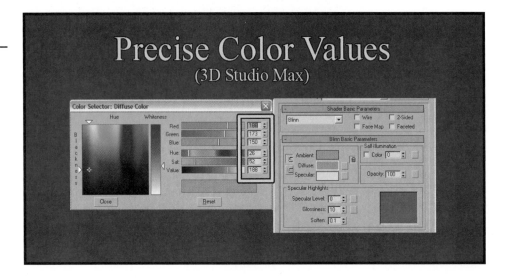

| NOTE |

To clone a specific color that is already being used within your scene, use the eye dropper icon located within the graphical color-picking interface. This will allow you to quickly grab another color and place it into the new shader.

The overall color of a material is not determined by a single HSV or RGB value. Much like the reflected light is compartmentalized within the shader algorithms, there are three color channels that can be adjusted within the material editor. The diffuse, ambient, and specular hues can be independently manipulated for increased customization.

Diffuse Color

The diffuse color is, to all intents and purposes, the true color of the object. It is the color that the object will appear to the viewer when it comes into direct contact with the scene lights. If you had only one color channel to work with, this is the one you would absolutely need.

By default, most programs will assign the diffuse color as a neutral gray color. You will notice as you adjust the diffuse color that the material icon will start to change colors within the material editor. Visual 8–33 illustrates the effects of changing the diffuse color to a deep red on the material icon.

Specular Color

The specular color controls the hue of the object's highlight. This color represents the light rays that are bounced directly back at the viewer off the object. Although the default specular color in most 3D software packages is a pure white, a real-world highlight is, more often then not, a lighter hue of the diffuse color, as seen in Visual 8–34.

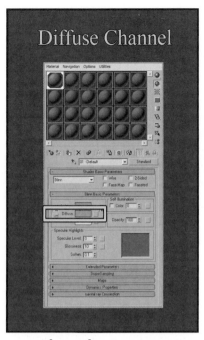

visual |8–32|

Diffuse Color Channel

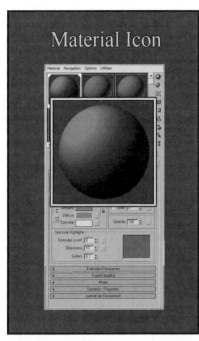

visual |8–33|

Material Icon – Diffuse Color Changed to Red

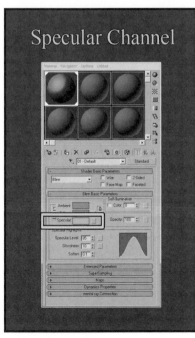

visual |8–34|

Specular Color Channel

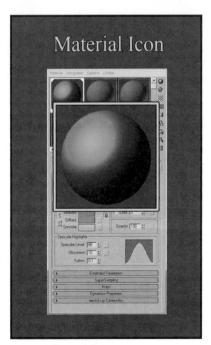

visual |8–35|

Specular Color – Lighter Version of
Diffuse Color

Ambient Color

The opposite of the diffuse channel, the ambient color represents the hue that is picked up from the indirect light in the scene or when it is in shadow. Often this color channel is locked to the diffuse color so that they are guaranteed to relate to each other.

Adjusting the ambient color dramatically away from the diffuse often can produce unwanted, computer-generated, or unrealistic looking results.

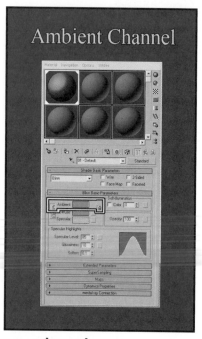

visual |8–36|

Ambient Color Channel

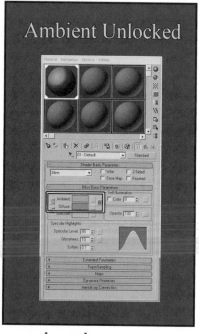

visual |8–37|

Ambient Color Unlocked from the Diffuse

Opacity/Tansparency

This parameter will determine how opaque or transparent the material will appear to the viewer. Typically adjusted on a scale from 0, completely transparent, to 100, fully opaque, the transparency channel is used when mimicking glass and plastic surfaces.

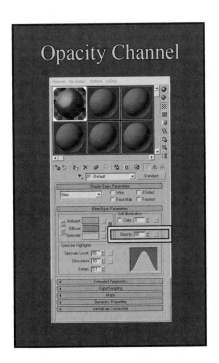

Opacity/Transparency
Channel

TEXTURE MAPS

Whereas the shading algorithm and common parameters are the foundation and framework for a material, the texture maps provide the finishing touches necessary detail to transform a piece of geometry into a believable and realistic object in your scene. Considering that there are very few objects in the real world that have uniform visual characteristics, texture maps are the gateway to providing very specific color and textural information.

Visual 8–39 shows a red sphere sitting on a ground plane. Only the first two steps of the material creation process have been applied; assigning the shader algorithm and adjusting the common parameters. Although there is some vital color and surface-type information being passed along to the viewer, the image seems unfinished and computer-generated.

visual |8–39|

Shading Algorithm and
Common Parameters –
Red Sphere and
Floor Plane

Visual 8–49 shows the exact same scene with the addition of texture maps. It is now clear that the red sphere is actually a rubber kickball and that it is sitting on a gymnasium floor. It is important to note that there is no extra geometry or lights being used in the render. The image has been enhanced solely with the use of texture maps within the material editor.

The detail on the ball and floor was created by assigning imagery to the specific pieces of geometry in the scene. These images, or maps, were used to affect the appearance of the color and texture of the object. Texture maps, which are generally far more efficient than modeling all of the minute details in 3D, can exist as either bitmap or procedural images, depending on what is needed for the shader.

Bitmap Textures

Bitmap textures rely on pixel-based, raster images to drive the output of the shader. Highly detailed and customizable, bitmaps encompass everything from digital photographs to custom imagery created in any number of graphic editing software packages, including Adobe Photoshop and Corel Painter. Bitmaps allow for nearly unlimited creative freedom for the digital artist. For this reason, bitmap textures are commonly used to create more highly photo-realistic textures.

Visual 8–41 shows the bitmap texture map used to create the hardwood floor seen in Visual 8–40. Notice that the image is approximately 640 × 480 pixels high.

This resolution is fine for the camera placement used in Visual 8–41. However, because there is always a finite amount of pixel information for bitmaps, camera location and render size can be an issue. For instance, if the camera is moved much closer to the kickball, the floor texture is quite blurry, as can be seen in Visual 8–42.

Therefore, it is always important to keep pixel size in mind when creating bitmap textures in 3D. You should always build textures according to the size needed at the camera's closest point. If the floor texture map is replaced with a higher resolution version, the resulting image will appear much more clean and crisp. Visual 8–43 demonstrates the rendering difference when upsizing the bitmap resolution from 640×640 to 1024×1024.

visual |8–42|

Close-Up of Bitmap Floor Texture – Too Little Pixel Information

visual |8–43|

Close-Up of Bitmap Floor Texture – Increased Pixel Information

Procedural Textures

Procedural textures, the opposite of bitmaps, are images that are created by complex mathematical algorithms internally within the 3D software package. They are infinitely scalable because they are not pixel-based but, rather, recalculated for each frame. Therefore, camera location and render size for procedural texture maps is a nonfactor. For instance, a simple procedural grid image has been mapped to the plane in Visual 8–44.

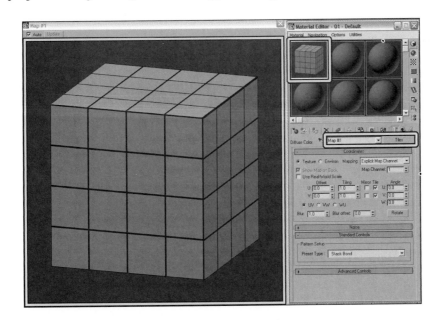

visual |8–44|

Procedural Texture Map – Tiles/Grid

| NOTE |

Some of the larger animation studios such as Blue Sky Studios in White Plains, New York, use only procedural texture maps when creating films such as *Ice Age* and *Robots*. They have developed custom tools to allow their digital artists to have the same creative control and freedom of bitmaps but with the quality and scalability of procedurals textures. This has allowed them to render out the films at IMAX size and quality without major adjustments to their texture pipelines.

However, when we move the camera to an extreme close-up of the plane, the image is recalculated on-the-fly, producing a crisp clean render without any degradation of the texture.

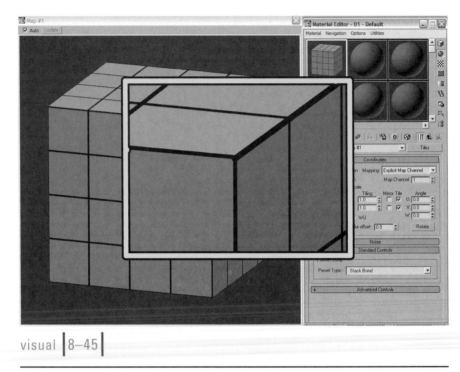

visual |8–45|

Procedural Texture Map – Extreme Close-Up of the Grid

Whereas mathematically driven procedural textures can easily create linear maps such as grids, checkers, and two-color gradients, they also can produce some very organic-looking imagery. Understanding that surfaces in the real world are not perfectly linear and clean, 3D software manufactures have devised a host of procedural textures that use varying degrees of randomness to calculate the maps. Examples of the most commonly used procedural texture maps can be seen in Visual 8–46.

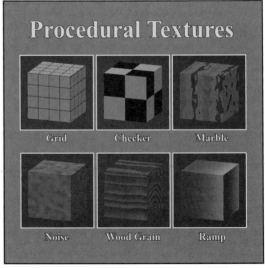

visual |8–46|

Procedural Texture Map Examples

MAPPING CHANNELS

Creating a texture map is only half the battle. Knowing how and where to place it, so that it affects your geometry correctly, is an art. Digging deeper in the 3D software's material portal, you will find a series of *mapping channels* that will allow you to customize your texture maps and the specific aspects of the surface they will manipulate. Some channels will be extremely straight forward as they will directly affect the appearance of the mapped object such as the color or surface texture. However, other channels will use textures to control more subtle aspects of the surface properties such as the specular reflection patterns. Although you could dedicate an entire textbook just to this subject, here are some of the more commonly used options that will allow the digital cinematographer to create more effective texture maps and materials.

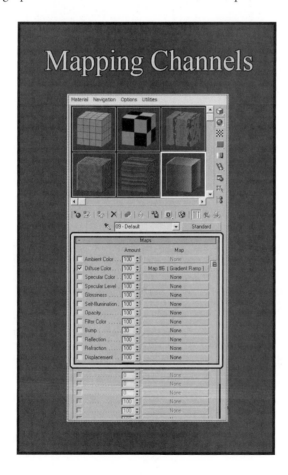

visual | 8–47 |

Mapping Channels
Within the Material Portal

Diffuse Maps

The most basic of texture maps is the diffuse mapping channel. It controls the color of the object as it appears in direct light within a scene. If you were wallpapering your 3D object, this is the channel on which you would put the wallpaper.

Diffuse Mapping Channel

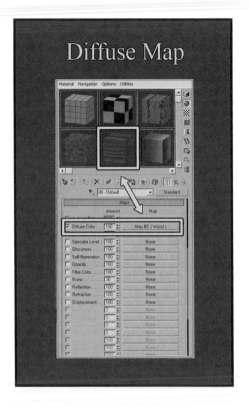

Visual 8–49 shows a side-by-side image of the diffuse texture map used and the resulting 3D render. Notice that the object's color and appearance is completely different, whereas the shape, surface texture, and light reflection are unchanged.

Diffuse Texture and
Render Example

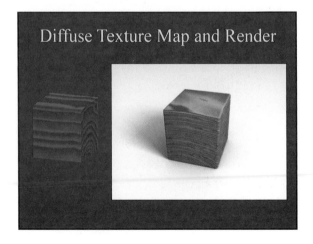

Ambient Maps

An ambient texture map will affect the look of an object or parts of an object that is in shadow. The default for most 3D packages is to have the ambient map locked with the diffuse map. This will ensure that there are not any dramatic color and texture shift across a single object.

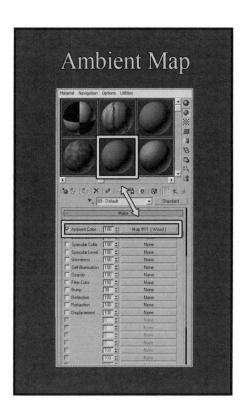

Visual 8–51 shows a side-by-side image of the ambient texture map used and the resulting 3D render. Notice that as the illumination moves past the terminator, the ambient map becomes more apparent.

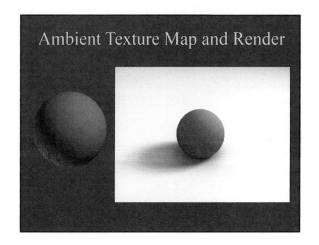

Specular Maps

The specular channels are used to control the look and intensity of an object's highlights or hotspots, depending on whether you map the color or the level. Both can be extremely useful when trying to customize the specularity of a more complex object.

Specular Mapping
Channel

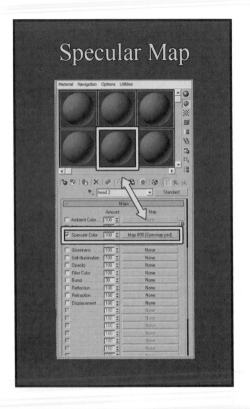

Specular Texture Map

Although a specular color map works in a similar way to a diffuse in that it affects the actual appearance of the highlight, a specular level map controls the intensity and placement. The specular level map, as with all mapping channels that deal with intensity and placement only, then only recognizes grayscale image information. The lighter or closer to white the texture map is, the more specularity that will appear on the object and vice versa. Visual 8–53, for example, is the specular level map for a human head. Notice that the image is intentionally divided up into specific areas of black and white. These areas will determine the specularity output of the shader.

For demonstration purposes only, let's place the image onto the diffuse map to see exactly what parts of the head it is affecting. Notice in Visual 8–54 that the white portions of the map are strategically placed on the parts of the face that are typically more shiny and oily, including the forehead, nose, and cheekbones.

visual |8–54|

Specular Texture Map on
the Diffuse Channel

Therefore, when we place that map into the intended specular level channel, it will create the illusion that certain parts of the face are shinier than the rest because of the increased highlights.

visual |8–55|

Specular Texture Map
Final Render

Bump Maps

Whereas diffuse, ambient, and specular maps affect the appearance of the surface, *bump maps* create the illusion that the surface shape itself has been altered. Typically used to create realistic surfaces variations such as woodgrain or fabric weaving, bump maps can save valuable production time because the original model is unchanged. Much like a specular level map, the bump channel only recognizes grayscale imagery. In fact, the color information in the texture image is creating a height map, which tells the software what and how the surface should be altered. For instance, Visual 8–57 shows a typical procedural noise map that has been placed into the bump channel.

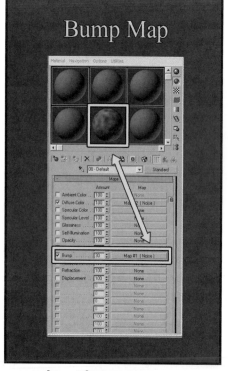

visual |8–56|

Bump Mapping Channel

visual |8–57|

Bump Texture Map

The software will calculate the amount of surface deviation, or bumping, directly from the color of the map. The default setting in most 3D packages is for white to represent relief, or an outward bump, whereas black will recess, or bump inward. Visual 8–58 shows the results of applying the texture map seen in Visual 8–57 to the bump channel of the material, which is applied to a sphere.

visual |8–58|

Bump Map Render

Displacement Maps

A sibling of the bump map, *displacement maps* also are used to create surface variation. The major difference, however, is that displacement maps physically change the surface geometry, whereas bump maps leave the objects unchanged. Therefore, displacement maps are used as more of a modeling tool, whereas bump maps are more of a traditional material and rendering tool.

Visual 8–59 shows the same texture map image used in Visual 8–57. However, this time, it has been placed into the displacement map channel.

This image will be used to alter the geometry by using the grayscale pixel information as a height map; white is relief and black is recess. Visual 8–60 shows a side-by-side comparison of the geometry pre- and postdisplacement mapping.

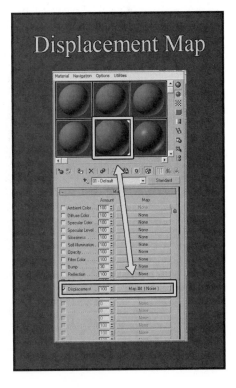

visual | 8–59 |

Displacement Mapping Channel

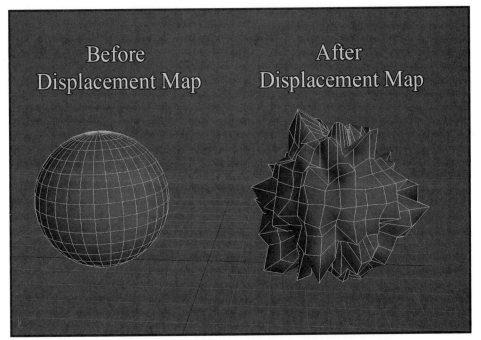

visual | 8–60 |

Surface Geometry – Pre- and Postdisplacement Mapping

Reflection Maps

In the real world, shiny objects with a high degree of specularity may wave reflections of the world around them. In digital filmmaking, it can be a render-intensive process to get highly accurate reflections. However, using *reflection maps*, although not as technically accurate, often can create the visually stunning results you are looking for.

visual |8–61|

Reflection Mapping
Channel

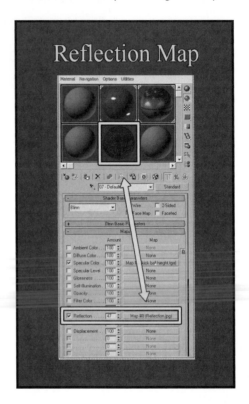

Let's use the red kickball as an example. The current texture mapping parameters reinforces the fact that it is supposed to be made primarily of rubber. What if we wanted this kickball to appear to be made out of thin shiny metal material similar to a Christmas tree ornament?

visual |8–62|

Rubber Kickball Render –
No Reflection

To achieve this, we can place a texture map into the reflection mapping channel. However, we must step back a moment to consider what it is exactly that the kickball should be reflecting. In reality, the ball should reflect what is behind the camera. In this particular case, and in most 3D environments, the artists do not model objects that are off-camera. Therefore, we will have to create an image that will mimic what would be there if we did model it. Visual 8–63 shows the texture map that was created for the reflection map. Notice that is contains part of the floor as well as the wall behind it.

Reflection Texture Map

When the scene is rendered again, notice that the kickball has a much different look and feel. Not only does the object seem hard and metallic, it gives the viewer some important visual cues as to its immediate environment.

visual |8–64|

Kickball with
Reflection Map

Opacity/Transparency Maps

Opacity maps are extremely useful when trying to create intricate transparency patterns across a single object. As with the bump and specular maps, the opacity channel recognizes only grayscale imagery because it deals with intensity and placement of the transparency.

Opacity/Transparency
Mapping Channel

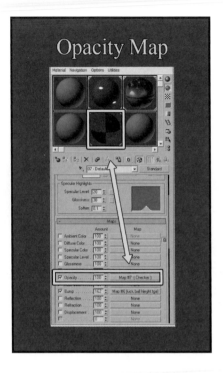

visual |8–66|

Opacity Texture Map

Using the kickball scene as an example, let's use an opacity map to create the illusion that half of the surface is created out of glass. However, to make things a little more complicated, let's use a checkerboard pattern as the texture image.

Visual 8–67 shows the resulting render. Notice that because the texture map was made up of 100 percent black and 100 percent white squares, there are hard edges between the fully opaque and fully transparent portions of the ball. However, if we put a slight Gaussian blur on the original checkerboard texture map and remap the object, the edges will appear much softer.

visual |8–67|

Opacity Map Render

visual |8–68|

Blurred Checkerboard Texture with Resulting Render

UV MAPPING

As important as the texture maps are is the manner in which they are applied or wrapped onto the 3D geometry. It is rather easy to visualize how you would apply wallpaper onto a flat wall. However, it can get quite tricky when you try to wrap a flat 2D image map onto a 3D surface. If you have ever tried to wrap a gift that was awkward in shape, you will know exactly what I mean.

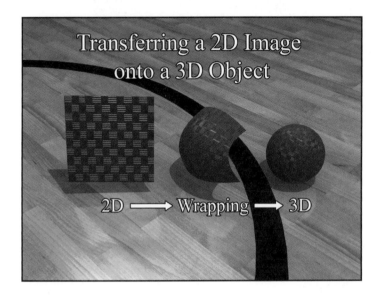

Transferring a 2D Image onto a 3D Surface

To accomplish this goal, a set of mapping coordinates were devised to help bridge the gap between the 2D and 3D worlds. As in the Cartesian XY system, 3D surfaces are assigned UV coordinates.

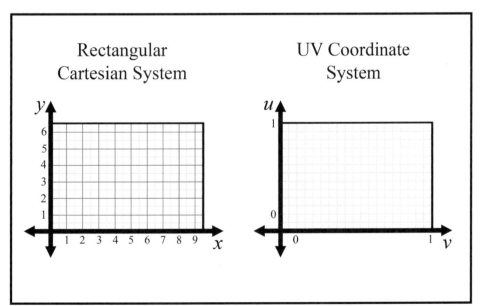

Rectangular Cartesian System and the UV Coordinate System

However, unlike the Cartesian XY system, which is fixed in space, UVs are local to the surface geometry and will not change depending on where the object is placed in the scene. The U-axis represents the horizontal direction, whereas the V represents the vertical axis. Visual 8–71 demonstrates how, ideally, the UVs would be laid out on some of the more common primitive objects.

visual |8–71|

UV Mapping Coordinates on Three Primitive Objects

| NOTE |

In some software packages, such as 3D Studio Max, you will see the mapping coordinates listed as UVW. The W refers to the third dimension, which relates directly to Z axis in the Cartesian XYZ system. However, the UVW system only applies to objects mapped with procedural textures in which there is an extra axis of data.

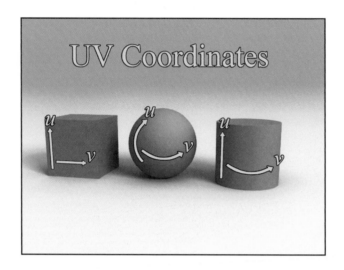

The real trick, however, is to accurately assign the UV coordinates onto the 3D geometry. In fact, most texture mapping woes stem from poor UV mapping on an object. Visual 8–73 shows an example of a simple grid texture that has been poorly mapped to the surfaces of three primitive objects; a cube, a sphere, and a cylinder. Notice that the grid, whose lines should be equidistant and at 90 degree angles, appears uneven and stretched out.

To help combat this UV mapping dilemma, 3D software programs have developed a set of mapping tools that allow the digital artist to project their texture maps on to the geometry in a variety of ways.

visual |8–72|

Poorly Mapped Primitives

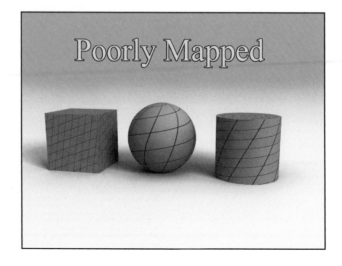

Planar Mapping

The most basic of the UV mapping tools, planar mapping is used best to project a 2D texture image onto a relatively flat 3D surface. Working in much the same way as a film projector works, the texture information is transmitted from a flat plane in space. Visual 8–74 shows planar mapping being used correctly to map an image onto a flat surface.

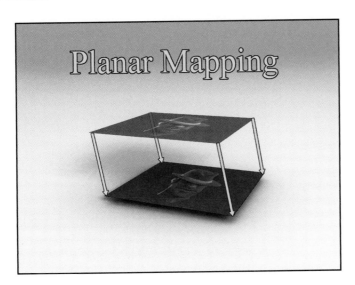

visual |8–73|

Planar Mapping

However, if you try to use the same planar mapping method on 3D cube, you will notice some rather unfortunate results. The software is unclear how to handle the texture image pixels for the sides of the cube because it is being projected from the flat surface. Therefore, the sides of the cube that are perpendicular to the planar map appear to be stretched and distorted.

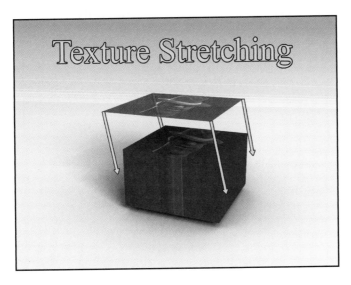

visual |8–74|

Incorrect Use of Planar Mapping

Box Mapping

To project a texture map onto a 3D cube, *box mapping* is your ideal choice. The image is projected from a flat surface, from multiple angles. Therefore, it is quick and easy to create a seamless texture for all six sides of a cube.

visual |8–75|

Box Mapping

However, if this method is used on a more organic shape, such as the sphere in Visual 8–76, the resulting texture looks uneven with obvious seams.

visual |8–76|

Incorrect Use of Box Mapping

Spherical Mapping

To handle the organic shape of a sphere, you'll want to apply a *spherical map* on to the surface to achieve the best texture mapping results. This projection system works by enveloping the sphere by wrapping a planar map around the surface and stitching it together from pole to pole.

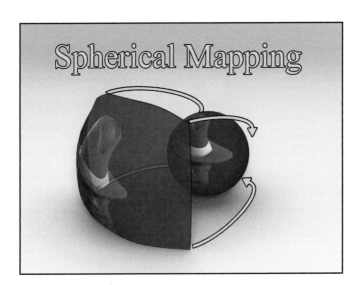

Spherical Mapping

This stitching creates a texture seam along the surface of the sphere. A seam is an important component to all types of mapping, in that it must be taken into consideration when developing the texture image. In this particular case, it is critical that the left edge of the image, seen in Visual 8–78, matches up perfectly with the right edge, as they will meet along the seam once it has been mapped onto the object.

Texture Image –
Matching Edges

For demonstration purposes, let's adjust the image so that the left edge does not match the right. The resulting texture map, seen in Visual 8–79, will produce unwanted results when rendered. Notice that the seam becomes an obvious eyesore on the surface of the sphere.

Texture Image –
Uneven Edges

Map with Obvious Seam

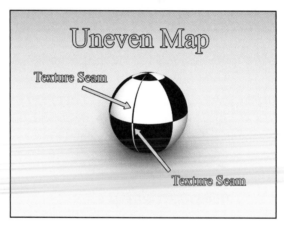

Cylindrical Mapping

A cross between a spherical and planar, the *cylindrical map* has three main projection components. The main portion of the surface is wrapped with a planar map that is stitched at the back of the cylinder. The other two components involve planar maps, which cover the flat top and bottom caps.

Cylindrical Mapping

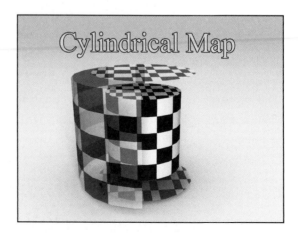

UV Unwrapping

This textbook is not designed to provide the enormous amount of detail needed to fully comprehend the *UV unwrapping* process. However, it is important that you understand how it works on a conceptual level. The unwrapping process, in general terms, allows the artist to deconstruct the existing object's UV coordinates and customize them for the texturing process. The ultimate goal is to flatten or unwrap the UVs, which are currently spread over the 3D object, so that they can be easily painted in a graphic editing program such as Adobe Photoshop. Visual 8–82 shows the diffuse map for the face of a humanoid character.

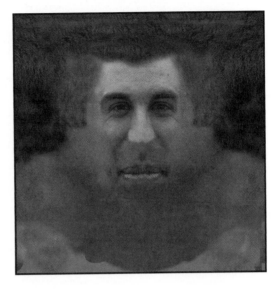

visual |8–82|

Face Diffuse Map

Notice that the texture map looks very awkward; it is extremely flat and distorted. However, this is the ideal way to create the most detailed and accurate texture maps for more advanced 3D surfaces. When you look at the UVs in Visual 8–83, you will see that that is exactly how this particular face flattened during the unwrapping process.

visual |8–83|

Unwrapped Face UV Map

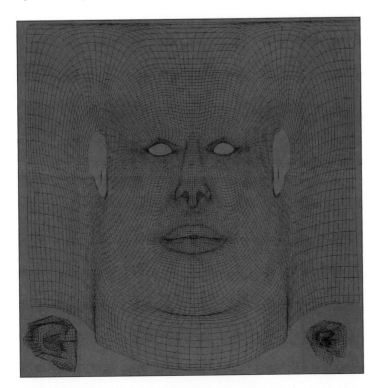

Overlay of Diffuse Map
and Unwrapped Face
UV Map

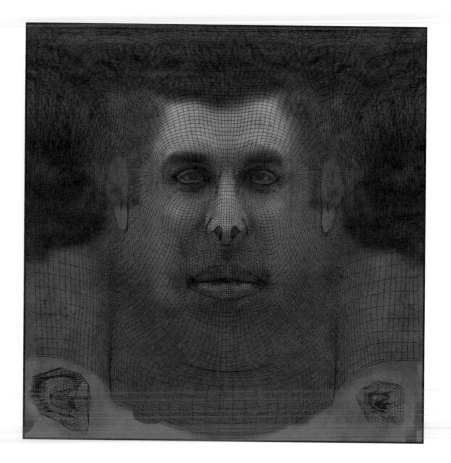

ADDING REALISM

One of the biggest giveaways that an image is computer-generated is the lack of real-world imperfections. Most beginner digital artists tend to model and texture objects as if they came right off the factory floor: perfect, shiny, and new. Although there may be some newer objects within any given scene, chances are that most have a little wear-and-tear.

Visual 8–86 shows a still from *Head Quarters,* a student film that I created at the Rochester Institute of Technology about ten years ago. At first glance, it appears to be a fairly average-looking environment that you might find in the basement of any public building such as a school or library.

However, there are some intentional real-world imperfections that were added to give it that lived-in, worn-out look. Visual 8–86 shows some close-ups of these details, which include stickers, dirt, and rust.

visual |8–85|

Head Quarters Image

visual |8–86|

Head Quarters Image – Close-Up of Imperfections

Layered Shaders

To achieve the type of subtle, and not-so-subtle, imperfections seen in Visual 8–86, multiple textures and materials were layered on top of one another. Each one of the components of the *layered shader* has a unique function and purpose, adding the realistic touches that will help sell your image to the viewer. Visual 8–87 demonstrates a layered shader, which includes a base material, stickers, dirt, and rust materials.

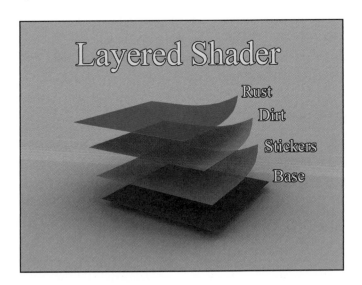

visual |8–87|

Layered Shader Diagram

Visual 8–88 demonstrates a metal teapot that contains only a base material. The base material is representative of what the teapot would look like when brand new. However, to add further realism, we want to add some personality and wear and tear.

Teapot with Base Material
– Brand New CG Look

Paint and Stickers

Creating personality and visual detail is an important part of the texturing process and incorporating paint and stickers can be great additions to your scene objects. Almost everything that is manufactured these days is branded in some way shape or form. Often, details such as logos, decals, stickers, warning labels, instructions, price tags, and barcodes are overlooked.

In the case of the new metal teapot shown in Visual 8–88, let's add a large painted logo on the front as well as a small warning sticker on the bottom. Because we are adding these layers on top of the base shader, we will have to create both a texture image and an opacity map. The opacity map will consist of a grayscale image that will tell the software to allow only the logo and sticker to appear and will allow the base material to show through the rest. Visual 8–89 shows the texture image that will be used to create the logo and warning sticker. The opacity map, seen in Visual 8–90, defines what will be opaque and which parts will be transparent.

visual |8–89|

visual |8–90|

Teapot Paint and Sticker Texture Map

Teapot Paint and Sticker Opacity Map

It is important to note that although both layers use the Phong shading algorithm, the paint and sticker layer's specular level was lowered. Visual 8–91 shows the rendered results of adding the layered shader on to the teapot.

visual |8–91|

Teapot Render with Additional Paint and Sticker Texture Layer

Dirt, Rust, and Gunk

The addition of the paint and sticker layer to the metal teapot gave it a welcome personal touch. The logo and warning label separated this particular teapot from all the other brands on the market. However, it is still looking very new and unused. To add some wear-and-tear onto the surface, we will place a *dirt map* on the next layer above the paint.

Visuals 8–92 and 8–93 show the dirt map and its corresponding opacity map. Dirt maps for the most part should be subtle hints of dirt, rust, and gunk. Do not go overboard with these maps, as too much dirt can make it look as unnatural as not putting any on at all.

visual |8–92|

Teapot Dirt Texture Map

visual |8–93|

Teapot Dirt Opacity Map

The dirt layer, which should not be shiny at all, was put into a Lambert material. Visual 8–94 shows the rendered results of the dirt map.

Teapot Render with
Additional Dirt
Texture Layer

RENDERING ALGORITHMS AND ENGINES

The culmination of all your hard work and labor within the 3D environment results in the rendering of your film. Technically speaking, the rendering process involves your chosen software package translating the 3D geometry, materials, lights, and animation into a 2D image or series of images. However, there are many different types of *rendering algorithms* to choose from. These options can vary widely in look and feel, learning curve, accuracy, and price. Let's take a look at some of the more common engines available on the market.

Wireframe to Render

Scanline

The default rendering algorithm for software packages such as 3D Studio Max, the *scanline renderer* is the fastest and easiest engine to use on the market. However, with that increased speed and usability comes a heavy downside. It is also the least accurate of all the rendering algorithms because it does not take light reflections and refractions into consideration when calculating the final image. The scanline rendering process sends a light ray out from the camera and calculates a final pixel as soon as it hits the first scene object. Also, it starts to calculate the image from the top left and works its way down, pixel line by pixel line.

Visual 8–96 shows a render produced by the scanline algorithm. Any reflections and refractions that are shown are created using maps and are not physically based.

visual |8–96|

Scanline Render Example

Raytracing

Building on the scanline algorithm, *raytracing* allows for more accurate renders because of its increased number of light bounce calculations. Instead of the pixel information being decided at first contact, it allows the light rays to continue to interact with the geometry in the scene to a user-defined number of bounces. This gives the digital artist the option for accurate reflections and refractions. Visual 8–98 shows the same scene that was rendered in Visual 8–96, using the raytracing engine. Although the image quality overall is much higher, the rendering speed has taken a dramatic hit. This may not be such a big deal for single images, but it could prove to be a larger production issue when creating a film (Petrov).

visual |8–97|

Raytracing Example

Mental Ray

Considered to be the first true production quality rendering engine, *Mental Ray* was among the first to incorporate both raytracing and GI into the renderer.

Once only available as a third-party renderer by the German-based software manufacturer Mental Images, Mental Ray has recently been incorporated directly into many of the top 3D animation packages such as Maya and 3D Studio Max. This gives anyone with the base software the capability to render extremely high-quality images. Previously, this only was reserved for the likes of Pixar and Industrial Light & Magic. Visual 8–98 shows the results of the Mental Ray rendering engine.

visual |8–98|

Mental Ray Example

SUMMARY

Digital lighting is as much about the objects it illuminates as it is about the source itself. Understanding how objects react and interact with light will determine the overall quality of the lighting and the quality of the digital cinematography in general. The many options for material and texture map creation within most 3D software applications will allow you ample opportunity to create highly accurate and photo-realistic renders. However, understanding these options and being able to determine which is the best fit for your particular needs is usually what separates the exceptional from the ordinary.

in review

1. What is a shader algorithm and how does it relate to lighting quality?

2. Explain the concept of light reflection.

3. What are the components to total reflected light?

4. What types of objects are best used with Phong shading?

5. What mapping channel would you use to affect the object's appearance in shadow?

6. Explain the difference between bitmap and procedural textures.

7. Explain the difference between bump and displacement maps.

8. What are UV coordinates and how do they relate to texture maps?

9. Name the three most common UV mapping tools.

10. What is a dirt map and how can it add reality to your imagery?

11. Explain the difference between the scanline rendering process and raytracing.

exercises

1. Using only a primitive cylinder and plane, create a plastic flyswatter. The cylinder should be used as the handle, and the plane will serve as the swatter head. Make sure to use the appropriate shader algorithm to achieve the plastic look as well as an opacity map to create the many holes on the swatter head.

   a. Without changing any of the geometry, transform the plastic flyswatter into a metal spatula by adjusting the shading algorithm and opacity map.

2. Using the metal spatula from the first exercise, create a reflection map from a digital photo so that it looks like the spatula is in a kitchen environment.

   a. Create the same effect using raytracing or Mental Ray, by placing the digital photo onto the diffuse map of an off-camera object. The raytracing or Mental Ray rendering engine should be able to calculate accurate reflections if the materials are set up correctly.

3. Using the same metal spatula, add some realistic touches by creating a logo that will appear on the handle.

   a. Create a dirt map so that it looks like the spatula has just been used to make scrambled eggs.

appendix

BIBLIOGRAPHY

Burns, Paul. "Chapter Fourteen 1890–1894." *The History of the Discovery of Cinematography*, 2006. Retrieved January 11, 2007.

Cinematographer Style. Dir. Jon Fauer. ASC, 2006.

Electro Optical Industries, Inc. "The Unit of Luminous Intensity: Candela (CD)." *Electro Optical Industries, Inc.* 2000.

Ford, Janet Lynn. "Color Theory: Overview." *Color Worqx*. November 2006.

Leggat, Robert. (1993). *Camera Obscura*. Retrieved January 13, 2006.

Millerson, Gerald. *Lighting for Television and Film*. Woburn, Massachusetts: Focal Press, 1991.

Petrov, Borislav. "Render FAQs." *Virtual Republic Boboland*, 2007.

index

abbreviations, framing heights, 78
absorption, light, 139
Acker, Shane, 276–281
Act I, 25
Act II, 26
Act III, 26
action
    axis of, 118–121
    inciting incident, 25
    rising, 26
    telling vs. showing, 38
active camera moves, 108
additive color system, 161
afterimages, 66
After You (Cordingley), 23–24,
    124–127
aim, 92
ambient color, 302
ambient maps, 308–309
amplitude, 134
analogous colors, 166
angle of light, 148–154
angle of refraction, 141
angle of view, 59–60
animated films, 6–11
animatics, 51
animation
    3D, 6–11
    future of, 11
    light, 155
animation schools, 20–21
animation styles, 39–40
animation tangents, 104–106
Animation World Network, 21
animators, qualities of
    successful, 7–9
Anistropic shading algorithm, 295
antagonists, 25
aperture, 57–59, 63
archetypes, 27–31
area lights, 196–197
Aristotle, 24
art direction, 38–40
artificial light, 185–190
aspect ratios, 109
assumed objects, 211–213
asymmetrical balance, 111
attenuation, 144–145, 235–237
audio description, 37

available light, 183–185
axis of action, 118–121

background color, 100
back lighting, 151–152
Back to the Future (film), 73
balance
    asymmetrical, 111
    image, 110–111
    symmetrical, 110–111
barn doors, 202
base camera, 92
bias, shadow, 250
bird's eye shots, 72
bitmap textures, 304–305
black-body radiator, 156
Blinn, James F., 298
Blinn shading algorithm, 293–294
blocking, 108–117
booms, 83
bouncers, 197–199
boxes, lighting schemes for,
    263–269
box mapping, 320
brainstorming, 22
brightness, of light, 142–144
Brillant, Edward, 10–11
bump maps, 311–312

Calahan, Sharon, 7
call to adventure, 30
camera angles, 71–73
    bird's eye shots, 72
    canted shots, 73
    high-angle shots, 71
    low-angle shots, 72
    over-the-shoulder shots, 73
    point of view shots, 72
camera cones, 96–98
camera icons, 92
camera moves, 69, 79–84
    within 3D environment,
        103–108
    active, 108
    with cranes and booms, 83
    dolly shots, 82
    empty moves, 107
    handheld shots, 83
    keyframes, 103–106

    meaning behind, 107–108
    pan, 79–80
    passive, 108
    physical, 79–83
    roll, 81
    steady cam, 83
    tilt shots, 80
    tracking shots, 81–82
    zooms, 83–84
camera obscura, 56
camera pan, 79–80
camera paths, 106–107
camera perspective, 69–71
camera rig, 45
camera roll, 81
cameras
    See also virtual cameras
    aperture, 57–59
    depth of field, 61–64
    directing. *See* direction
    lens, 59–61
    overview, 56–57
    shutter, 64–65
    still vs. film, 65–66
camera setups, basic, 67–69
camera shake, 121–122
camera shots, 66–67
    angles of, 71–73
    blocking conventions,
        113–117
    close-up shots, 76–77
    cut-away shots, 78
    dolly shots, 82, 83–84
    exterior shots, 115–116
    framing of, 73–78
    full shots, 75
    handheld shots, 83
    insert shots, 77
    interior, 116–117
    long shots, 74–75
    master shots, 114–115
    medium shots, 75–76
    pan, 79–80
    pivot shots, 119
    rack focus shots, 85
    setting up, 108–113
    tilt shots, 80
    tracking shots, 81–82
    zolly, 84
    zooms, 83–84

camera target, 92
camera tracking, 123
camera type, 94
Campbell, Joseph, 27
canted shots, 73
card reflectors, 197–199
Cartesian coordinate system, 81, 317–318
cartoony style, 39
cast shadows, 203, 205–207
character design, 40–42
    model sheets, 41–42
    sketches, 40–41
character development, 25, 27–31, 40–41
character lighting, 257–261
characters
    archetypes, 27–31
    limited, 22–24
    telling vs. showing by, 38
    too many, 38
cinematics, 12–13
cinematographer, responsibilities of, 5
cinematography
    in gaming industry, 12–13
    history of, 4–5
    introduction to, 4–5
climax, 26
clipping planes, 96–99
closed framing, 113
close-up shots, 76–77
CMYK colors, 162
color channels, 301
colored light, 137
color palettes, 165–167
color parameters, 299–302
color(s)
    ambient, 302
    analogous, 166
    complimentary, 165
    cool, 172
    diffuse, 300
    harmony among, 165–167
    hue, 167–168
    of light, 156, 234–235
    meanings and symbolism, 171–173
    monochromatic, 171
    of objects, 299–302
    primary, 163
    saturation, 168
    secondary, 164
    shade, 170
    shadow, 209–211
    specular, 300–301
    split complimentary, 167

terminology, 167–171
    tertiary, 164
    tint, 170
    tone, 171
    triadic, 166
    value, 168–169
    warm, 171–172
    white balance, 157–159
color schemes, 165–167
color shifts, 222–223
color systems, 160–162
    additive, 161
    subtractive, 162
color temperature, 156–159
color theory, 156, 160
color values, numeric, 300
color wheels, 162–164
combo shots, 84
combustion light, 184–185
complimentary colors, 165
composition, image, 109–112
cone angles, 195–196, 239–241
cones, 96–98
conflicts, 25
contact shadows, 205
continuity, 118–121
contrast, 146–148
cookies, light, 211–213
cool colors, 172
Cordingly, Christopher, 24, 124–127
coverage, light, 154–155
cranes, 83
creative process, 19–24
    idea generation, 19–22
    parameters for, 22–24
creativity, spark of, 20
cubic decay, 236
cucoloris, 212
cut-away shots, 78
cylindrical mapping, 322

daylight, 192–193
decay, of light, 235–236
default lighting, 229, 231–232
depth maps, 247–249
depth of field (DOF), 61–64, 100–102
Descartes, Renè, 81
design research, 42
dialogue, 38
diffuse color, 300
diffuse maps, 307–308
diffuse reflection, 290–291, 292
digital cinematographer, 6–7
digital lighting. See 3D lights/lighting

digital production process, 8–11
digital shadows, 246–250
direct illumination, 178–179
direction, 65–85
    camera angles, 71–73
    camera moves, 79–84
    camera perspective, 69–71
    camera setups, 67–69
    camera shots, 66–67
    in digital filmmaking, 107
    framing, 73–78
    staging and blocking, 108–113
    visual continuity, 118–121
directional lights, 191–193, 242–243
Director of Photography (DoP)
    in animation, 7
    responsibilities of, 5
displacement maps, 313
dolly shots, 82, 83–84
dolly zoom, 84
Donati Theorem, 22–23
double rim lights, 220
dramatic structure, 24–27
dynamic cameras, 122

edges, 255–256
Einstein, Albert, 139
electromagnetic energy, 138
electromagnetic radiation, 133–134, 135
empty moves, 107
establishing shots, 74–75
exposure, 57
exterior lighting schemes, 269–274
exterior shots, 115–116
extreme close-up shots, 77
extreme long shot, 75
eye, 58, 66

falloff, 144–145, 195, 240
15mm lens, 95
50mm lens, 95–96
fight scenes, 37
fill light, 214, 217–218, 220–222
film, 57, 66
filmmaking process
    See also direction; preproduction process
    animated vs. live-action, 6, 10–11
film cameras, directing, 65–85
film complexity, time constraints and, 23–24
film direction. See direction

film exposure, 57
filmmaking, depth of field and, 61–64
filter range, of shadow, 250
Final Fantasy (film), 39
final lighting, 229–230
final storyboards, 48–49
Finding Nemo (film), 7
first-person point of view, 32
fish-eye lens, 59
flash, 150
fluorescent lights, 185, 189–190, 191
focal lengths, 59–61
focal parameters, 102
focal points, 101
four-camera layout, 90–91
frames, 66
frames per second (fps), 65–66
framing, 73–78
    closed, 113
    close-up shots, 76–77
    cut-away shots, 78
    full shots, 75
    insert shots, 77
    long shots, 74–75
    medium shots, 75–76
    open, 113
framing heights, 78
free camera, 94, 95
frequency, 134–135
front lighting, 150
Front view, 90
F-stops, 58–59, 63
full shots, 75

gaming industry
    future of, 11
    role of cinematography in, 12–13
geometry, lighting and, 253–256
global illumination (GI), 181–182
    faking, 270–272
gobos, 201
Godfather, The (film), 4, 13
Golden Rectangle, 111–112
Green Screen technology, 123
ground plane, 181

halogen lights, 185, 188–189
handheld shots, 83
hard lighting, 146–147
headshots, 258–261
herald, 29
hero, 28

Hero's Journey, 27–31
Hero with a Thousand Faces, The (Campbell), 27
high-angle lighting, 153–154
high-angle shots, 71
highlights, 309–311
Hitchcock shot, 84
hotspots, 195, 240, 309–311
HSV (hue, saturation, and value) color model, 169
hue, 167–168
human eye, 58, 66
hyperrealism, 39

icons, 49–50
idea generation, 19–22
illuminance, 142–145
illumination
    defined, 178
    direct, 178–179
    global, 181–182, 270–272
    indirect, 180–181
illustration, 12
image balance, 110–111
image composition, 109–112
image planes, 59, 99–100
imagery, 42–43
IMAX format, 66
incandescent lights, 136, 185, 186–188
inciting incident, 25
indirect illumination, 180–181
infinite lights, 191–193
inmost cave, 31
insert shots, 77
inspiration, 19–22, 42–43
intensity, of light, 142–144, 233–234
interior lighting schemes, 261–269
interior shots, 116–117
inverse square law, 145, 235

Jackson, Peter, 18–19

Kelvin scale, 156–157, 186–187, 189, 190
keyframes, 103–106
key light, 214, 215–217, 220–222
key-to-fill ratio, 221–222

Lambert shading algorithm, 294–295
Lasky, Jeremy, 7
layered shaders, 325–328
"Leeds Bridge Traffic" (Le Prine), 4

lenses, 57, 59–61, 83, 94–96
Le Prine, Louis Aime Augustin, 4
light, 57
    See also 3D lights/lighting; lighting
    absorption, 139
    angle of, 148–154
    animation, 155
    attenuation, 144–145, 235–237
    characteristics of, 142–156
    colored, 137
    color of, 156, 234–235
    combustion, 184–185
    contrast, 146–148
    coverage, 154–155
    electromagnetic radiation, 133–134
    intensity, 142–144, 233–234
    interaction of, with objects, 138–141
    introduction to, 131–133
    photography and, 57–58
    photon theory of, 139–141
    reflection, 139–140
    refraction, 141
    scattering, 140–141
    surface reflection and, 289–293
    transmission, 141
    visible spectrum, 133–135
    white, 136–137, 138
    white balancing, 157–159
light cookies, 211–213
light energy, 138–139
lighting
    See also 3D lights/lighting; light
    in 9, 276–281
    area lights, 196–197
    back, 151–152
    character, 257–261
    direct illumination, 178–179
    directional lights, 191–193, 242–243
    exteriors, 269–274
    front, 150
    geometry and, 253–256
    global illumination, 181–182
    hard, 146–147
    for headshots, 258–261
    high-angle, 153–154
    indirect illumination, 180–181
    interiors, 261–269
    introduction to, 132–133
    low-angle, 152–153
    omni-directional lights, 193–194, 243–244

product, 256–257
production lights, 191–197
role of, 178
shadows and, 202–213
side, 151
soft, 147–148
spotlights, 148–149, 194–196
three-point, 213–223
lighting accessories, 197–202
barn doors, 202
bouncers, 197–199
gobos, 201
reflectors, 197–199
scrims, 201
softboxes, 199–200
umbrellas, 199–200
lighting decisions, 230
lighting production
introduction to, 178
phases of virtual, 229
production lights, 191–197
shadows and, 202–213
three-point lighting, 213–223
lighting setup, 45
light inventory, 262
light setups, 132
light sources, 160, 182–190
artificial light, 185–190
fluorescent lights, 189–190
halogen lights, 188–189
incandescent lights, 186–188
natural light, 183–185
linear decay, 236
location design, 42–43
lock-off camera setup, 67–68
long shots, 74–75
Lord of the Rings (film), 18–19
low-angle lighting, 152–153
low-angle shots, 72
lux, 142

main spotlight, 238–239
mapping channels, 307–316
master shots, 114–115
match moving, 123
material editor, 298
materials
color, 299–302
common parameters for, 298–303
introduction to, 286–289
mapping channels, 307–316
opacity/transparency parameters, 302–303
production flow for, 287–289
properties, 286

realism of, 324–328
shader algorithms, 293–298
surface reflection, 289–293
texture maps, 303–316
UV mapping, 317–324
material transparency, 248–249
Maya, 298
medium shots, 75–76
Méliès, George, 4
Mental Ray, 330
mentor, 28, 30
mid-day light, 192–193
modeling, with light, 213–223
model sheets, 41–42
monochromatic colors, 171
moving cameras, 69
multi-layer shading algorithm, 295–296
multilister, 298

natural light, 183–185
faking, 269–274
time of day and, 267–269, 272–274
negative lights, 252–253, 280
Newton, Isaac, 136–137, 145, 160
9 (Acker), 276–281
nonrenderable objects, 92

objective point of view, 32
objective viewpoint, 69–70
object modeling, with light, 213–223
objects
adding real-world imperfections to, 324–328
color of, 299–302
surface edges, 255–256
off-camera objects, 91
omnidirectional lights, 193–194, 243–244
180 degree rule, 120–121
opacity, 288
opacity maps, 315–316, 326–327
opacity/transparency parameters, 302–303
open framing, 113
Opticks (Newton), 160, 162
ordeal, 31
ordinary world, 30, 31
Orean-Naynar-Blinn shading algorithm, 296
orthographic views, 92–93
outline, 34
overhead schematics, 45–46
over-the-shoulder shots, 73

pan, 79–80
parallax, 79
passive camera moves, 108
perceived intensity, 143–144
persistence of vision, 66
perspective
camera, 69–71
objective, 69–70
points of view, 32
subjective, 69, 70–71
perspective views, 90, 93
Phong, Bui Tuong, 298
Phong shading algorithm, 294
photography, 56
See also cameras
depth of field and, 61–64
light and, 57–58
photometers, 142
photon theory of light, 139–141
physical camera moves, 79–83
pivot shots, 119
Pixar Animation Studio, 7, 39
Pixar Web site, 21
pixel size, 304–305
planar mapping, 319
point lights, 243–244
point of view shots, 72
points of interest, 112
points of view (POVs), 32
positives, 59
power points, 112
preliminary sketches, 40–41
preproduction process
art direction, 38–40
character design, 40–43
character development, 27–31
scripting process, 34–37
storyboarding, 44–50
story development, 24–34
story reels, 51
presets, 94
primary colors, 163
prisms, 136
procedural textures, 305–306
production lights, 191–197, 229
area lights, 196–197
directional lights, 191–193
omni-directional lights, 193–194
spotlights, 194–196
product lighting, 256–257
protagonists, 25, 28
pull focus, 85
Purple Rose of Cairo, The (film), 4

quadratic decay, 235–236
quality, light, 146–148

rack focus shots, 85
radiosity, 181
    faking, 265–267
ray bias, 250
raytraced shadows, 249
raytracing, 329
realism, 39, 324–328
reflection, 139–140
    diffuse, 290–291, 292
    on mixed surfaces, 291–293
    specular, 289–290, 292
    surface, 289–293
reflection maps, 314–315
reflectors, 197–199
refracted light, 136
refraction, 141
refusal of the call, 30
rendering, 57
rendering algorithm, 328–330
rendering cameras, 91
rendering engines
    Mental Ray, 330
    raytracing, 329
    scanline, 329
research
    design, 42
    role of, in idea generation,
        20–22
resolution, 26
resurrection, 31
reward, 31
RGB colors, 161
rim light, 214, 218–222
rising action, 26
road back, 31
roll, 81
roughs, 48
rounded edges, 255–256
rule of thirds, 111–112
running time, 22–24

sample range, of shadow, 250
saturation, color, 168
scanline renderers, 329
scattering, of light, 140–141
scenes, 66
schematic views, 50
scrims, 201
script format, 35
scripting process, 34–37
secondary colors, 164
set design, 42–43
shader algorithms, 287, 293–298

shaders
    common parameters for,
        287–288
    layered, 325–328
shades, color, 170
shadow area, 205
shadow bias, 250
shadow casting lights, 237
shadow casting objects,
    204–205, 211
shadow edge, 205–206
shadow maps, 247–249
shadows, 29, 202–213
    3D lights and, 237
    assumed objects, 211–213
    cast shadows, 203, 205–207
    color, 209–211
    components of, 203–207
    digital, 246–250
    hard-edged, 206
    hard lighting and, 146–147
    raytraced, 249
    sample range of, 250
    soft-edged, 206–207
    soft lighting and, 147–148
    as spatial cues, 207–209
    throw, 211
shapeshifter, 29
sharp edges, 256
shots. *See* camera shots
shutter, 64–65
shutter speeds, 64–65
side lighting, 151
Side view, 90
sketches, 40–41, 47
skylight, 192–193, 245–246
slug lines, 36
softboxes, 199–200
soft lighting, 147–148
spark-generation, 20–22
spatial cues, from shadows,
    207–209
special effects, 39, 123
specular color, 300–301
specularity, 288
specular maps, 309–311
specular reflection, 140,
    289–290, 292
spheres, 253–255
spherical mapping, 320–322
split complimentary colors, 167
spotlights, 148–149, 194–196,
    237–241
Square Enix, 13
staging, 108–113
Stahlberg, Steven, 13

standard lights, 232–237
    See also spotlights
steady cam, 83
story beats, 33–34, 47
storyboarding
    basic, 44
    content for, 45–46
    finals, 48–49
    process, 46–49
    roughs, 48
    symbols and icons, 49–50
    thumbs, 47
storyboard templates, 49
story concept, expanding on,
    32–33
story development, character
    development and, 40–41
story ideas, sources of, 19–22
storymen, 44
story outline, 34
story reels, 51
story structure, 24–27
storytelling, 18
    See also visual storytelling
student films, parameters on,
    22–24
student mistakes, 37–38
styles, 39–40
subjective viewpoint, 69, 70–71
subsurface scattering, 140–141
subtractive color system, 162
sunlight, 191, 192–193
sunset, 137, 193
surface edges, 255–256
surface reflection, 289–293
    diffuse reflection, 290–291
    mixed surfaces, 291–293
    specular reflection, 289–290
surfaces. *See* texture maps
symbols, 49–50
symmetrical balance, 110–111

Tammaro, Louis, 12–13
target, 92, 238–240
target camera, 94
telephoto lens, 59–60
telling vs. showing, 38
templates, storyboard, 49
terminators, 204
tertiary colors, 164
textual information, 46
texture maps, 288–289, 303–306
    ambient maps, 308–309
    bump maps, 311–312
    diffuse maps, 307–308
    displacement maps, 313

mapping channels, 307–316
opacity maps, 315–316
reflection maps, 314–315
specular maps, 309–311
transparency maps, 315–316
textures
bitmap, 304–305
procedural, 305–306
real-world, 324–328
third-person point of view, 32
35mm, 60
three-act structure, 24–27
3D animation, 6–7
future of, 11
production process, 8–11
similarity to real-world
production, 10–11
3D animators. *See* animators
3D cameras. *See* virtual cameras
3D lights/lighting, 230–231
character lighting, 257–261
default lighting, 231–232
directional lights, 242–243
exclusion and inclusion,
250–252
exterior lighting, 269–274
interior lighting, 261–269
introduction to, 228
negative lights, 252–253, 280
omnidirectional lights,
243–244
parameters for, 232–237
product lighting, 256–257
radiosity faking with, 265–267
shadows and, 246–250
skylights, 245–246
spotlights, 237–241
standard lights, 232–237
volume lights, 244–245
3D modeling, 286–289
See also materials
3D Studio Max, 298, 299
three-headed monster
concept, 7–9
three-point lighting, 213–223
color shifts, 222–223
fill light, 214, 217–218,
220–222
key light, 214, 215–217,
220–222
key-to-fill ratio, 221–222
rim light, 214, 218–222
threshold guardian, 29, 30

throw shadows, 211
thumbnail sketches, 47
thumbs, 47
tilt shots, 80
time limitations, 22–24, 38
time of day, 267–269, 272–274
tint, 170
tone, 171
toon shaders, 296–297
Top view, 90
total reflected light, 291–293
Toy Story (film), 23
tracking, 123
tracking shots, 81–82
transmission, light, 141
transparency handling, 248–249
transparency maps, 315–316
transparency parameters, 302–303
triadic colors, 166
trickster, 29
"Trip to the Moon, A" (Méliès), 4
tungsten light bulbs, 158
turning points, 26
200mm lens, 96
Two-Minute/Two-Character
principle, 23–24

umbrella diffuser, 147
umbrellas, 199–200
UV coordinate system, 288,
317–318
UV mapping, 317–324
box mapping, 320
cylindrical mapping, 322
planar mapping, 319
spherical mapping, 320–322
UV unwrapping, 323–324

value, color, 168–169
Vertigo shot, 84
viewport configuration, 92–93
viewports, 91
views
orthographic, 92–93
perspective, 93
virtual cameras, 6
advanced techniques,
121–123
base camera, 92
camera moves, 103–108
camera type, 94
clipping planes, 96–99

cones, 96–98
depth of field, 100–102
four-camera layout, 90–91
functions of, 90–91
image planes, 99–100
introduction to, 89–90
lenses, 94–96
orthographic views, 92–93
parameters, 94–100
perspective views, 93
target, 92
virtual lighting. *See* 3D
lights/lighting
virtual sets
lighting for exterior, 269–274
lighting for interior, 261–269
visible light, 133–135
vision, persistence of, 66
visual continuity, 118–121
visual description, 36
visual information, 45–46
visualization industry, 39
visual storytelling
art direction, 38–40
character design, 40–42
character development, 27–31
common student mistakes
in, 37–38
creative process, 19–24
introduction to, 17–19
points of view, 32
scripting process, 34–37
set design, 42–43
storyboarding, 44–50
story reels, 51
story structure, 24–27
Vogler, Christopher, 27–28, 29
volume lights, 244–245

Walt Disney Studios, 44
warm colors, 171–172
wavelengths, 134–135
white balance, 157–159
white light, 136–138
wide-angle lens, 60, 95
Willis,Gordon, 4
Writer's Journey, The (Vogler),
27–28

zolly, 84
zoom lens, 83
zooms, 83–84

IMPORTANT-READ CAREFULLY: This End User License Agreement ("Agreement") sets forth the conditions by which Delmar Learning, a division of Thomson Learning Inc. ("Thomson") will make electronic access to the Thomson Delmar Learning-owned licensed content and associated media, software, documentation, printed materials and electronic documentation contained in this package and/or made available to you via this product (the "Licensed Content"), available to you (the "End User"). BY CLICKING THE "I ACCEPT" BUTTON AND/OR OPENING THIS PACKAGE, YOU ACKNOWLEDGE THAT YOU HAVE READ ALL OF THE TERMS AND CONDITIONS, AND THAT YOU AGREE TO BE BOUND BY ITS TERMS CONDITIONS AND ALL APPLICABLE LAWS AND REGULATIONS GOVERNING THE USE OF THE LICENSED CONTENT.

1.0 SCOPE OF LICENSE

1.1   Licensed Content. The Licensed Content may contain portions of modifiable content ("Modifiable Content") and content which may not be modified or otherwise altered by the End User ("Non-Modifiable Content"). For purposes of this Agreement, Modifiable Content and Non-Modifiable Content may be collectively referred to herein as the "Licensed Content." All Licensed Content shall be considered Non-Modifiable Content, unless such Licensed Content is presented to the End User in a modifiable format and it is clearly indicated that modification of the Licensed Content is permitted.

1.2   Subject to the End User's compliance with the terms and conditions of this Agreement, Thomson Delmar Learning hereby grants the End User, a nontransferable, non-exclusive, limited right to access and view a single copy of the Licensed Content on a single personal computer system for noncommercial, internal, personal use only. The End User shall not (i) reproduce, copy, modify (except in the case of Modifiable Content), distribute, display, transfer, sublicense, prepare derivative work(s) based on, sell, exchange, barter or transfer, rent, lease, loan, resell, or in any other manner exploit the Licensed Content; (ii) remove, obscure or alter any notice of Thomson Delmar Learning's intellectual property rights present on or in the License Content, including, but not limited to, copyright, trademark and/or patent notices; or (iii) disassemble, decompile, translate, reverse engineer or otherwise reduce the Licensed Content.

2.0 TERMINATION

2.1   Thomson Delmar Learning may at any time (without prejudice to its other rights or remedies) immediately terminate this Agreement and/or suspend access to some or all of the Licensed Content, in the event that the End User does not comply with any of the terms and conditions of this Agreement. In the event of such termination by Thomson Delmar Learning, the End User shall immediately return any and all copies of the Licensed Content to Thomson Delmar Learning.

3.0 PROPRIETARY RIGHTS

3.1   The End User acknowledges that Thomson Delmar Learning owns all right, title and interest, including, but not limited to all copyright rights therein, in and to the Licensed Content, and that the End User shall not take any action inconsistent with such ownership. The Licensed Content is protected by U.S., Canadian and other applicable copyright laws and by international treaties, including the Berne Convention and the Universal Copyright Convention. Nothing contained in this Agreement shall be construed as granting the End User any ownership rights in or to the Licensed Content.

3.2   Thomson Delmar Learning reserves the right at any time to withdraw from the Licensed Content any item or part of an item for which it no longer retains the right to publish, or which it has reasonable grounds to believe infringes copyright or is defamatory, unlawful or otherwise objectionable.

4.0 PROTECTION AND SECURITY

4.1   The End User shall use its best efforts and take all reasonable steps to safeguard its copy of the Licensed Content to ensure that no unauthorized reproduction, publication, disclosure, modification or distribution of the Licensed Content, in whole or in part, is made. To the extent that the End User becomes aware of any such unauthorized use of the Licensed Content, the End User shall immediately notify Delmar Learning. Notification of such violations may be made by sending an Email to delmarhelp@thomson.com.

5.0 MISUSE OF THE LICENSED PRODUCT

5.1   In the event that the End User uses the Licensed Content in violation of this Agreement, Thomson Delmar Learning shall have the option of electing liquidated damages, which shall include all profits generated by the End User's use of the Licensed Content plus interest computed at the maximum rate permitted by law and all legal fees and other expenses incurred by Thomson Delmar Learning in enforcing its rights, plus penalties.

6.0 FEDERAL GOVERNMENT CLIENTS

6.1   Except as expressly authorized by Delmar Learning, Federal Government clients obtain only the rights specified in this Agreement and no other rights. The Government acknowledges that (i) all software and related documentation incorporated in the Licensed Content is existing commercial computer software within the meaning of FAR 27.405(b)(2); and (2) all other data delivered in whatever form, is limited rights data within the meaning of FAR 27.401. The restrictions in this section are acceptable as consistent with the Government's need for software and other data under this Agreement.

7.0 DISCLAIMER OF WARRANTIES AND LIABILITIES

7.1   Although Thomson Delmar Learning believes the Licensed Content to be reliable, Thomson Delmar Learning does not guarantee or warrant (i) any information or materials contained in or produced by the Licensed Content, (ii) the accuracy, completeness or reliability of the Licensed Content, or (iii) that the Licensed Content is free from errors or other material defects. THE LICENSED PRODUCT IS PROVIDED "AS IS," WITHOUT ANY WARRANTY OF ANY KIND AND THOMSON DELMAR LEARNING DISCLAIMS ANY AND ALL WARRANTIES, EXPRESSED OR IMPLIED, INCLUDING, WITHOUT LIMITATION, WARRANTIES OF MERCHANTABILITY OR FITNESS OR A PARTICULAR PURPOSE. IN NO EVENT SHALL THOMSON DELMAR LEARNING BE LIABLE FOR: INDIRECT, SPECIAL, PUNITIVE OR CONSEQUENTIAL DAMAGES INCLUDING FOR LOST PROFITS, LOST DATA, OR OTHERWISE. IN NO EVENT SHALL DELMAR LEARNING'S AGGREGATE LIABILITY HEREUNDER, WHETHER ARISING IN CONTRACT, TORT, STRICT LIABILITY OR OTHERWISE, EXCEED THE AMOUNT OF FEES PAID BY THE END USER HEREUNDER FOR THE LICENSE OF THE LICENSED CONTENT.

8.0 GENERAL

8.1   Entire Agreement. This Agreement shall constitute the entire Agreement between the Parties and supercedes all prior Agreements and understandings oral or written relating to the subject matter hereof.

8.2   Enhancements/Modifications of Licensed Content. From time to time, and in Delmar Learning's sole discretion, Thomson Thomson Delmar Learning may advise the End User of updates, upgrades, enhancements and/or improvements to the Licensed Content, and may permit the End User to access and use, subject to the terms and conditions of this Agreement, such modifications, upon payment of prices as may be established by Delmar Learning.

8.3   No Export. The End User shall use the Licensed Content solely in the United States and shall not transfer or export, directly or indirectly, the Licensed Content outside the United States.

8.4   Severability. If any provision of this Agreement is invalid, illegal, or unenforceable under any applicable statute or rule of law, the provision shall be deemed omitted to the extent that it is invalid, illegal, or unenforceable. In such a case, the remainder of the Agreement shall be construed in a manner as to give greatest effect to the original intention of the parties hereto.

8.5   Waiver. The waiver of any right or failure of either party to exercise in any respect any right provided in this Agreement in any instance shall not be deemed to be a waiver of such right in the future or a waiver of any other right under this Agreement.

8.6   Choice of Law/Venue. This Agreement shall be interpreted, construed, and governed by and in accordance with the laws of the State of New York, applicable to contracts executed and to be wholly preformed therein, without regard to its principles governing conflicts of law. Each party agrees that any proceeding arising out of or relating to this Agreement or the breach or threatened breach of this Agreement may be commenced and prosecuted in a court in the State and County of New York. Each party consents and submits to the non-exclusive personal jurisdiction of any court in the State and County of New York in respect of any such proceeding.

8.7   Acknowledgment. By opening this package and/or by accessing the Licensed Content on this Website, THE END USER ACKNOWLEDGES THAT IT HAS READ THIS AGREEMENT, UNDERSTANDS IT, AND AGREES TO BE BOUND BY ITS TERMS AND CONDITIONS. IF YOU DO NOT ACCEPT THESE TERMS AND CONDITIONS, YOU MUST NOT ACCESS THE LICENSED CONTENT AND RETURN THE LICENSED PRODUCT TO THOMSON DELMAR LEARNING (WITHIN 30 CALENDAR DAYS OF THE END USER'S PURCHASE) WITH PROOF OF PAYMENT ACCEPTABLE TO DELMAR LEARNING, FOR A CREDIT OR A REFUND. Should the End User have any questions/comments regarding this Agreement, please contact Thomson Delmar Learning at delmarhelp@thomson.com.